PRAISE FOR 1

MW00777806

"This book provides an in-depth look at the relationships between culture and evaluation/research. Prepare yourself for a reading that will transform your practice!"
—Sebastian Galindo, *University of Florida*

"This is one of those rare texts which can serve both as an introduction and as an advanced consideration of evaluation."
—Arthur E. Hernandez, *University of the Incarnate Word*

"The desperate need for a book that provides empirical approaches to culturally responsive approaches in evaluation cannot be understated. Theories, principles, and frameworks are more known than the empirical practices and applications and this book provides a plethora of substantive studies that exist. What a treasure chest! Chouinard and Cram are the authors who can and should open these dialogues to a wider audience and this book will make an indelible contribution to the evaluation field."
—Rodney Hopson, *University of Illinois at Urbana-Champaign*

"Everyone conducting social scientific research should have this essential resource on their shelf."
—Frances Kayona, *Saint Cloud State University*

"This is a well-done and much-needed text on an important topic in program evaluation."
—Raymond Sanchez-Mayers, *Rutgers University*

"This book can guide evaluators to create a future for evaluation that could lead to improved responsiveness to the needs of members of marginalized communities, and increase the transformative contribution of evaluation to improved social justice in the world."
—Donna M. Mertens, *Gallaudet University*

Sara Miller McCune founded SAGE Publishing in 1965 to support the dissemination of usable knowledge and educate a global community. SAGE publishes more than 1000 journals and over 800 new books each year, spanning a wide range of subject areas. Our growing selection of library products includes archives, data, case studies and video. SAGE remains majority owned by our founder and after her lifetime will become owned by a charitable trust that secures the company's continued independence.

Los Angeles | London | New Delhi | Singapore | Washington DC | Melbourne

Culturally Responsive Approaches to Evaluation

Evaluation in Practice Series

Christina A. Christie & Marvin C. Alkin, Series Editors

1. *Mixed Methods Design in Evaluation,* by Donna M. Mertens

2. *Facilitating Evaluation: Principles in Practice,* by Michael Quinn Patton

3. *Collaborative Approaches to Evaluation: Principles in Use,* Edited by J. Bradley Cousins

4. *Culturally Responsive Approaches to Evaluation* by Jill Anne Chouinard and Fiona Cram

Culturally Responsive Approaches to Evaluation

Empirical Implications for Theory and Practice

Jill Anne Chouinard
University of Victoria

Fiona Cram
Katoa Ltd.

Los Angeles | London | New Delhi
Singapore | Washington DC | Melbourne

FOR INFORMATION:

SAGE Publications, Inc.
2455 Teller Road
Thousand Oaks, California 91320
E-mail: order@sagepub.com

SAGE Publications Ltd.
1 Oliver's Yard
55 City Road
London, EC1Y 1SP
United Kingdom

SAGE Publications India Pvt. Ltd.
B 1/I 1 Mohan Cooperative Industrial Area
Mathura Road, New Delhi 110 044
India

SAGE Publications Asia-Pacific Pte. Ltd.
18 Cross Street #10-10/11/12
China Square Central
Singapore 048423

Printed in the United States of America

ISBN: 978-1-5063-6853-5

This book is printed on acid-free paper.

Acquisitions Editor: Helen Salmon
Editorial Assistant: Megan O'Heffernan
Production Editor: Astha Jaiswal
Copy Editor: Diane DiMura
Typesetter: Hurix Digital
Proofreader: Ellen Brink
Indexer: Maria Sosnowski
Cover Designer: Dally Verghese
Marketing Manager: Shari Countryman

19 20 21 22 23 10 9 8 7 6 5 4 3 2 1

BRIEF CONTENTS

List of Appendices, Figures, Tables   ix

About the Authors   xi

Volume Editors' Introduction   xiii

Acknowledgments   xv

Chapter 1 • Introduction   1

Chapter 2 • A Conceptual Framework for Inquiry   19

Chapter 3 • Methodology and Descriptive Overview of Selected Studies   33

Chapter 4 • The Indigenous Context   39

Chapter 5 • The Western/North American Context   71

Chapter 6 • The International Development Context   95

Chapter 7 • A Discussion of the Conceptual Framework Across Domains of Practice   119

Chapter 8 • Concluding Thoughts   135

References   139

Appendices   163

Index   203

DETAILED CONTENTS

List of Appendices, Figures, Tables   ix

About the Authors   xi

Volume Editors' Introduction   xiii

Acknowledgments   xv

Chapter 1 • Introduction   **1**

Overall Background to Book   1
    History of Culturally Responsive Evaluation   3

Social Inquiry as a Cultural Product   9
    Philosophical Legacy and Roots   9
    Extensions Into Geographic and Cultural Contexts   13

This Book   15
    Purpose of This Book   15
    Overview of The Book   17

Chapter 2 • A Conceptual Framework for Inquiry   **19**

Defining Culture   19

Dimensions of Culture and Cultural Context   24

Chapter 3 • Methodology and Descriptive Overview of Selected Studies   **33**

Description of Studies   33
    Selection Approach   33

Sample Characteristics   35

Strategy for Analysis   37

Limitations   38

Chapter 4 • The Indigenous Context   **39**

Overview of Chapter   39

Description of Sample   43
    Selection   43
    Characteristics   43

Review and Integration of Selected Studies   45
    Descriptive Analysis   45
    Integration and Synthesis   46
    An Ecological View of Program Context   46
    Understanding the Importance of Local Programming   49
    The Indigenous World Is a Kinship World   51
    Evaluators as Both Insiders and Outsiders   55
    Co-Production of Evaluation Design and Implementation   57
    A Power-Sharing Evaluation Methodology   60
    Evaluator Accountabilities to Community   63

Critical Discussion and Implications for Practice   65

Chapter Summary   67

Extending Inquiry   68
    Bibliography of Further Readings   68
    Exercises Based on Case Examples   68
    Discussion Questions   69

Chapter 5 • The Western/North American Context   71

Overview of Chapter   71

Description of Sample   73
    Selection   73
    Characteristics   74

Review and Integration of Selected Studies   75
    Descriptive Analysis   75
    Integration and Synthesis   76
    Interpretation of Culture   76
    Manifestations of Power   78
    Complexities of Language   80
    The Variety of Identities   82
    The Dimensionality of Time   83
    The Cultural Appropriateness of Evaluative Measurements   85
    The Use and Influence of Evaluative Findings   87

Critical Discussion and Implications for Practice   89

Chapter Summary   92

Extending Inquiry   92
    Bibliography of Further Readings   92
    Exercises Based on Case Examples   92
    Discussion Questions   93

Chapter 6 • The International Development Context   95

Overview of the Chapter   95

The International Development Context in Evaluation   97

Description of Sample   98
   Selection   98
   Characteristics   98

Review and Integration of Selected Studies   99
   Descriptive Analysis   99
   Integration and Synthesis   100
   Contextual Complexity   100
   Temporal Dimensionality   102
   Participatory Strategies   104
   Methodological Dissonance   107
   Going Beyond the Spoken Word   109
   Cultural Translation   110
   Ethical Imperative   112

Critical Discussion and Implications for Practice   113

Chapter Summary   117

Extending Inquiry   117
   Bibliography of Further Readings   117
   Exercises Based on Case Examples   118
   Discussion Questions   118

**Chapter 7 • A Discussion of the Conceptual
Framework Across Domains of Practice   119**

The Epistemological Dimension of Cultural Practice   120

The Ecological Dimension of Cultural Practice   122

The Methodological Dimension of Cultural Practice   124

The Political Dimension of Cultural Practice   125

The Personal Dimension of Cultural Practice   127

The Relational Dimension of Cultural Practice   128

The Institutional Dimension of Cultural Practice   130

The Axiological Dimension of Cultural Practice   131

The Ontological Dimension of Cultural Practice   132

Concluding Remarks   133

Chapter 8 • Concluding Thoughts   135

References   139

Appendices   163

Index   203

LIST OF APPENDICES, FIGURES, TABLES

List of Appendices

Appendix 1 • A Summary of Sample Studies in Indigenous Context (n=31) 163

Appendix 2 • A Summary of Sample Studies in Western Context (n=24) 179

Appendix 3 • A Summary of Sample Studies in International
Context (n=25) 191

List of Figures

Figure 1.1 • Culturally Responsive Evaluation Framework 8

Figure 3.1 • Total Number of Studies Across Three Domains of Practice 36

Figure 3.2 • Program Contexts Across Domains of Practice 37

Figure 4.1 • Number of Articles Published by Year, 2000–2017 44

Figure 4.2 • Conceptual Framework for the Northern Territories
Emergency Response Program Logic 48

Figure 5.1 • Number of Publications Selected by Year, 2000–2017 74

Figure 6.1 • Number of Publications Selected by Year 99

List of Tables

Table 2.1 • Conceptual Framework for Inquiry: Locations of
Culture in Research and Evaluation 26

Table 4.1 • Criteria for Identifying Indigenous and Tribal Peoples 39

Table 8.1 • A Summary of Themes Across Domains of Practice 136

To Blake and Matthew—because without love we have nothing

For Pat and Gwen—outstanding parents and excellent human beings

ABOUT THE AUTHORS

Jill Anne Chouinard was an associate professor in the Department of Educational Research Methodology at the University of North Carolina at Greensboro. As of January 2020, she is an associate professor in the School of Public Administration at the University of Victoria in British Columbia. She is currently the associate editor of the *Canadian Journal of Program Evaluation*. Her main interests are in cross-cultural/culturally responsive approaches to research and evaluation, participatory research and evaluation, and evaluation and public policy. She has extensive experience working on evaluations at the community level in the areas of education and training, social services, public health, and organizational learning and change. She positions evaluation as a catalyst for learning, collaboration, social justice, and community change.

Fiona Cram has tribal affiliations with Ngāti Pāhauwera and is the mother of one son. She is currently director of Katoa Ltd., a Kaupapa Māori (by, for, and with Māori) research and evaluation organization in Aotearoa New Zealand and is editor-in-chief of *Evaluation Matters—He Take Tō Te Aromatawai*. Fiona has over 20 years of Kaupapa Māori research and evaluation experience with Māori tribes, organizations, and communities, as well as government agencies, district health boards, and philanthropics. A large portion of this work involves the use of mixed or multiple methods in the pursuit of decolonization, tribal sovereignty, and societal transformation.

VOLUME EDITORS' INTRODUCTION

Rightfully so, attention to diversity, equity and inclusion has been of increasing concern among evaluators for some time. Nearly 15 years ago, the American Evaluation Association (AEA) began to develop a statement on cultural competence in evaluation. After six years of work, in 2011, AEA released the statement, emphasizing the importance of diversity and cultural competence for the field of evaluation. The statement addresses the role of culture and cultural competence in evaluation, why cultural competence is imperative to quality evaluation, and describes some practices for evaluators to pursue. The statement concludes by observing that:

> "Evaluators have the power to make a difference, not only directly to program stakeholders but also indirectly to the general public. This is consistent with the Guiding Principle that obliges evaluators to consider the public interest and good in the work they do. In a diverse and complex society, cultural competence is central to making a difference."

Given the importance of conducting evaluation in a manner that respects and honors the culture and cultural practices and norms of the communities with which evaluators engage, a book in this series that addresses this topic is essential. In *Culturally Responsive Approaches to Evaluation*, Chouinard and Cram offer a deeper discussion of cultura in evaluation and reflect on how to effectively integrate culturally responsive approaches to evaluation into practice. In particular, students and practitioners who are engaged in evaluation with indigenous communities, Western contexts, or the international development context will greatly benefit from the lessons embedded in this text.

The book opens with a far-reaching and engaging introduction to culturally responsive approaches. An overview of the philosophical and historical origins of culturally responsive evaluation offers an important introduction to the subject. Then, a conceptual framework for inquiry is introduced, organized along nine dimensions of cultural practice, including epistemological, ecological, methodological, political ontological, axiological, relational, institutional and personal. For each dimension, clarifying questions to be considered during analysis and implications for methodological decisions are specified. The remainder of the book describes how culturally responsive approaches have been used in evaluations across three program contexts:

indigenous, Western and international development. Readers are introduced to 81 peer-reviewed publications. Analysis of these publications, guided by the conceptual framework shared in chapter 2, reveals essential lessons and implications for students and practitioners of evaluation. Chouinard and Cram guide readers through extant literature on culturally responsive evaluation and identify findings that will benefit evaluation students, emerging practitioners and established evaluators interested in reflecting on their professional practice.

Chouinard and Cram highlight the importance of and benefits to valuing local communities and approaches in evaluations across all three contexts. For example, in working with indigenous communities, culturally responsive evaluators prioritize relationship building so that community members can be meaningfully engaged in the evaluation from the outset. Findings from their analysis of evaluations in the international development context challenge evaluators to reflect on the tension between local knowledge and Western methodologies that may be more valued, particularly by funders.

The review of evaluations detailed in this book highlight that "...there is nowhere evaluators can go that will not require them to be culturally responsive" (p.119). This text is essential for evaluators who strive to better understand how and why honoring local contexts and cultures makes for better evaluation practice.

Alana R. Kinarsky, Christina A. Christie,
and *Marvin C. Alkin*

ACKNOWLEDGMENTS

Though the act of writing is solitary, the silences and spaces are filled with the voices of so many others whom we have met, shared, and conversed with throughout our lives that we would be remiss in not acknowledging them.

Jill would like to thank her students and colleagues at the University of North Carolina at Greensboro for their support, assistance and, above all, their inspiration. A special thank you to Jeremy Acree, for his assistance with research and for believing that this book tells an important and necessary story. And a special thank you to all of my other graduate students at the University of North Carolina at Greensboro, who have patiently listened to my theories and participated in book clubs and class sessions and late-night discussions. This book is really for all of you. I would like to acknowledge my colleagues at the university (in particular Ayesha Boyce) and those in the field of evaluation (and beyond) for setting such a high standard and providing incredible inspiration and hope that, together, we can tackle injustice and create a more equitable society for all. In particular, I would like to acknowledge Jennifer Greene, whose work inspired me to pursue a PhD in evaluation. I owe a debt of gratitude to my two graduate advisors: Martin Barlosky for believing in me and encouraging me to continue graduate work beyond my masters, and Brad Cousins for helping me find my voice and being a great friend, mentor, and colleague. I would also like to thank Doug Dollinger for his editing expertise and for helping me to think through some of my most deeply held assumptions. Most of all, I would like to acknowledge and thank my husband, Blake Walters, for always allowing me the space to write and for reminding me that the academic and creative voice are one.

Fiona would like to thank so many people that she's a little hesitant to start this paragraph for fear of leaving someone out. I owe a debt to my PhD supervisor and employer across many social science research projects, Sik Hung Ng, who encouraged me to learn research methods. With this in mind, my PhD and research experience became opportunities to practice so that I might become useful to my people. I acknowledge the support and friendship of wāhine toa (strong women) at Te Rōpū Rangahau Hauora a Eru Pōmare, University of Otago, Wellington—Papaarangi Reid, Bridget Robson, Vera Keefe, Ruruhira Rameka and others—who brought me in, got me to sit and talk about methodology, and made me feel useful. Many thanks to Auntie Sophie Keefe who guided and provoked my cultural knowledge and practice. I acknowledge Linda Tuhiwai Smith for her guidance and for encouraging me to write about methodology. I have worked with many more amazing Māori women and even occasionally amazing Māori men, as well as non-Māori allies and friends.

It has also been my joy to be drawn out of Aotearoa New Zealand by my Hawaiian elder—Morris Lai—and to meet evaluators from many places around the world. You have all nourished me, and many of you have provided friendship and great nights of entertainment and dancing (yes, I'm thinking of you, Donna Mertens). And mostly I'd like to express my love and thanks to David Wignall and Tk Price for filling me with the energy and courage to leave home.

SAGE and the authors are grateful for input from the following reviewers:

Linda Pursley, *Lesley University*

Donna Mertens, *Gallaudet University*

Tiffany J. Davis, *University of Houston*

Frances Kayona, *Saint Cloud State University*

Sebastian Galindo, *University of Florida*

Arthur E. Hernandez, *University of the Incarnate Word*

Raymond Sanchez Mayers, *Rutgers University School of Social Work*

Rodney Hopson, *University of Illinois at Urbana-Champaign*

1 INTRODUCTION

"As long as we conceptualize the issues of knowledge processes in terms of information transfer without giving sufficient attention to the creation and transformation of meaning at the point of intersection between different actors' life-worlds, and without analyzing the social interactions involved, we shall have missed the significance of knowledge itself" (Long, 1992, p. 274).

OVERALL BACKGROUND TO BOOK

Program evaluation is a systematic process of data collection and analysis designed to address issues of program improvement, measure program effectiveness and the attainment of outcomes, and serve decision-making and accountability purposes. Many of the programs we evaluate are designed to address multifaceted and often intractable sociopolitical and economic issues, referred to by many as "wicked problems" or even "super-wicked problems." Our news is dominated by such problems. Every day, we hear stories of racial inequities, perilous migrations, indigenous land protests, health and natural disasters, and ongoing religious strife. These problems are located close to home as well as further abroad and impact children, families, and communities. It is against this sociopolitical backdrop that the discussion of culturally responsive evaluation practice begins.

One of the key assumptions behind culturally responsive evaluation practice is the idea that culture is an integral part of the context of evaluation, not only in terms of the program and community context but also in terms of the methodologies and methods evaluators use in their work (SenGupta, Hopson, & Thompson-Robinson, 2004). As Hopson (2003) points out, it is important to recognize that "cultural differences are not merely surface variations in style, preference and behaviour, but fundamental differences in how people experience social life, evaluate information, decide what is true, attribute causes to social phenomena and understand their place in the world" (p. 2). The fundamental point is that contextual factors and cultural considerations include not only demographic descriptions of communities and programs but, more importantly, diversity in values and the less vocalized issues of power, racism, class, and gender that continue to shape our societies (Senese, 2005; SenGupta et al., 2004).

Although evaluators have been working in diverse communities for over 50 years, evaluations that explicitly endeavor to be more responsive to culture and cultural context are a more recent phenomenon. While we have opted to use the moniker of "culturally responsive" practice, responses to culture have also been referred to as culturally competent, culturally consistent, culturally sensitive, tribally driven, transformative, culturally anchored, indigenous, values based, multicultural or cross-cultural—to list just a few of the descriptors used. Each of these approaches has a distinct history and its own political roots, ideological rationales, and geographic foci (Hood, Hopson, & Kirkhart, 2015). The important connector between them is the recognition of, and the commitment to, evaluation that responds to people's cultural context. The field of evaluation has also grown to include a vast and diverse collection of theoretical and practical approaches designed to address the increasing complexities and challenges of program and community contexts. These approaches are grounded in philosophical and social justice commitments to equity, democracy, and—for indigenous peoples and their supporters—decolonization. They privilege the inclusion and engagement of the program community, and position culture and cultural context as key variables in the process of evaluation.

The most recent shift in terminology has been from *cultural competence* to *culturally responsive* evaluation (CRE), from a focus on the cultural *competency* of evaluators (SenGupta et al., 2004) to culturally responsive *practice*, denoting practical strategies and frameworks for evaluation (e.g., Frierson, Hood, & Hughes, 2002; Hood et al., 2015; Hopson, 2009). Culturally responsive approaches are most often rooted in a political concern for personal empowerment and societal transformation to enhance social inclusion, with attention given to the specific needs and cultural dimensions of a program's participants and their wider community (Frierson et al., 2002). As Hopson (2009) explains, "CRE is a theoretical, conceptual, and inherently political position that includes the centrality and attunedness to culture in the theory and practice of evaluation" (p. 431). Culture is therefore central to the assessment of a program's value, worth and merit (Askew, Beverly, & Jay, 2012). Along with this is the explicit recognition that culture is a methodologically and epistemologically relevant and vibrant construct that requires specific and focused attention within evaluation design, process, and implementation (Chouinard & Hopson, 2016). As Hood et al., (2015) state, culturally responsive approaches unequivocally recognize that "culturally defined values and beliefs lie at the heart of any evaluative effort" (p. 284).

In this book, we adopt the term *culturally responsive approaches* as it captures the intent of strategies and frameworks to ensure the centrality and inclusion of culture in evaluation theory and practice. Our research *on* culturally responsive approaches to evaluation, as well as our work as practitioners working in diverse communities with and among, and most importantly *for,* culturally and historically marginalized populations, provides the motivation to explore the myriad ways in which culture informs and influences the evaluation context, both at home and across the globe. Whether the focus is on an after-school program with local teens in Chicago, a smoking cessation program in a remote First Nations community in Canada, a health initiative in Appalachia, or a needs assessment involving Cambodian women in Southeast Asia, culture is central. We argue that every evaluation context is a cultural context; there is no place where evaluation is culture-free, although there are places where culture goes unnamed (see below, Philosophical Legacy and Roots). While the spotlight on cultural responsiveness has revealed gaps in evaluation practice for poor, minority, and marginalized peoples, we need to consider how cultural responsiveness can be explicitly recognized so that everyone's worldview is treated as a product of their cultural embeddedness. As we cannot explore every cultural context, our goal in this book is to critically explore culturally responsive approaches to evaluation across three culturally distinct program contexts (indigenous, Western, and international development), with a specific focus on areas of commonality, difference, and "dynamic dissonance."

The purpose of this first chapter is to introduce culturally responsive responses to evaluation. We then turn to describe its historical background. Following this, we delve into social inquiry as a social and cultural product, including a description of the philosophical roots of culturally responsive approaches to evaluation. While historical and philosophical backgrounds intersect in intricate and evolving ways, for simplicity and clarity, we discuss them separately. We then examine how critical geography can inform and enrich our understanding of culturally responsive approaches to evaluation. The third and final section presents our fivefold purpose for writing this book, followed by an overview of the remaining chapters contained within this volume.

History of Culturally Responsive Evaluation[1]

We can trace the beginning of cultural responsiveness to a small group of African American researchers and evaluators who, from the 1930s to the 1950s, adopted evaluation methods and approaches that were responsive and sensitive to African American experiences during racial segregation (Hood, 2009; Hood & Hopson, 2008). The "Nobody Knows My Name" Project, spearheaded by Stafford Hood and Rodney Hopson, honors the legacy of these African American contributors to culturally and socially responsive educational research and evaluation. These courageous pioneers, working during the pre–*Brown* era, were motivated by an unfaltering belief in democracy, equity, equality, and justice and argued for the need to expand evaluative thinking beyond simple technical considerations. Their work foreshadowed the later work of Robert Stake, Barry MacDonald, Egon Guba and Yvonna Lincoln (Hood & Hopson, 2008).

---

[1] As a side note, we acknowledge the impossibility of doing justice to all of the many influences in our field and acknowledge that history is narrated from one or another perspective. All historical translation is, at best, partial. While we attempt to convey the breadth of our field, we were not yet born when these issues were being discussed, though we do recognize being present is no guarantee of historical accuracy. Our narration is not an indicator of "the way it was" but an invitation to an ongoing conversation that seeks to build linkages and connections, both with our past and with the many voices and perspectives across the globe.

In the mid-1960s, Robert Stake was signaling the need for education evaluators to pay close attention to individual differences among students and background conditions, to search for relationships among variables, and to include perspectives other than their own. In "The Countenance of Education Evaluation," Stake (1967) writes, "My attempt here is to introduce a conceptualization of evaluation oriented to the complex and dynamic nature of education, one which gives proper attention to the diverse purposes and judgments of the practitioner" (p. 524). As Stake (1975) describes almost a decade later, we need to develop "a reporting procedure for facilitating vicarious experience. We need to portray complexity. We need to convey holistic impression, the mood, even the mystery of the experience" (p. 23). Out of this early work came an emphasis on what Stake came to refer to as "responsive evaluation," which Hood (1998) identified as one of the few approaches where cultural diversity was considered central to the evaluation. In Stake's (2004) own words,

> Being responsive means orienting to the experience of personally being there, feeling the activity, the tension, knowing the people and their values. It relies heavily on personal interpretation. It gets acquainted with the concerns of stakeholders by giving extra attention to program action, to program uniqueness, and to the cultural plurality of the people. Its design usually develops slowly, with continuing adaptation of evaluation purpose and data gathering in pace with the evaluators' becoming well acquainted with the program and its contexts. (p. 86)

Within education evaluation, they also pay tribute to the work undertaken by Gloria Ladson-Billings (1995) on culturally relevant pedagogy. She has challenged the reliance of the educational system on so-called "culturally neutral," generic pedagogical models that actively fail African American students, arguing instead for a pedagogy responsive to the unique experiences of these students. In doing so, she challenges racist assumptions of African American inferiority. Her advocacy for antiracist teacher education also has significance for evaluators entering a culturally diverse and at times complex context (Ladson-Billings, 2000).

Stake's earlier reflections on responsiveness, which emphasized a constructivist perspective, building relationships with communities, and understanding the program and community context and cultural context, along with Ladson-Billing's work on culturally relevant pedagogy, were taken up by a group of primarily African American evaluators (see Frierson et al., 2002; Hood, 1998; Hopson, 2003) (see more below).

On the other side of the Atlantic, a group of educational evaluators, led by Barry MacDonald out of the Centre for Applied Research in Education (CARE), University of East Anglia, began exploring alternative approaches to evaluation outside of the 1970s mainstream paradigm of outcomes and standards-based practices. Throughout the '70s and '80s, this group of evaluators held invited seminars at Cambridge University, where they explored "non-traditional modes of evaluation," (MacDonald & Parlett, 1973, p. 74). These modes were anthropological, naturalistic, contextualized, inclusive of a diverse range of perspectives, focused on qualitative methods, and they offered a flexible, *responsive* approach to evaluation. For MacDonald (1976) and his group, evaluation was considered a public good that should be taken out of the hands of policy makers and shared with the broader public, thus guaranteeing their "right to know" while ensuring a more democratized citizenry. As MacDonald (1976) states,

> In a society such as ours, educational power and accountability are widely dispersed, and situational diversity is a significant factor in educational action. It is also quite clear that our society contains groups and individuals who entertain different, even conflicting, notions of what constitutes educational excellence. The evaluator therefore has many audiences who will bring a variety of perspectives, concerns and values to bear upon his presentations. (p. 39)

This democratic, values-based vision of evaluation led MacDonald and colleagues (see Kushner, 2000; Simons, 2012) to explore the use of case studies as a practical means of apprehending, through observation, listening, and questioning, the project experience of participants across different institutional settings.

In 1985, Michael Quinn Patton edited a volume of *New Directions for Program Evaluation*, in which he explored the cultural dimensions of evaluation practice, as he felt that evaluators often remained unaware of the influences of culture on their practice. Patton was particularly concerned with the influence of evaluation at the global level. For Patton (1982, 1985), effective evaluation practice requires a genuine sensitivity and openness to cultural and contextual complexities to ensure what he refers to as "situational responsiveness." According to Patton (1985), "evaluators find that the anthropological concept of culture ceases to be a theoretical construct and becomes a matter of practical, first-hand experience" (p. 1). Like Stake and MacDonald before him, Patton encouraged evaluators to gain a genuine understanding of the cultural context in which they were working.

A few years later, Anne Marie Madison edited a volume of *New Directions for Program Evaluation* (1992a) titled "Minority Issues in Evaluation." She defined this as "a new direction in program evaluation in that it links methodological, moral, and ethical evaluation issues to the minorities who have the highest stake in the attainment of social policy and program goals" (p. 1). For Madison, evaluators have an ethical obligation to examine the approaches and techniques they adopt for use in racial and ethnic minority and poor communities. In other words, evaluators should seek alternative approaches better suited to the inclusion of minority populations, and they should ensure their approaches are commensurate with the principles of social justice. In her own article in that volume, Madison (1992b) identifies the need for evaluation to focus on cultural context, culturally congruent methods, the active inclusion of community members, the perspective of the evaluator, shared construction, cultural bias and the responsibility of evaluators. Madison also identifies Stake's responsive evaluation model as a culturally appropriate approach for use in minority populations.

Karen Kirkhart's presidential address at the 1994 American Evaluation Association (AEA) conference challenged attendees to explore the multicultural influences on their work as evaluators, highlighting the dynamic nature of culture and the implications of intersectionality (e.g., in terms of race, gender, class, ethnicity). In her address, Kirkhart used the concept of multicultural validity to frame and help make sense of the convergence of culture, theory, method, and practice. As Kirkhart (1995) states, "While we acknowledge the impossibility of getting outside our cultural contexts we have not come to grips with the full implications of that fact for evaluation theory, method and practice" (p. 8).

Donna Mertens used her 1998 AEA presidential address to speak about the role of evaluation in transforming society, and her time as president to lead national and international diversity initiatives. Her focus on societal transformation rather than individual empowerment has been central to her transformative paradigm for research and evaluation (e.g., Mertens, 2009, 2014). Her commitment to this paradigm arose largely out her querying of social justice and human rights when she was growing up and her subsequent culturally responsive evaluation practice with those marginalized by poverty, gender and/or disability, particularly those in the deaf community. Although now retired from Gallaudet University, Mertens continues to be in demand around the world to teach and practice transformative evaluation.

In 1998, Stafford Hood presented a paper at the Robert Stake Retirement Symposium weaving the story of the *Amistad* slave ship revolt, including the slaves' imprisonment upon landing in New York and subsequent exoneration, as a way to portray the key dimensions of responsive evaluation. His talk focused on Robert Stake's responsive evaluation and underscored the importance of "understanding," the interpretation of which is strongly influenced by the culture of stakeholders, a critical point for Hood in the evaluation of programs in culturally diverse community contexts. He also discussed the need for interviewing and observation to achieve understanding from multiple perspectives and subject positions, as well as the need to achieve cultural familiarity and knowledge of the community and of its language.

The 1990s also saw moves by indigenous peoples to mark out a territory for themselves within the field of evaluation. At the far end of the Pacific, there was sea-change in Aotearoa New Zealand. The 1989 Public Sector Finance Act introduced *outputs* and *outcomes* into bureaucratic language, while the governmental purchaser–provider split in the early 1990s opened opportunities for Māori (indigenous) nongovernmental organizations (NGOs) to deliver services and programs within communities. Linda and Graham Smith were also socializing Kaupapa Māori (by Māori, for Māori) theory and practice within the academy at this time, so a move to develop Kaupapa Māori evaluation enabled Māori NGOs to meet funder accountability requirements from within their cultural context (Cram, 2005). The culmination of the 1990s was Linda Smith's (1999, 2012) foundational book, *Decolonizing Methodologies*, in which she presented the potential of research to be culturally responsive and a tool for decolonization.

In the United States, the work of Joan LaFrance and Richard Nichols helped reframe evaluation as a culturally responsive tool for indigenous peoples. They have documented the efforts of the American Indian Higher Education Consortium

(AIHEC)—a consortium of 34 American Indian colleges and universities—to consult, research and then develop an "Indigenous Evaluation Framework" (LaFrance & Nichols, 2009). The purpose of this work is to support indigenous student achievement in science, technology, engineering, and mathematics (STEM). Community and tribal sovereignty are core principles in this framework, touching on indigenous knowledge creation, the importance of place, the centrality of community and family, personal sovereignty, and tribal sovereignty. Their work also documented the researchers and writers who preceded them into Indian Country, and whose work informed the development of the framework (LaFrance, 2004; LaFrance & Nichols, 2010).

Much like the work of Hood and Hopson, LaFrance and Nichols' work has been pivotal to ensuring that the work of their evaluation elders is not forgotten. The early 2000s also saw *hui* (gatherings) between Māori and Hawaiian evaluators to talk story and build both capacity and courage (Kawakami, Aton, Cram, Lai, & Porima, 2007). Māori evaluators also answered the call to share their skills with Native Alaskans, as indigenous evaluators engaged in what Chino and DeBruyn (2006) in public health have called capacity building of "Indigenous models for Indigenous communities."

In the early 2000s, the AEA formed a taskforce to review the *Program Evaluation Standards* (of the Joint Committee) from a culturally competent standpoint. After significant input, recommendations were approved for future revisions to the *Program Evaluation Standards* (American Evaluation Association, Diversity Committee, 2004). In 2011, the final draft of the *Statement on Cultural Competency* (AEA, 2011) was approved by the AEA membership, culminating work that had been initiated in 1999 by the American Evaluation Association and the W. K. Kellogg Foundation. The *Statement* is comprehensive in its treatment of culture and the need for cultural competence in evaluation, referring to it as an "ethical imperative" tied to the validity of our work and findings, and acknowledging the dynamics of power, the complexity of cultural identity, the need for self-knowledge and understanding, and the biases inherent in language. As the *Statement* reads, "Cultural competence in evaluation theory and practice is critical for the profession and for the greater good of society."

Recent work on culturally responsive evaluation has focused on translating the theoretical principles of cultural responsiveness to practice (see Frierson et al., 2002; Frierson, Hood, Hughes, & Thomas, 2010; Hood et al., 2015), with additional online sources and in-person workshops offering guidance to help evaluators navigate the challenges of addressing culture and cultural context in their evaluation practice (see Appendices). The focus on practice locates cultural responsiveness at nine identified phases of an evaluation, from initial preparation and engagement of stakeholders all the way through to disseminating and using the results (see Figure 1.1 below).

Consideration is given to ensuring that the composition of the evaluation team is representative of the community, that team members have self-awareness and a deep understanding of the program's context and the cultural context of the community, that there is an acknowledgment of differences in power and status and a stress on collaborative approach to evaluation, and that evaluation instruments are culturally appropriate.

FIGURE 1.1 ■ Culturally Responsive Evaluation Framework

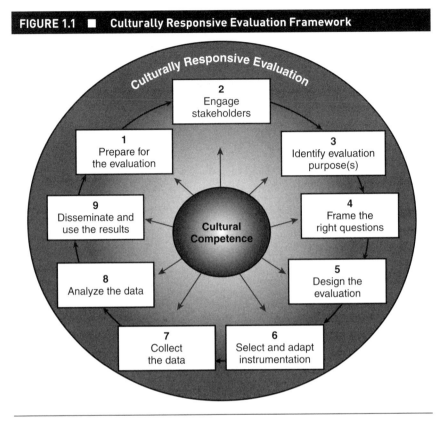

Source: Frierson et al. (2002), Hood et al. (2015).

The practice of culturally responsive indigenous evaluation (CRIE) has emerged to align itself with culturally responsive evaluation. The practice components of CRE (Figure 1.1 above) have been aligned with the Mohican/Lunappe medicine wheel, and the practices interrogated for their cultural responsiveness in Indian Country and other indigenous evaluation contexts. This process was informed by other indigenous theories, including Tribal Critical Race Theory (Brayboy, 2005; Writer, 2008), Decolonization Theory (Smith, 2012), and Kaupapa Māori Theory (Cram, Kennedy, Paipa, Pipi, & Wehipeihana, 2016). The Eastern Door, where evaluators enter a community, is where trust relationships are built. Evaluators must follow cultural protocols for first encounters and seek to codesign the evaluation from the start. Tribal sovereignty must be recognized and the needs, priorities, and aspirations of local people explored. The Southern Door is where theories of change are built and responsive methods selected to investigate these changes. The Western Door is about potential and perseverance, and is where evaluators gather and analyse credible evidence with a strength-based lens to understand success and the structural barriers to it. The Northern Door is about understanding lessons and seeking new beginnings. Here evaluators involve the community in reflection, reporting, and dissemination, as well as in strengthening community capacity for advocacy (also see Bowman, 2018; Bowman & Dodge-Francis, 2018). It is important to note that while the transformative goal of indigenous evaluation, namely decolonization, is often aligned with social justice and equity, it can also be in sharp relief as agendas collide (see Cram & Mertens, 2016).

Prior research (e.g., Chouinard & Cousins, 2007, 2009) has also identified central themes that capture strategies, consequences, and organizing conditions and influences across culturally responsive evaluation contexts: the use of collaborative approaches, the development of culturally specific measures to ensure validity of instrumentation, the emergent conceptualizations of culture from emic definitions to broader considerations, the focus on evaluator and stakeholder relationships, consideration given to the evaluator perspective and role, the identification of a "cultural translator" to help facilitate cultural understanding, and the challenges adapting methods and instruments to the cultural context. Overarching these themes and the practices they encompass are the lesson from those African American evaluators in the first half of the 20th century, namely, the necessity of building authentic relationships to gain insight into the lives and cultural contexts of those with whom we are undertaking an evaluation. Frierson, Hood, and Hughes (2010) go a step further to argue that someone on an evaluation team should have a "shared lived experience with the stakeholders" (p. 84), an essential step for those collecting and analyzing evaluative data.

These themes together capture the dynamic range and multifarious manifestations of culture in culturally responsive evaluation practice as featured in these earlier studies. Chapters 4, 5, and 6 together expand our understanding of this earlier work, helping broaden our knowledge of what it means to conduct culturally responsive approaches across three distinct cultural contexts (indigenous, Western, and international development).

SOCIAL INQUIRY AS A CULTURAL PRODUCT

Philosophical Legacy and Roots

Despite the fact that evaluators have been working in culturally diverse communities for many years, the recognition that social inquiry is a historically, culturally, economically, and politically mediated construction is more recent. Taking up Ladson-Billings' (2000) invitation to acknowledge the epistemological ground upon which we stand and to interrogate the "truths" our epistemology illuminates and the "truths" it occludes, we turn to an exploration of the myriad intersections between culture and applied research in the social sciences.

C. Wright Mills (1959) talks about the "sociological imagination" as a reminder that biography, history, and society are intertwined; not only are our personal biographies and stories shaped by broader historical and cultural forces, but, more importantly, so too are the social sciences a product of human cultural history. The imagination required is a critical understanding that methodological practices are historical and cultural artifacts. The West's storehouse of organized, classified, and arranged knowledge (Smith, 1999, 2012) is what Foucault (1972) has referred to as a "cultural archive." This cultural archive reflects the recognized and acknowledged past, histories, and biographies and reflects the stories, accepted translations of the past, and normalized "rules of " (Foucault, 1972), and as such, it often remains unexamined, and taken for granted; we use it to reflect and look at ourselves. The philosopher Roland Barthes coined the term *ex-nomination* to refer to the anonymity of economic (and other) determinants of a society. Through ex-nomination, dominant groups remain invisible and benefit undisturbed from the unequal distribution of goods (e.g., wealth) and services (e.g., education) in our societies. To put this more bluntly, "whiteness is constructed as natural, innocent and omnipresent" (Spencer, 2006, p. 16), while other groups fall short by comparison as they are nonnatural, noninnocent and are subsequently forced to the margins of society. To disrupt this traditional understanding, and thereby the status quo, we need to be as W. E. B. Du Bois (1920) when he wrote about the souls of White Folk: "Of them I am singularly clairvoyant. I see in and through them" (p. 184).

Otherwise, the universality of research concepts and methodologies, and the thinking emerging from those in privileged cultural positions will remain unchallenged and unnamed. Lifting this "invisible veil" (Katz, as cited in Sue & Sue, 1999), will shine a light on social science methodologies and processes as socially constructed and, in fact, highly contestable and contested. We need to fine-tune our "sociological imagination," that is, our awareness of how our personal experiences connect and relate to the society we live in and to the stories we create (Mills, 1959). We will then be able to think beyond our personal and cultural history and, in the words of Maxine Greene (1994), to "become awake to the process of our own sense making" (p. 440).

The social sciences, long-considered neutral, objective, and unbiased, are born out of a racialized history that underrepresents, misrepresents, distorts, and ignores the diversity of cultural perspectives, geographies and histories of so many of the world's non-white and non-male gendered population. According to Smith (1999), Westernized research methods "are underpinned by a cultural system of classification and representation, by views about human nature, human morality and virtue, by conceptions of space and time, by conceptions about gender and race" (Smith, 1999, p. 44), all of which serves to potentially misrepresent (and underrepresent) the very communities that we seek to understand and work with. Scheurich and Young (1997) refer to this as "civilizational racism," a level of racism that contains our deepest and most profound assumptions about the nature of the world, about reality, and about what counts as valid knowledge. This form of racism is unconscious and perceived as normative or natural, resulting in the erroneous belief that our more dominant paradigms are somehow outside of history and, therefore, not socially constructed. This form of racism is reflected in the history of the social sciences and in the privileged and dominant paradigms that continue to dominate our field. Linda Smith (1999) writes about the impact of this on Indigenous peoples:

> The ways in which scientific research is implicated in the worst excesses of colonialism remains a powerful remembered history for many of the world's colonized peoples. It is a history that still offends the deepest sense of our humanity . . . It galls us that Western researchers and intellectuals can assume to know all that is possible to know of us, on the basis of their brief encounters with us. (p. 1)

Culturally responsive approaches to evaluation bring "culture" back into our sociological and methodological theories and practice, back into our constructions of knowledge (epistemologies), our perspectives about reality (ontologies), and our considerations of ethics and values (axiologies). This is the language of paradigms that Mertens (e.g., 2009) has found so useful to describe her transformative research and evaluation inquiry and that has been taken up by indigenous researchers and others to promote discussion and debate (Meyer, 2001; Wilson, 2008). As Patton (2015) explains, a paradigm represents a worldview and a way of thinking about the world, and is therefore "deeply embedded in the socialization of adherents and practitioners . . . [it] tell[s] us what is important, legitimate, and reasonable . . . [it] is also normative, telling the practitioner what to do without the necessity of long existential or epistemological consideration" (p. 89). Scheurich and Young (1997) point out that these assumptions we hold about the world are shaped by Euro-American modernist notions that are themselves based on principles of White racial supremacy. These "racially biased ways of knowing" (Scheurich & Young, 1997, p. 4), what Gordon, Miller, and Rollock (1990) refer to as "communicentric bias" (p. 15) are thus interwoven into the fabric of our social and cultural histories. As Banks (1993) explains,

> Although many complex factors influence the knowledge that is created by an individual or group, including the actuality of what occurred, the knowledge that people create is heavily influenced by their interpretations of their experiences and their positions within particular social, economic, and political systems and structures of a society. (p. 6)

The positions, perspectives and worldviews of the many peoples whose cultural and ethnic histories remain outside of the dominant Euro-Western White, male view (what we have come to know as the Western canon) have simply been ignored, distorted, or demeaned. As Stanfield (1999) has concluded, "The social sciences and evaluation research are products of an American society with deeply racialized roots" (p. 420). This has been reinforced by a generalized forgetfulness about the evaluation work of peoples of color, including those African American scholars described above who Hopson and Hood have had to almost exhume to bring their expertise back into our field.

Foucault's (1972, 1980) notion of discourse may help elucidate and extend our discussion of what he terms *legitimized knowledge* (e.g., dominant, globalizing, and privileged) and *subjugated knowledge* (e.g., naïve, regional, and located lower on the hierarchy). For Foucault, discourses can help us make sense of the social world, in terms of how we produce knowledge, how we represent others (and ourselves), and how discourses can influence and inform our practice and our inscriptions of meaning, of what we consider dominant and more subjugated perspectives and voices. As Montgomery (2005) points out, discourses "enable and delimit fields of knowledge and consequently govern not only the truth about a field, but also what can be said, thought, and done within any field" (p. 29). As such, discourses do far more than simply structure "reality" and what is considered valid knowledge, as they actually legitimate and create it (Foucault, 1972). One of the dangers of discourse is that what is circulated as "truth" is a mere representation (Said, 1978), often reflecting the interests of dominant groups in our society.

Foucault (1980) uses the concept of genealogy to describe how dominant discourses structure reality, shape and normalize personal identities, and regulate society. As Best and Kellner (1987) point out, Foucault uses genealogy to "liberate suppressed voices and struggles in history from the dominant narratives that reduce them to silence" (p. 273). By returning more traditionally subjugated knowledge into his concept of genealogy, Foucault means to disturb and disrupt the more accepted and dominant forms of knowledge. As Foucault (1980) clarifies, "There is not one but many silences, and they are an integral part of the strategies that underlie and permeate discourses" (p. 27). Foucault's concept of genealogy thus enables a better understanding of how power and knowledge function within discourses to create unequal systems of dominance and subservience. Knowledge and knowledge construction (what we might refer to as history making) thus become, in Lather's (1991) words, "inherently culture-bound and perspectival" (p. 2), making it imperative that evaluators move beyond a mere awareness of plurality to a more enhanced understanding of the historical and systemic processes in our social histories that have brought us to this point. Culture, within this broader understanding, thus becomes thought of less as a local manifestation and more as a concept within a larger system of domination (Hall, 1996a, Hall 1996b).

Evaluation is never a neutral activity, as it is underpinned by basic assumptions about the world, about knowledge and its social construction, and includes fundamental questions about privilege, inclusion, and meaning. While we can recognize the more overt forms of racism, prejudice, and bias in our society, it is much more challenging for us to recognize implicit and covert forms of bias that underlie the theoretical and epistemological foundations of our approaches to social inquiry, what Scheurich and Young (1997) refer to as "epistemological racism." This type of racism is unconscious and perceived as normative or natural, rather than as a "historically evolved social construction" (Scheurich & Young, 2002, p. 58), resulting in the mistaken belief that our more dominant paradigms are somehow outside of history and, therefore, not socially constructed. As Stanfield (1999) reminds us, "Logics of inquiry are cultural and political constructs" (p. 33), the exploration of which requires enhanced understanding of what it means to conduct culturally responsive evaluation in diverse cultural settings.

Cultural responsiveness is an interdisciplinary approach to evaluation informed and influenced by multiple critical discourses and liberatory philosophies, defined by a *bricolage* (Denzin & Lincoln, 2000) of emergent critical representations and constructions played out within dynamic, shifting, and evolving contexts of practice. Grounded in an epistemology of complexity (Kincheloe & McLaren, 2005), culturally responsive practice sits at the intersection of critical discourses that challenge the dynamics of class, race, gender, sexuality, and issues of inequity, poverty, and diversity that define our society. Typologies have positioned culturally responsive practice as an ideologically and democratically oriented approach to evaluation (Greene, 2005), aligned with social justice (and transformative) approaches (Mertens & Wilson, 2012) and at the intersection of indigenous, critical theories and epistemologies of race, and social justice and advocacy models (Hopson, 2009). In common across all typologies is an explicitly ideological and political stance; a focus on power, privilege, democracy, and social transformation; and a belief that no knowledge (and its construction) is ever disinterested.

Our understanding of culturally responsive theory and practice is informed by indigenous epistemologies, critical theoretical approaches (e.g., postmodernism, critical geography, critical ethnography, critical race theories), postcolonialism, participatory research, feminist studies, qualitative approaches, cultural sociology, cultural studies, and anthropology, all of which provide a critical orienting lens to better situate our evaluation practice in the cultural context of the program community.

Extensions Into Geographic and Cultural Contexts

The underlying ethos, or spirit, of our work as evaluators, teachers, and researchers is a belief in, and a positioning of, culturally responsive social inquiry as a practice profoundly embedded in relationships and context. This is not news for indigenous peoples, whose world is relationships (Wilson, 2008). This includes kinship relationships with people, as well as relationships with the natural environment and the cosmos (Cram et al., 2015). Cajete (2000) writes, "People understood that all entities in nature—plants, animals, stones, trees, mountains, rivers, lakes, and a host of other living entities—embodied relationships that must be honored" (p. 86). When indigenous peoples meet, they engage in "rituals of encounter" that clear a spiritual or metaphorical space for their gathering (e.g., see Salmond, 1975). These rituals honor history, people, place, and the purpose of the gathering. In this section, we explore a similar concept of relational and contextual space.

Our focus on culture, and on issues of race, class, gender, and sexuality, is informed by a critical research tradition, where the emphasis shifts to a pluralistic and relational conception of knowledge construction, and the privileging of a multiplicity of voices and perspectives to make visible the social, cultural, and political dynamics of place, space, and history. This critical stance emphasizes the interplay and connection between relationships and context, which we conceive of as dynamically bound by "space," a concept we borrow from critical geography, as it reimagines and reanimates context in compelling and culturally dynamic ways. From this perspective, there is an almost performative quality to space (Dilley, 2002), as it is depicted as a social process (Harvey, 1973; Massey, 2005)—a "co-production" (Lefebvre, 1991; Thrift, 2003)— very much shaped by the interactions among people and by the historical process of continual construction amidst the shift and flow of meaning (Gregory, 2009). De Certeau (1984) defines space as a "practiced place" constructed by the operations that produce, orient, situate, and temporize it.

We borrow the metaphor of space (or the spatial) from critical geography as it integrates geography and sociology (Harvey, 1973), highlighting relationships between program contexts and people and communities, and helps to capture the relational and potentially "transformational dynamic" (Soja, as cited in Blake, 2002) of the evaluation process. The spatial metaphor constructively and creatively reframes our thinking about the dynamic connection between the relational and contextual, between the material and the social, in spaces and places where we create meaning in relationship with one another. Spaces are not considered neutral, unstructured places, but as sites saturated with multiple, often competing and often contested cultural, political, historical, and social narratives. As Cornwall (2004) states, spaces are "infused with existing relations of power [where] interactions within them may come to produce rather than challenge hierarchies and inequalities" (p. 82). It is precisely the connection between power, knowledge, and geography that ultimately transforms how human geography has conceptualized the idea of space (Gregory, 2009). Space is thus not defined as a static, homogenous, or empty place, but as a socially constructed process that also foregrounds space as a historical process of continual construction, a flow and a performance. As Foucault (1986) describes,

> The space in which we live, which draws us out of ourselves, in which the erosion of our lives, our time and our history occurs, the space that claws and gnaws at us, is also, in itself, a heterogeneous space. In other words, we do not live in a kind of void, inside of which we could place individuals and things. We do not live inside a void that could be colored with diverse shades of light, we live inside a set of relations that delineates sites which are irreducible to one another and absolutely not superimposable on one another. (p. 23)

In their re-animation of space, critical geographers have opened up our "geographical imagination[s]" (Harvey, 1973, p. 14), shifting our perception of space and place in our own stories and biographies, helping us reimagine our relations to others and to the spaces that surround us, helping us recognize both the transformative and everyday potential and meaning of space as a practiced, historicized place. Critical geographers have thus moved from asking "what is space?" to "how is it that human practices create and make use of distinctive conceptualizations of space?" (Harvey, 1973).

In culturally responsive practice in evaluation, the concept of space enables a reframing of context as a more expansive, dynamic, political, interconnected, spiritual, fluid, emergent, ethical, and performative place, a "produced" place (Lefebvre, 1991), always in the process of becoming (Crang & Thrift, 2000), of the "near and far, of the side-by-side, of the dispersed" (Foucault, 1986). Within this shifting space, relations are understood as "embedded practices" (Massey, 2005, p. 10), a place where the local and global are "mutually constituted" (p. 184) and etched with traces of production and its "generative past" (Lefebvre, 1991, p. 110). As Massey (2005) asks, "Where would you draw the line around the lived reality of your daily life?" (p. 184). Space thus takes on an ontological dimension, as it situates us within a fluid landscape within which we come to understand the shifting spaces that define our lives, or as Massey (2005) might say, our "stories-so-far" (p. 9). The concept of space (or the spatial) thus provides a theoretical framing in which to position our understanding of the relational, ecological, and cultural dimensions of evaluation practice across Western, indigenous, and international geographic and social locations.

THIS BOOK

Purpose of This Book

Our purpose in writing this book is fivefold.

First, we live in a dynamic cultural and political period, as the social, economic, and political effects of neoliberal policies and globalization, ethnic and religious conflict, and environmental devastation continue to mount. Our epoch can be defined by a transmigration of people and ideas and a shifting of borders and walls. It is a time in which maps of our cultural, political, and geographic landscape are being redefined on an almost daily basis. As evaluators who work in communities, schools, and organizations across the globe, we cannot avoid the turbulent and unstable realities of this era. Implicit in our work as evaluators are numerous cultural and methodological assumptions concerning the purpose of evaluation, the role of evaluators, the principles of practice, the nature and limitations of the inquiry process, and ongoing disputes regarding evidentiary standards. Our book aspires to explore what it means to design and conduct culturally responsive evaluations within these shifting cultural and political contexts. We also seek to examine the role of evaluation and evaluators within the broader unstable global context.

Second, while there is now significant interest in culturally responsive approaches to evaluation, and the knowledge base is indeed growing, we still have gaps in our knowledge about how to integrate notions of cultural context into our evaluation theory and practice (SenGupta, Hopson, & Thompson-Robinson, 2004), not to mention gaps in our knowledge about how to conduct and implement culturally responsive approaches to evaluation in communities that have traditionally been underserved, underrepresented, colonized, and/or marginalized (Chouinard & Cousins, 2007; Hood et al., 2016). As the requirement for culturally responsive approaches to evaluation continues to grow across all sectors (e.g., social, health, educational, international), so too do the knowledge, skills, and resources needed to shift the concept of cultural responsiveness from theory to meaningful and engaged practice.

Third, our focus in this book is restricted to a systematic review of empirical studies across three program domains (indigenous, Western, and international development), as we agree with others (e.g., Christie, 2003; Cousins, 2004; Henry & Mark 2003; Smith, 1993) that understanding the empirical research is essential in our field, especially as it can shed light on the often elusive relationship between theory and practice. As Lather (2015) has stated, "The best theory comes out of empirical work."

Fourth, despite similarities, our prior research suggests that culturally responsive approaches to evaluation are expressed and experienced in three distinct ways in international, indigenous, and Western contexts (Hood et al., 2015). Through an analysis of the empirical literature spanning the past 17 years, we critically explore culturally responsive approaches to evaluation across these three specific domains of practice: (1) international development context[2]; (2) First Nations and Inuit contexts in Canada, American Indian/Native American contexts across the United States, and Māori contexts in New Zealand; and (3) Western contexts, including STEM, Latin American, immigrant, and other minoritized populations.

Fifth, while approaches to evaluation have evolved over the years to include approaches that are more inclusive and responsive to local contexts, methodological questions and debates about method choice continue to dominate the field, remaining one of the most persistent issues in evaluation (Smith, 2008). Despite the rich selection of methodological choices currently available, evaluators nonetheless work in a public climate where the current gold standard of program evaluation is defined as an impartial, objective, and evidence-based methodology (Chouinard, 2013; Greene, 2005). Thus, while there continues to be significant discussion and debate among evaluation scholars and practitioners about evaluation methodology and method use, evaluations that give preference to experimental and quasi-experimental designs and quantitative methods are still considered more credible and valid, and thus more likely to receive federal or international funding (Chouinard, 2016). One of our goals in this book is to highlight the multiple connections between culture and validity (American Evaluation Association, 2011) and between culture and the inferences we make in evaluation and to integrate Kirkhart's (1995) notion of "multicultural validity" into our analysis of the empirical literature across the three domains of practice. As Nelson-Barber, LaFrance, Trumbull, and Aburto (2005) have explained, "A lack of awareness for cultural differences can result in erroneous assumptions about program implementation and program outcomes. Understanding 'place' in the equation is crucial" (p. 75).

---

[2] While we recognize evaluation does take place in international settings (e.g., "made in Africa"), our focus in this book is specifically on evaluation in the international development context.

Overview of the Book

Our analysis will be based on a conceptual framework that locates culture in social inquiry along nine dimensions (epistemological, ecological, methodological, political, personal, relational, institutional, ethical, and ontological), which we use as a lens to analyze empirical studies across the three distinct cultural domains mentioned earlier. Chapter 2 provides a description of this conceptual framework, as well as a comprehensive description of culture and its many intersections with other domains of inquiry. Our goal is to provide a thorough understanding of culture to enable an appreciation of its history and use in the social sciences, and its many concomitant interconnections with our methodological practices. Chapter 3 describes our research methodology, selected sample, and approach to data analysis. We also provide a descriptive picture of the empirical studies included for analysis in our book. The main chapters of the book, Chapters 4, 5, and 6, each provide a comprehensive description and thematic analysis of the studies in each of the three identified domains of practice. A discussion follows, as do questions for further discussion. Chapter 7 is summative in design and provides a comparative analysis of culturally responsive approaches across all of the three culturally responsive domains. To enable our analysis, we use the conceptual framework described in Chapter 2 to highlight the lessons drawn from these chapters and to try to push evaluators to extend their current thinking and culturally responsive practice. Chapter 8, our final chapter, revisits some of the key themes from the earlier chapters, with questions raised for practitioners of culturally responsive practice.

2 A CONCEPTUAL FRAMEWORK FOR INQUIRY

"Key to the ancient and enduring concept of culture is the relatively modest, yet enormously consequential doctrine that if people think and feel differently about the world, they are not demented or stupid. Instead, they simply are making different assumptions and using different categories to make sense of the world they inhabit and find meaning in it" (Rosaldo, 2006, p. ix).

In this chapter, we provide a conceptual framework that locates culture in research and evaluation contexts along nine dimensions (epistemological, ecological, methodological, political, personal, relational, institutional, ontological, and axiological). This framework was originally conceptualized in earlier work (e.g., Chouinard & Cousins, 2009; Chouinard & Hopson, 2016; Chouinard & Milley, 2016) and has been recently enhanced through further re-visioning and discussion (see Cram & Mertens, 2015, 2016). Teaching culturally responsive approaches to research and evaluation alongside evaluation work in diverse communities led to the addition of clarifying questions and methodological implications for each identified dimension. Before we begin this, however, we need to explore the concept of culture: how it is understood now, and how it has been defined over time. Our conceptualization of culture[1] sets the stage for our framework, which we describe as a lens for the critical analysis of studies across geographic and cultural domains.

DEFINING CULTURE

The concept of culture has a contested history and remains the subject of much debate and discussion across academic and popular forums, in fields including anthropology, sociology, architecture, psychology, leisure studies, biology, geography, business, and the arts. Its migration and use across a diverse range of disciplines has led to a plethora of definitions, applications, critiques, and debates. As a multidimensional and fluid concept, culture can refer to a people, a nation, a way of life, beliefs and customs, organizations,

---

[1] The definition of culture used in this book is defined exclusively on the basis of race/ethnicity/indigeneity. We knowledge that definitions of culture can also include groups identified on the basis of disability, deafness, gender, or religion. As such, the book does not touch on issues of intersectionality, itself a form of critical inquiry and critical praxis (Collins & Bilge, 2016), and the recent theme of the Fifth International Center for Culturally Responsive Evaluation and Assessment (CREA) Conference in Chicago in March 2019.

art forms, and activities and can serve as a noun, adjective, or verb depending upon its context of use. According to Williams (1983), a leading cultural theorist, "Culture is one of the two or three most complicated words in the English language" (p. 87).

Etymologically, the word "culture" comes from the Latin *colere*, meaning "to the till the ground," and from the German *kultur*, meaning "agricultural development" (Baldwin, Faulkner, & Hecht, 2006). Over time, the concept of culture has evolved from its use to designate the cultivation of land and crops in the early 16th century, to a shift from plants and animals to more abstract things, such as the human mind, and to notions of "high" culture, civilization, and the arts. In 1605, Francis Bacon described culture as individual attributes of manners and knowledge (Bolaffi, Bracalenti, Braham, & Gindro, as cited in Baldwin et al., 2006). By the 1900s, the definition of culture was extended to include shared meanings, knowledge, values, morals, and customs (of people or nations) and to describe practices that produce a system of shared meanings. While these latter definitions have had the most influence on the social sciences (Bocock, 1992), the term has migrated to many different fields and, in the process, has been shaped and reshaped and continuously debated in the context of differing and conflicting social analyses (Rosaldo, 2006).

Building on the work of Kroeber and Kluckhohn, 1952 (Baldwin et al., 2006) locate over 300 definitions of culture (post-1952) that span academic disciplines and countries of origin. They have compiled and analyzed these to develop an understanding of the range of definitions, and to identify themes and relationships across definitions. They identify seven themes: (1) culture defined as a structure/pattern in terms of a system of ideas, behaviors, or symbols; (2) culture as an instrument or tool for a specific purpose; (3) culture as an ongoing process and social construction; (4) culture as a product consisting of artifacts; (5) culture as an individual or group refinement of intellect or morality; (6) culture as a function of group-based power or ideology; and (7) culture conceived as group membership in terms of place or belonging. While each theme is considered distinct, there is significant overlap between and among themes, highlighting the multifaceted, evolving, and dynamic nature of culture, and the varied lenses in which it can be understood historically and geographically as well as across disciplines. The themes draw attention to the relational nature of culture (Fischer, 2007), to the notion that cultures are passed down from one generation to the next (Guzman, 2003), that cultures are learned (Rosaldo, 1989), that they are socially constructed through historical and political processes (Rosaldo, 1989), that they are not static but dynamic (Willging, Helitzer, & Thompson, 2006), that they are related to language and to the production of knowledge (Gordon, Miller, & Rollock, 1990), and that they are implicated in the politics of power and privilege (Seidman, 2004). The notion of culture thus moves beyond a mere demographic marker to a socially, politically, and historically vibrant and embedded construct, implicating and entwining our epistemological and ontological questions in the social, political, and cultural assumptions, norms, and values that govern our society. Given its multifaceted use across such a broad range of disciples, its meaning and application remains provisional and fluid, depending upon its context of use.

To ground our understanding of culture in our work as methodologists and evaluators, and to ask the fundamental question "Why does culture matter?", we need to provide a descriptive overview of four key philosophical shifts in the concept and meaning of culture over the past 50 years. All four shifts emphasize the role of language and discourse in transmitting, shaping, and constructing culture, with a heightened concern given to the "process" of culture (Baldwin et al., 2006). The first shift, credited in large part to Clifford Geertz (1973), is interpretive, or a view of culture as semiotic, focused on the anthropological study of how people make meaning within their own cultural perspectives, languages, and contexts. As Geertz (1973) describes,

> man is an animal suspended in webs of significance he himself has spun, I take culture to be those webs, and the analysis of it to be therefore not an experimental science in search of law but an interpretive one in search of meaning. (p. 5)

A semiotic approach to culture opens the door to an understanding of these "webs of significance," a potential access to other cultural worlds as a way to somehow apprehend and "read" cultural meanings. Geertz borrows the term *thick description* from Gilbert Ryle to denote the kind of intellectual effort required to study these cultural worlds, to get beyond the limitations of our own interpretations of other people's experiences, and to develop some knowledge, although incomplete, of other people's lives. Cultural analysis, however, remains incomplete, contestable and, in the words of Geertz (1993), "marked less by a perfection of consensus than by a refinement of debate" (p. 29).

The next shift in culture is termed the *intergroup perspective* (Baldwin et al., 2006) and is focused on group membership, community, and identity. On the surface, this shift describes how people identify as members of a group, community, or nation; how groups or nations identify themselves based on membership and constructs of belonging (we can be in or out); and how membership can serve to separate and create distance between groups, members, and nations. While there are advantages to group membership and strong community, there is also evidence of people's willingness to disadvantage themselves to maintain intergroup differences and status differentials (e.g., Henry Tajfel and John Turner's work in the 1970s on social identity theory [Tajfel, 1982]). This work emerged out of the laboratory and into real life in Mick Billig's 1978 book, *Fascists: A Social Psychological View of the National Front.* In this book, Billig analyzes the ideology of the ultra–right wing political group, the National Front. He shines a light on the belief system, or culture, the National Front presents in propaganda for new recruits, while at the same time highlighting an organizational core that is strongly anti-Semitic.

Benedict Anderson's influential book *Imagined Communities* (1983) is a further reminder that these communities are social constructions that can serve to create walls and borders, to shut out historically "minoritized" populations and control immigration, and to create categories of difference that manifest based on locations of birth, religion, race, sexuality, gender, or class. The notion of "intergroup perspective" thus takes on a more vibrant, powerful, and potentially more menacing meaning today, especially in light of debates about immigration, race, religion, and ethnicity, for example, that are dominating our politics and our media.

The third shift in the concept of culture, albeit one with many epistemic implications, moves away from the anthropological definition to a "critical turn" (Baldwin et al., 2006), where the analysis of culture moves from a focus on what culture is, and where it comes from, to a critique of cultural practices (what culture does). This approach, influenced by cultural studies and critical theory, is based on a neo-Marxist analysis focused on the symbolic effects of culture, defined as a politicized construct shaped by the dynamics of power and ideology. This distinctly political shift in focus was rooted in an attempt to understand the sociology of culture, to understand why things, words, signs, or people acquire certain meanings, value, and status (and not others), and how these meanings interrelate; it is the connection between cultural meanings and social conditions that becomes salient (Seidman, 2004). Hall's (2016) story is quite illustrative here:

> An imperial country, which has destroyed hundreds of cultures around the world and negotiated its way in and through them, certainly knows what the concept is! It may have a slightly "up-country, bush helmet" sort of conception: "the native culture." But if you were a colonial administrator, you were perfectly well aware that something "cultural" was going on when, even in scorching heat, you nevertheless dressed for dinner. There is obviously something symbolic going on there! And you had to understand as well that there was a clash of cultures. After all, on the other side as it were, was some other culture which, somehow, you had managed to absorb or which you had to administer but which had its own way of life. You had to administer between two systems of law, between two ways of resolving disputes, between two kinds of marriage, et cetera. (pp. 15–16)

The notion of culture thus shifts from defining and clarifying group membership to problematizing group membership and criteria of inclusion and exclusion, and revealing the tensions, disruptions, contradictions, and treatment of those who sit at the margins and periphery of history (Baldwin et al., 2006). Our focus is precisely this shift in the conceptualization of culture, from the aesthetic to the political, to a notion of culture as a site of contestation, deeply implicated in the construction and re/production of knowledge.

A postmodern perspective, which may be considered a fourth shift, adds a key element of critique to our epistemological assumptions, to our notions of truth and the construction of meaning. As Kincheloe and McLaren (1998) explain, "The thrust [of postmodernism's] critique is aimed at deconstructing Western metanarratives of truth and the ethnocentrism implicit in the European view of history and the unilinear progress of universal reason" (p. 271). In rejecting the belief in a single, monolithic criterion of truth, postmodernism opens up the possibility of a culturally relevant approach to social inquiry that does not privilege one worldview over others, and that recognizes the contextual and localized nature of knowledge construction, thus giving priority to the inclusion of diverse voices in the field. As Bauman (1992) explains,

> The main feature ascribed to 'postmodernity' is thus the permanent and irreducible pluralism of cultures, communal traditions, ideologies, 'forms of life' or 'language games' (choice of items which are 'plural' varies with theoretical allegiance) . . . No knowledge can be assessed outside the context of the culture, tradition, language game, etc. which makes it possible and endows it with meaning. (p. 102)

The recognition of multiple, localized, and partial truths (over one universal meta-truth) thus means that no one group has a monopoly on the truth (Howe, 1994) and that knowledge (and its construction) must be understood and appraised within its own cultural and social context. Postmodernism thus moves research toward a less reductionist and more pluralistic conception, toward the recognition that knowledge can be defined only by the plurality of perspectives and the multiplicity of subject positions (Agger, 1991). As Howe (1994) points out, "The full participation of all those involved in decisions about what is going on and what should be done is the only way to determine non-oppressive, culturally pertinent truths and working, practical judgments" (p. 525). Thus, in acknowledging the multiplicity of voices, postmodernism helps to make visible the many and varied social, political, and cultural forces that guide our social inquiry methods and practices (Giroux, 2005).

Gone with postmodernism is an Enlightenment notion of identity that sees individuals as their essential selves throughout their lifetimes, with an "inner core" present within them from the time of their birth. This changed slightly when symbolic interactionists within sociology, such as G. H. Mead, posited this inner core as formed and modified in relation to, and through engagement with, the worlds they inhabited, that is, by their culture (Hall, 1996a, 1996b). This push to connect people with their outer world was extended in the postmodern subject. Individuals are seen as situated within power relations that have been defined by history, economics, and the environment. Our identity is therefore not so much in "crisis" as it is a production and a positioning that is always in process and never completed. As Hall (1996b) describes, "Identity becomes a 'moveable feast': formed and transformed continuously in relation to the ways we are represented or addressed in cultural systems which surround us" (p. 598). Our identities thus overlap and intertwine across cultural, class, gender, and racial divides and across political, economic, and social histories that are saturated with unequal status, power, and privilege. The many points of inclusion and exclusion, of being a part of and being outside, underscore the very complexity and range of identities.

As program evaluators working in diverse local and global communities, and in program contexts that are designed to address increasingly intractable social, health, economic, and environmental issues, we must ground our understanding in the culture and cultural context of the program communities in which we work. As SenGupta, Hopson, and Thompson-Robinson (2004) explain,

> Culture is an undeniably integral part of the diverse contexts of evaluation, and therefore an integral part of evaluation. Culture is present in evaluation not only in the contexts in which programs are implemented but also in the designs of these programs and the approach, stance, or methods evaluators choose to use in their work. (p. 6)

Conveyed in this description is a sense of culture that is inscribed and shaped by the evaluator, making it more generative, more grammatalogical, and less fixed conceptually (Clifford & Marcus, 1986). Culture thus takes on a relational focus, as it is situated and embedded in a far more symbolic, discursive, and political environment (Fortun, 2009). As evaluators or researchers working in the field, culture is not something that we discover or locate somewhere out there, something found, but something that we create, that essentially, we write (Clifford & Marcus, 1986).

As evaluators, our role at a very basic level involves judging the merit, worth or significance of a program or policy. Whether or not we involve program and community stakeholders in a collaborative process, our role is one of passing judgment or establishing merit or significance. On what basis to do we frame assessments? Who decides what or whom to include or exclude? How do we decide? Whose ideas and perspectives structure the design and reporting framework? Who narrates and writes the final report? As Fortun (2009) explains, writing culture "also happens in the *performance* of analysis" (p. xi). From this perspective, culture is not something that exists external to us, but something that we participate in the production and in the creation of through the work that we do. As Hood, Hopson, and Kirkhart (2016) argue, "Culturally defined values and beliefs lie at the heart of any evaluative effort" (p. 284). In other words, there are no culture-free evaluations, as culture itself remains a socially, politically, and historically vibrant and embedded construct fundamentally constitutive of the values and norms that govern society.

DIMENSIONS OF CULTURE AND CULTURAL CONTEXT

In earlier empirical research, we explored how evaluation is conceptualized and practiced within culturally diverse program contexts (see Chouinard & Cousins, 2009; Chouinard & Hopson, 2016; Chouinard & Milley, 2016). This initial research was focused on an analysis of the empirical literature, interviews with evaluation scholars and practitioners, and focus groups with community members to look at how culture is conceptualized and how it is thought to influence the program and evaluation context (Chouinard, 2010). Through this research, we identified seven interconnected dimensions of culture (epistemological, ecological, methodological, political, personal, relational, and institutional) that are implicated in evaluation and, more specifically, in the contexts in which evaluation takes place. The inclusion of indigenous peoples under the umbrella of Donna Mertens's transformative inquiry paradigm led to discussions between Cram and Mertens (2015, 2016) about the responsiveness of the transformative paradigm to the cultural context, concerns, and aspirations of indigenous peoples. One outcome of these discussions is the extension of the conceptual framework outlined here to include axiological and ontological dimensions. We consider these nine dimensions as dynamic and overlapping, interweaving throughout the evaluation and very much framed by the boundaries, positions, and possibilities within the specific program and community context.

Table 2.1 provides a conceptual framework for inquiry that further expands upon the nine dimensions of cultural practice, with guiding questions related to evaluation practice and methodological implications. We consider that these nine dimensions of practice, guiding questions, and methodological implications shed light on the contours, shapes, parameters, and dynamics of practice.

The *epistemological dimension* reflects the diverse approaches to knowledge construction and highlights the flow and co-creation of knowledge between evaluators and stakeholders and among stakeholders themselves, as well as the evaluator's role and positioning amid what are often a multiplicity of competing paradigms (e.g., constructivism, positivism, critical social theory). A key concern for evaluators is often whose voices and languages are included and whose are excluded in the encounters that take place, as the dynamics of inclusion and exclusion comprise the knowledge co-construction processes and ultimately also the evaluation outcomes. Evaluators must recognize that, historically, social science knowledge of marginalized populations has demeaned characteristics, distorted interpretations of conditions and potential, and remained limited in its capacity to inform efforts to understand and improve life chances of historically disadvantaged populations (Ladson-Billings, 2000).

The *ecological dimension* provides a conception of context that is temporal, highlighting the need for evaluators to look at the evaluation not as a fixed process in time and space, but as a set of relations connected to larger sociopolitical systems that act on and influence the local setting, and, with it, the program, in myriad ways, historically, politically, culturally, and economically. This dimension represents what Guzman (2003) might refer to as a "hierarchy of social forces" (p. 174) that interweave throughout the evaluation, calling attention to the multiple levels of influence at play in an evaluation.

The *methodological dimension* describes the range of philosophical approaches to knowledge construction and highlights the point that these methodologies, collaborative though they might be, nonetheless remain social, cultural, economic, and political constructions (Chouinard & Cousins, 2015; Hopson, 2003), and as such cannot be considered neutral. This dimension has a strong cultural dynamic in terms of methodological justifications of validity (Kirkhart, 1995, 2005) and commensurability with the local cultural community and context. We are drawn to Reagan's (1996) notion of "epistemological ethnocentrism" as a way to describe the assumptions and biases of a field, a description that underscores the point that knowledge is a contestable construct mediated by social, political, and cultural influences, all of which are involved in the process of social inquiry.

TABLE 2.1 ■ Conceptual Framework for Inquiry: Locations of Culture in Research and Evaluation

Dimensions of Cultural Practice	Key Questions Guiding Analysis	Methodological Implications
Epistemological • approaches to knowledge construction • Western versus local/indigenous paradigms • evaluator role/positionality • frames of representation and meaning	• Which forms of knowledge are privileged? • Which forms are dominant? • Which are excluded? • Whose perspectives are used in the design of the evaluation? • Whose voices and perspectives frame the analysis? Whose are excluded? • What role does the evaluator/stakeholder play in the evaluation? • To what extent is the evaluator/stakeholder engaged in the process?	• stakeholder selection (whom to include/exclude) • evaluator selection (reflective of community or not) • Reflect on your role in the setting, as it is multifaceted (educator, facilitator, conflict manager, translator, storyteller). • Understand different paradigms (e.g., positivist, constructivist) • Be aware of prevalent discourses that shape meaning, norms, and values. • Appreciate stakeholders as local experts and gatekeepers of knowledge.
Ecological • culture and contextual clarity and understanding • community history, culture, and background • broad social, historic, and economic history and influences	• What is the history of the program community? • To what extent does the history, culture, and background of the community inform the evaluation design, process and consequences? • In what ways are the community's social, historical, and economic realities taken into account?	• Determine boundaries of program community (ecological model). • Acquire knowledge of community and spend time in context. • Understand history and current influences. • Understand rules of protocol (e.g., who can speak). • Identify what is culturally salient in context and what is not (inferences); this varies among programs. • View community members as experts and keepers of local knowledge.

Dimensions of Cultural Practice	Key Questions Guiding Analysis	Methodological Implications
Methodological • range of philosophical approaches • multicultural validity/ definitions of data quality • method and instrument development • local adaptation and cultural commensurability	• To what extent are methods commensurate with/reflective of the local culture? • Do they reflect diverse needs of the population? • Who in the community participates in the evaluation? • What factors are considered in the formation of the evaluation team? • Who interprets, writes up, reports, and uses the findings? • Whose language is used/ translated in evaluation documentation? • Is validity defined in culturally appropriate ways?	• Use of collaborative approaches enhances data quality and increases validity/ trustworthiness. • Evaluative data needs to be understood in terms of community realities. • Knowledge/familiarity with community increases validity of findings. • Privileging one approach is problematic; need to consider pluralistic methods. • Develop transparent processes of inclusion. • Recognize potential cultural incommensurability of Western methodological approaches. • Need to identify culturally and contextually congruent methods and instruments within each setting. • Need to be flexible in trying things that might not seem culturally congruent. • Attend to culture and context in all formal aspects of evaluation (question development, data instruments, data collection and analysis, and reporting). • Bring up issues of race, power, inequity, diversity, and culture for dialogue in meetings, e-mails, and conversations.

(Continued)

TABLE 2.1 ■ (Continued)		
Dimensions of Cultural Practice	**Key Questions Guiding Analysis**	**Methodological Implications**
Political • power and privilege • diversity of values, worldviews, and dominant discourses • governing professional norms • conflicting policies and agendas • levels of inclusion/ exclusion	• What expressions of power can be observed in the evaluation? • Who holds power? Who doesn't? • Whose values dominate? • To what extent is the evaluation driven by external norms and standards of accountability? • How do issues of power and privilege inform the evaluation design and process? • What is the rationale for the evaluation (e.g., accountability, learning, social justice)? • Whose views are represented, by whom and how? • Whose are excluded?	• Consider connections between evaluation, values, policy, and politics. • Recognize conflicting priorities and unequal power and privilege among stakeholders, sponsors, and evaluators. • Recognize dominant knowledge systems. • Evaluate approaches promote equity, access, and social justice. • Create spaces for dialogue among and between stakeholders.
Personal • "critical"/reflexivity and self-awareness • values and personal biases • openness and learning • researcher social and cultural location and background	• Are cultural similarities/ differences observed? • To what extent are evaluators aware of their own cultural location and values? • How does their position inform their work and their understanding of context and approach? • How open are they to learning about the cultural context? • In what ways do their self-reflections and awareness inform their evaluation approach?	• Reflect on evaluator's cultural norms, personal beliefs, identity, biases, values, and privileges. • Be open to learning. • Be humble; go in with an open mind; make no assumptions. • Identify evaluator's cultural positioning.

Dimensions of Cultural Practice	Key Questions Guiding Analysis	Methodological Implications
Relational • situational identity (insider/outsider) • co-constructions of knowledge • understanding and trust • communication style or approach • time spent in community	• How much focus is given to building relationships with community members and other stakeholders? • How is knowledge framed and constructed within the evaluation process? • How much time is spent in the program community building relationships and becoming familiar with community norms, values, and customs?	• Note heterogeneity and intracultural variability within groups. • Be wary of simplistic insider/outsider dichotomies. • Invite a cultural interpreter or translator as a bridge between evaluator and community. • Need to spend time in the community to build relationships with community. • Make no assumptions about people and groups.
Institutional • policies and political agendas • evaluation purpose/ rationale • program and information needs (and balance with community) • professional norms and ideologies • time and resources • program foundations	• Which policies/political agendas guide practice? • What is the guiding rationale behind approach and evaluation purpose? • How are community and funder needs balanced/ counter-balanced? • How much time and how many resources are dedicated to project? • Are dedicated resources feasible? • Whose professional norms and ideologies guide practice? • How are these norms balanced with local practices? • How are local and external information needs balanced?	• Need to balance between what are often conflicting needs and priorities of community stakeholders and agency funders. • Seek clarity around research purpose and relevance for multiple stakeholders. • Identify specific program and community needs. • Find balance between meeting demands of evidence-based practice and meeting community needs. • Recognize length of time required to do this work. • Recognize institutional and policy, racism, and discrimination.

(Continued)

TABLE 2.1 ■ (Continued)		
Dimensions of Cultural Practice	**Key Questions Guiding Analysis**	**Methodological Implications**
Axiological • frames ethical engagement with, and treatment of, evaluation communities and stakeholders • subject to cultural interpretations, particularly in relation to collective vs. individual ethical considerations	• What ethical framing guides evaluation practice? • Is the ethical framing compatible with the cultural context? • What risks arise for the safety of evaluation participants because of the ethical framing used?	• Acquire knowledge of history, values, beliefs, and norms, etc. • Understand rules of engagement. • Strengthen relationships with stakeholders. • Share knowledge, skills, and connections. • Acknowledge and implement collective ethical structures if warranted. • Promote knowledge creation that is of benefit to the community.
Ontological • Western, Eastern, indigenous differences • frames interpretation of reality and what counts as knowledge • potential dismissal of knowledge that is outside Western understandings	• Whose reality informs the knowledge available to be inquired about in the evaluation? • What impact does what is considered real have on validity and accountability? • How is a community's reality maintained? (e.g., though language, ceremony, relationships) Is this understood and considered in the evaluation? • What is the understanding of culture and race/ethnicity?	• Acquire ontological knowledge to ensure completeness of evaluative inquiry. • Understand ontological hierarchies that marginalize some realities and privilege others. • Recognize and understand how the community's understanding of the world is expressed and maintained.

The *political dimension* takes into account the multiple connections between evaluation and politics (Cronbach, 1980; House, 1993; Weiss, 1993) and brings the focus to the politics in policy formation, both through the relationships that we develop, and through the selection of our methodological approaches. This dimension is particularly salient within diverse and complex cultural contexts, as well as in communities that have a history of exploitation, marginalization, and dependence. This dimension also takes into account the connection between evaluation and politics (Weiss, 1993), from evaluation as part of the fabric of political decision making, to the politics surrounding the multiple relationships within an evaluation. Evaluation thus enters the political realm at the level of policy, where decisions are made about which programs to evaluate and why, whether for decision-making purposes, accountability, or program improvement.

The *personal dimension* refers to evaluators' positioning within the program context, to their "critical subjectivity" (Heron & Reason, 1997) a form of self-reflection related to the values and personal biases that guide their personal and professional practice. Acknowledgment and awareness of one's culture and social location ("the ground upon which we stand") is also identified in this dimension. Symonette (2004) describes the need to cultivate multilateral self-awareness, a concept that encompasses the self as a cultural being and an understanding of the self as positioned within the dominant and privileged Western paradigm.

The *relational dimension* is attuned to relationships within the evaluation context and to the predominance of collaborative approaches and constructivist forms of knowledge construction. This dimension also highlights the need for openness and rapport, not to mention the need for immersion in the program community. This dimension is considered a complex construct in culturally responsive settings, as encounters occur across cultural, class, gender, and racial divides that are often saturated with unequal status, power, and privilege.

The *institutional dimension* brings focus to the overarching professional norms, ideologies and institutional policies and practices that inform the project and the evaluation. This dimension also provides a sense of the interplay between the community and the program funder needs, with attention given to the use of culturally appropriate methodological approaches required by funding agencies. In international contexts, the challenge is often one of insufficient time or resources to develop the kinds of relationships and understanding required to conduct evaluations in complex and diverse communities. This challenge can be further exacerbated by program funders who view evaluation as a technocratic exercise in accountability and control over community needs that value local knowledge and the inclusion of community voices and perspectives.

The *axiological dimension* is concerned with the nature of ethics within an evaluation context. (We note that axiology is also about aesthetics and religion, but leave these aside for another time.) This dimension speaks directly to the relationship space conceived of by the evaluators writing about cultural responsiveness (Chapter 1). For evaluation to be valid, genuine relationships must be forged between evaluators and stakeholders, including program participants and their communities. These relationships are then the vehicle for evaluators to gain insight into the cultural context of the evaluation. For many indigenous peoples, trusting relationships are built during face-to-face meetings, where verbal and nonverbal communication can occur. Cram and Pipi (2000, p. 14) wrote, "This form of consultation allows the people in the community to use all their senses as complementary sources of information for assessing and evaluating the advantages and disadvantages of becoming involved." These meetings are guided by protocols of engagement, exchange, and sharing that demonstrate respect for the land evaluators are on, and the cultural context they are in.

The *ontological dimension* speaks to the nature of reality as multifaceted, with evaluators needing to explore the sources and rationale for diverse versions of reality—because diversity does not mean equality (Mertens, 2014). Those with power in a society have the ability to privilege their own reality and marginalize other realities. Understanding this is key to a critical analysis of disparities and inequities. Evaluators need to interrogate how the nature of reality within a context has been shaped by internal forces, as well as by external political and power relationships (Guba & Lincoln, 2005). For example, a capitalist "economy of exploitation" favors commerce and profit over people and place. Contrasting with this, Smith (2012) and Chilisa (2012) both speak of indigenous realities being relationships—with one another, with the environment, and with the cosmos—that are maintained and strengthened through language and ceremony. This speaks to an "economy of affection" (Henry & Pene, 2001).

3 METHODOLOGY AND DESCRIPTIVE OVERVIEW OF SELECTED STUDIES

The purpose of this book is to critically explore culturally responsive approaches to evaluation across three culturally distinct program contexts, with a specific focus on areas of commonality and difference. In this chapter, we describe the studies we selected for inclusion in each of the three domains. As culturally responsive practice is still a fairly new and evolving construct, and there is a dearth of knowledge about how to integrate culture into the evaluation of social and community-based programs, our focus in this book is on providing a comprehensive analysis of the empirical literature across the three domains of practice (indigenous, Western, and international development).

In this chapter, we describe the studies we have selected for inclusion, our selection criteria, and our approach to analysis. All of the selected studies are reflective case narratives based on the authors' experiences of implementing culturally responsive evaluation, either alone or in combination with other approaches. We consider these studies empirical as they each describe the evaluation and program context in some detail, the approach used, and reflections on their experiences. Most of the studies were written by the evaluators either alone or in partnership with other stakeholders.

DESCRIPTION OF STUDIES

Selection Approach

We confined our search criteria to evaluation studies of community-based programs that considered culture a key variable of interest and that were based primarily on original empirical research, reported and written primarily as critical or reflective narratives. We considered culture a key construct in studies that included a culturally framed rationale or evaluation focus, or in those that highlighted culturally based approaches, findings, or lessons learned. The research included not only traditional social science methods (e.g., case studies, mixed method inquiry), but also reflective case narratives based on participant experiences within one or more program contexts. Reflective narratives were considered empirical insofar as they incorporated observations based on the experiences of evaluators working on specific programs and evaluations with specific populations. We also searched special edited volumes for further study samples. Given that our search criteria were limited to studies that privileged culture, we did not limit our selection to what might be termed *best practices*. As a result, our selected studies provide a broad range of experience with culturally responsive practice in what can only be described as "complex ecologies," as each author focuses on including culture in his or her evaluation design, planning, and implementation.

All of the selected studies were identified through (1) an electronic search of well-known educational and social science databases, (2) manual searches of specific peer-reviewed journals, (3) an edited volume (Estrella et al., 2000), (4) bibliographic follow-up, and (5) discussions with colleagues who have worked in culturally responsive evaluation contexts or conducted research in these domains of practice. All of the studies we located were subject to peer review and, in most cases, on a double-blind basis. Search terms or key words included *cross/cultural evaluation*, *culturally responsive evaluation*, *cultural context*, *culturally competent evaluation*, *anthropological evaluation*, and *development evaluation*. For the indigenous studies, indigenous peoples (indigenous, native, Māori, Aboriginal, First Nations, Métis, Native Hawaiian, Inuit, American Indian, Alaska Native) had to be the main focus of an evaluation study.

To augment our search of the literature, we included databases that would provide a broad selection of studies in journals related to evaluation in each of the specified domains of practice. Although our sample is likely overrepresented by North American, European, and Australasian, as well as English-language journals, we did search though international development, indigenous and health-focused databases as well. In our effort to be comprehensive, our search included the following databases: Educational Resources Information Clearinghouse (ERIC), ProQuest Central, PsychARTICLES, PubMed, Medline, PsychINFO, Social Work Abstracts, Sociological Abstracts, and Medline. We also looked through recent issues of leading evaluation journals published between 2000 and 2017:

- *American Journal of Community Psychology*
- *American Journal of Evaluation*
- *Canadian Journal of Program Evaluation*
- *Educational Evaluation and Policy Analysis*
- *Evaluation*
- *Evaluation and the Health Professions*
- *Evaluation and Program Planning*
- *Evaluation Journal of Australasia*
- *Evaluation Matters—He Take Tō Te Aromatawai*
- *Evaluation Review*
- *Journal of Multidisciplinary Evaluation*
- *New Directions for Evaluation*
- *Social Science and Medicine*
- *Studies in Educational Evaluation*

The reference lists of located articles were also scanned for other relevant papers, and follow-up was done of citations of key articles and other articles written by key authors and evaluators.

The abstracts of located articles were read, and full papers located when the abstract indicated the use of culturally responsive approaches. The primary reason for the exclusion of full papers was often the lack of an explicit description of cultural responsiveness. While we are aware of the possibility that some evaluation studies in indigenous, Western, and international development contexts may have been overlooked, we are confident that the range of evaluation practices within our final sample provides a comprehensive overview of what has been happening recently in the practice of culturally responsive approaches to evaluation, at least insofar as concerns the published and peer-reviewed literature.

Peer review was used as a quality assurance mechanism for papers to ensure that a range of evaluation methods was canvassed. This meant that evaluation studies that responded to community demands could be included (e.g., the nonrandomization of participants in a case control study, the inclusion of local indigenous methods). Articles that provide reflective case narratives have not been included in the papers reviewed but have been retained as key overviews of the field that are often well cited by authors undertaking evaluations in indigenous contexts. Evaluations that have been reported on in non-peer-reviewed journals have also been omitted.

SAMPLE CHARACTERISTICS

As noted, through our comprehensive review of the literature, we ultimately identified 81 empirical studies (32 in the indigenous context, 24 in the Western context, and 25 in the international development context), all of which involved a culturally responsive approach to evaluation published between 2000 and 2017. Thirty two of the 81 articles (40%) were published between 2000 and 2006; 21 (26%) of the articles were published between 2006 and 2011; and 28 articles (34%) were published between 2012 and 2017. The greatest decrease in published studies is in the Western context, where we note only three studies published between 2012 and 2017, down from a high of 14 studies between 2000 and 2005. Figure 3.1 depicts the total number of studies each year across all three domains of practice (indigenous, Western, international development).

Program contexts for our sample of studies ranged across a number of program fields, with health/mental health and wellness the most frequently identified (35%), followed by education (25%), community development (20%), social services (6%), agriculture/environment (6%), science/technology (2%), legal (2%) and other (2%). In the indigenous context, over 62.5% of the studies were located in the health/mental health and wellness sectors versus 17% in the Western context and 16% in international development. In the Western context, 42% of the studies were located in the education sector, with only 16% in the indigenous context and 20% in the international development context (see Figure 3.2 below).

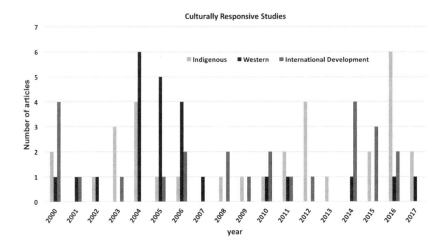

FIGURE 3.1 ■ Total Number of Studies Across Three Domains of Practice

While not all studies identified a specific evaluation or methodological approach, we were nonetheless able to identify a range of approaches (or multiple approaches) for most of the studies. The most prevalent approach across all studies was collaborative or participatory evaluation (e.g., participatory action research, democratic deliberative evaluation, or community-based participatory research), cited by 43 (53%) of the studies. Twenty-seven studies (33%) identified a culturally specific approach (e.g., culturally sensitive, anthropological, culturally valid, critical race theory, culturally competent, culturally relevant democratic inquiry, multicultural validity, indigenous methodologies, and culturally responsive evaluation). Other approaches cited included outcome mapping, Delphi method, values engaged, narrative inquiry, social justice, and phenomenological and process-oriented evaluation.

All the articles describe evaluations of a program or intervention implemented in either a single site or across multiple sites. Some articles present two evaluations to draw out lessons learned. These have been included when authors have described the evaluation methodology in detail. Papers in which the methodology was not fully described were excluded but retained for referencing in the critical discussion. Taken together, the vast majority of the studies were based on reflective case narratives grounded in the experiences of evaluators working in the field. From our reading, all but a few studies were written from the perspective of the primary evaluators, rather than from the perspective of both evaluators and program stakeholders or from the perspectives of only stakeholders themselves. As such, our understanding of the evaluation experience must be considered partial, especially given the positioning of storytelling, representation, and meaning making within culturally responsive frames (Chouinard & Cousins, 2009; Chouinard & Hopson, 2016). We acknowledge this partiality in our analysis and retelling of the stories.

FIGURE 3.2 ■ Program Contexts Across Domains of Practice

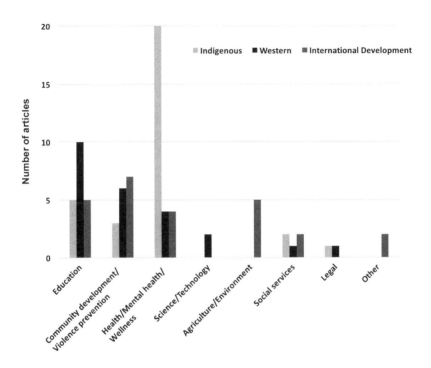

Culturally Responsive Studies

STRATEGY FOR ANALYSIS

Our reading and subsequent analysis of the empirical literature was guided by our conceptual framework for inquiry and its nine locations of culture in research and evaluation practice: epistemological, ecological, methodological, political, personal, relational, institutional, axiological, and ontological. We also used the "key questions guiding analysis" to focus our analysis on the key cultural dimensions of evaluation practice (see Table 2.1 in Chapter 2). Our reading and analysis of these studies also informed our conceptual framework, which we discuss comparatively across the three contexts in Chapter 7.

While each of the authors took the lead on the reading, summarizing, analyzing, and coding for specific domains of practice (whether indigenous, Western, or international development), each author followed the same protocol: Each study was read closely with one-page notes taken for each, all of which was subsequently summarized further for inclusion in individual tables (see Appendices A, B, and C). Given our interest in focusing our analysis on culture and implications for practice, our tables were organized by study, sample/context, approach stated/theoretical orientation, rationale, implications for practice (e.g., methods used for inclusion), and cultural considerations, implications, critiques, and connections to the framework. These summaries were read and analyzed by each author to ensure consistency in depth and coverage. They provide a relatively concise summary of each of the empirical studies included in our review and analysis.

After reading through each of the studies in our respective domains of practice, each author used the conceptual framework for inquiry as a lens in which to identify patterns, categories, and cross-cutting themes in each domain. Chapter 4 provides a thematic analysis of the indigenous context, Chapter 5 an analysis of the Western context, and Chapter 6 an analysis of the international development context. Utilizing our conceptual framework, Chapter 7 looks across each of these three chapters to provide a comparative and integrated analysis of the identified themes as a way to further our understanding of culturally responsive approaches in each domain, further our understanding about the similarities and differences across contexts, and further ground our conceptual framework in a comprehensive review and analysis of the empirical literature.

LIMITATIONS

We acknowledge at least three limitations on the articles reviewed. First, as the articles were sourced from peer reviewed academic journals, we have potentially bypassed a wealth of information on culturally responsive evaluation practice in the gray literature of evaluation reports and other, internal agency evaluation documents (e.g., proposals, plans, progress reports). Second, as we have included only English-language peer reviewed journal articles, we have potentially overlooked the culturally responsive evaluation practices described in non-English language journals. Third, and noted above, because of the way we have defined culture we may have excluded the culturally responsive evaluation practices of evaluators working in cultural contexts defined by, for example, gender, religion, (dis)ability or age, as well as how culturally responsive evaluation practices fully engage with issues of intersectionality.

4 THE INDIGENOUS CONTEXT

OVERVIEW OF CHAPTER

The question of who is indigenous seems to vex nonindigenous peoples around the world, with many authors beginning their discussions of indigenous research and evaluation with some discourse about there being no standard definition of indigenous peoples. By contrast, the International Labour Organisation (ILO) Convention No.169 takes a pragmatic approach and provides subjective and objective criteria for identifying indigenous peoples and tribal peoples (Table 4.1). The ILO also acknowledges the many other names that indigenous and tribal people are known by.

Indigenous and tribal peoples are also very clear about who they are. Their spiritual connections to place and people shape their world; they know how knowledge is

TABLE 4.1 ■ Criteria for Identifying Indigenous and Tribal Peoples

	Subjective Criteria	Objective Criteria
Indigenous peoples	Self-identification as belonging to an indigenous people	Descent is from populations who inhabited the country or geographical region at the time of conquest, colonization, or establishment of present state boundaries. They retain some or all of their own social, economic, cultural, and political institutions, irrespective of their legal status.
Tribal peoples	Self-identification as belonging to a tribal people	Their social, cultural, and economic conditions distinguish them from other sections of the national community. Their status is regulated wholly or partially by their own customs or traditions or by special laws or regulations.

Source: International Labour Organisation (2013, p. 2).

created; and they hold cultural protocols for polite and respectful engagement with one another, with the environment, and with the cosmos (Brant Castellano, 2004; Kennedy et al., 2015). Bagele Chilisa (2012), for example, talks about "indigenous practices and values on connectedness and relational ways of knowing" (p. xx). Similarly, Shawn Wilson (2008) describes the indigenous world as relationships. This may be why a nonindigenous researcher found that she was talking with an indigenous community jury about who she was and where she was from, rather than about the research she was seeking their approval to conduct in their community (Bond, Foley, & Askew, 2016). Many evaluators in indigenous contexts will also find that the assessment of their integrity is a community's priority, with the nature of their evaluation work in the community being secondary. Just as indigenous people know themselves, they also seek to know others.

Surprisingly, perhaps, there are many recent evaluations with indigenous peoples that give only the briefest nod to cultural context (e.g., evaluations of some health navigator initiatives) (Browne, Thorpe, Tunny, Adams, & Palermo, 2013; Schmidt, Campbell, & McDermott, 2016). Many evaluators talk little about being responsive and even less about if and how they are well placed to respond to the indigenous context they are working in. In this chapter, we bypass the minefield of trying to authenticate who and who is not indigenous and sidestep second-guessing whether evaluators might have been culturally responsive behind the scenes when they do not write about it in their published work. Instead, we examine formal evaluations in which the evaluators have explicitly exhibited cultural responsiveness.

We confined our search for culturally responsive evaluation to four developed countries—United States, Canada, Australia, and New Zealand. This recognizes the similarities these countries have in being colonized by the British, who brought disease, warfare, an alien and aggressive religion, family disintegration, and the stealing of land—among other strategies—to disrupt indigenous people's connection with their faith, with their traditional territories, and with one another (Brant Castellano, 2004). LaFrance (2004, p. 39) refers to "outsider populations" who have claimed indigenous homelands as their own, new home. The restriction of this chapter to these four countries should not be taken as any indication of there being little need for culturally responsive evaluation approaches in indigenous and tribal contexts in the remainder of the world or that other indigenous and tribal homelands have been more or less colonized. Some of the learnings described in this chapter may be helpful in these other territories. In addition, Chapter 6 of this volume, on culturally responsive evaluation in the international development context, includes indigenous contexts in these other places.

Before going into the lessons and implications that these studies hold for culturally responsive indigenous evaluation, the first part of this chapter will provide case examples, followed by an overview of our sample of 31 studies.

CASE EXAMPLE 1: The "Community Indian Resources for Community and Law Enforcement" (CIRCLE) Project and its evaluation have been guided by Lakota methodologies. The CIRCLE project, funded by U.S. Department of Justice, reflects the commitment of the Oglala Lakota people on the Pine Ridge Reservation to overcoming colonial oppression through the reinvigoration and practice of Lakota ways and spiritual laws. Tribal justice planners were initially incentivized to connect and coordinate otherwise disjointed elements of their justice system (e.g., police, courts) in order to improve responsiveness to crime and social issues. Then, when local ownership of the CIRCLE Project was facilitated by the project coordinator, people began to see the possibilities of the project to rebuild justice institutions to reflect community culture and respond to community needs. This was seen as a pathway to improving the administration of criminal justice in communities and supporting nation building. *Nation building* is defined as "the process of promoting Indian self-determination, self-governance, and sovereignty—and, ultimately, of improving tribal citizens' social and economic situations of governance" (Robertson, Jorgensen, & Garrow, 2004, p. 500). The project partners described this goal as "raising the tipi," a phrase laden with cultural meaning and teachings about the importance of family responsibility and tribal duty. The evaluators, in turn, wanted to ensure that their federally mandated evaluation of the CIRCLE Project was useful to the Oglala people. Their use of participatory action research and empowerment evaluation enabled them to align their evaluation with Lakota approaches to research and evaluation and to support nation building. The evaluators partnered with Oglala Lakota College to fund local researchers who were in the "driver's seat" for the design and implementation of the quantitative evaluation, with a shared aim of transforming the justice system through the sharing and use of evaluation findings. As the authors write, "The upending of a typical externally driven process opens up a space for 'a critical and spiritual form of research'" (Smith, 1997, p. 173) and for the recovery of Indigenous processes of research" (Robertson et al., 2004, p. 520).

CASE EXAMPLE 2: Launched in 2005, the aim of Nigawchiisuun (in Cree) or COOL (Challenging Our Own Limits) was to cater to the needs of parents in the Cree nation of Wemindji, Quebec, for an after-school care program and also increase student retention rates in school. The program was funded by Wemindji, overseen by a community committee, and based on Cree customs, values, and traditions. This "made COOL a distinctly homegrown, autonomous, self-determined Cree program" (Jordan, Stocek, Mark, & Matches, 2009, p. 74). The participatory evaluation of COOL is indebted to the principles of participatory action research (i.e., it is non-positivist, qualitative, openly political, and engages critical theory). Central to the participatory evaluation was indigenous self-determination and self-governance of the evaluation process, alongside a commitment to the useful-ness of the evaluation results for informing people's decision making and future actions (rather than judgment making). The focus of the evaluation was therefore on outcomes that mattered to the community, aligned with processes of decolo-nization. Over the four years of evaluation, evaluators sustained an ongoing dia-logue and trust relationship with Wemindji and helped build the community's capacity for research and evaluation. The varying literacy and educational levels of the program's facilitators were accommodated through the use of primarily visual evaluation methods (e.g., photovoice), and the facilitators were trained in participatory evaluation methods. The evaluation took a "talking back" approach based on the recovery of indigenous voices and the assertion of self-determination, alongside a critical examination of indigenous people's struggle with colonization. As the authors conclude, participatory evaluation "provides a counter-hegemonic methodology that not only works against the (neo)colonialist agenda of mainstream program evaluation, but articulates with broader processes of self-determination and decolonisation being explored in Indigenous communities" (Jordan et al., 2009, p. 81).

CASE EXAMPLE 3: A Healthy Eating Healthy Action health promotion program, Project REPLACE, implemented in six communities in Aotearoa New Zealand, aimed to improve the health of Māori by fostering practices and environments that support healthy lifestyles. For example, people were encouraged to do regular exercise (replace a short drive with a walk); lose weight (replace a takeaway meal with a home-cooked one); and cut out smoking (replace a cigarette with a glass of water). In each of the six communities, a community-based Māori health agency received funding for the program and was encouraged to set its own goals and tailor the program for its local community. The role of the evaluation team was to document the program's implementation in each community and any short-term outcomes. Its Kaupapa Māori (by, for, and with Māori) evaluation required face-to-face engagement and relationship building with participating communi-ties, using methods that allowed participants and other stakeholders to report their experience of the program. Program outcomes were explored at the individual, family, community, and tribal levels. The evaluation team reciprocated people's sharing of information by sharing food with them and providing feedback about other program successes. Six community case studies were developed based on the qualitative information gathered, and common themes were identified across the six sites. Many of the activities in the communities were family based or com-munal (e.g., community gardens), and health changes made by people impacted their physical, mental, spiritual, and family health. Culturally informed initiatives were most highly valued by participants, with the consequent health changes seen as the most sustainable. As the authors write, "In the Māori communities who participated in Project REPLACE . . . success should be measured . . . by the sustained community-led changes that have incorporated Māori values and practices into health promotion activities" (Hamerton, Mercer, Riini, McPherson, & Morrison, 2012, p. 68).

DESCRIPTION OF SAMPLE

Selection

Multiple electronic databases were searched (including ProQuest Central, PsychARTICLES, PubMed, Medline) for evaluation studies in indigenous contexts. The search covered 2000 through 2017. Indigenous peoples (indigenous, native, Māori, Aboriginal, First Nations, Métis, Native Hawaiian, Inuit, American Indian, Alaska Native) had to be the main focus of an evaluation study. The initial search was followed by searches of key evaluation journals. The reference lists of located articles were also scanned for other relevant papers, and follow-up was done of citations of key articles and other articles written by key authors or evaluators.

The abstracts of located articles were read, and full papers were located when the abstract indicated potential use of culturally responsive evaluation approaches. Fifty-two full papers were then more fully reviewed and 31 retained in the final sample.[1] The reason for the exclusion of full papers was the lack of an explicit description of cultural responsiveness. While we are aware of the possibility that some evaluation studies in indigenous contexts may have been overlooked, we are confident that the range of evaluation practices within our final sample provides a representative look at what has been happening in the field of culturally responsive indigenous evaluation.

Peer review was used to ensure that a range of evaluation methods was canvassed. This meant that evaluation studies that responded to community demands could be included (e.g., the nonrandomization of participants in a case control study, the inclusion of local indigenous methods). Reflective case narratives have not been included but have been retained as key overviews of the field that are often well cited by authors undertaking evaluations in indigenous contexts. Evaluations reported on in non-peer-reviewed journals have also been omitted.

Characteristics

All the articles describe evaluations of a program or intervention implemented in an indigenous context (communities, schools, organizations), either at single or across multiple sites. Some articles present two evaluations to draw out lessons learned. These have been included when authors have described the evaluation methodology in detail. Similar papers where the methodology is not fully described were excluded but retained

---

[1] Two papers by Jordan and colleagues (Jordan, Stocek, Mark, & Matches, 2009; Jordan, Stocek, & Mark, 2013) were retained, giving a total of 32 papers, but as these two papers are identical, they are counted here as one paper.

for referencing in the critical discussion. The evaluations described were undertaken by nonindigenous and by indigenous evaluators, and often by teams involving both.

The publication of papers was spread across 2000 through 2017. No papers were found in 2001, 2007, or 2014 (see Figure 4.1). Six of the papers were published in 2016. Two papers in the final sample are from Canada, with the others spread across the United States (N = 11), Australia (N = 9), and New Zealand (N = 9).

Target populations included Aboriginal and Torres Strait Islanders in Australia; Native Americans, Alaska Natives, and Native Hawaiians in the United States; Māori in New Zealand; and Aboriginal and First Nations in Canada. The domains include interventions focused on smoking, drug, or alcohol use; health lifestyles (including substance abuse prevention, diabetes prevention, healthy eating, gardening, exercising); after-school care, safety, and well-being (including family wellness); primary care (including training and deployment of lay health advisors); mental health; educational achievement; and justice. The age ranges targeted by interventions were from preschoolers through to adults. There were no interventions focused on elderly indigenous peoples, although elderly participants were actively included in community-based interventions.

The cultural responsiveness of the evaluations described in the articles ranges from the employment of local people as interviewers to the use of indigenous evaluators in close collaboration with indigenous communities. Most articles described working in participatory or collaborative ways with indigenous peoples. The issues addressed by initiatives were at times seen by the evaluators as isolated within a cultural context. So issues such as binge-drinking among young people (Jainullabudeen, et al., 2015), cervical screening (Watts, Christopher, Streitz, & McCormick, 2005), community development (Letiecq & Bailey, 2004), diabetes (Potvin, Cargo, McComber, Delormier, & Macaulay, 2003; Willging, Helitzer, & Thompson, 2006), obesity (Boulton & Kingi, 2011), substance abuse (Chong, Hassin, Young, & Joe, 2011), teen dating violence (Richmond, Peterson, & Betts, 2008), and values education and educational

FIGURE 4.1 ■ Number of Articles Published by Year, 2000–2017

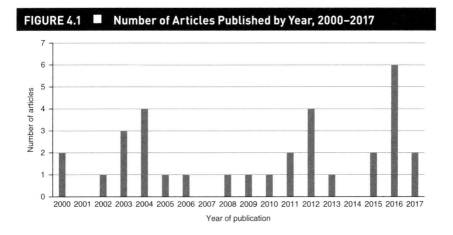

underachievement (Mackey, 2012) were seen as "the problem," with little or no unpackaging of why these issues are prevalent among indigenous peoples. Other evaluators linked issues to histories of colonization, racism, and marginalization and contextualized the programs being evaluated as part of community development, nation building and tribal sustainability, and self-determination.

At least one rejected article thanked the indigenous peoples in the community for their help with the design of the evaluation methodology, but this process was not described in the article (Tsey & Every, 2000). The rejection of articles should not be taken as a sign that the evaluators did not use culturally responsive evaluation approaches, but rather that they did not describe them in their reporting of their evaluation. Another rejected article fully described their engagement with the indigenous community in which they were working but focused on what this meant for program delivery and students' final course assessments and did not describe the program evaluation in spite of a promising abstract (Woodley, Fagan, & Marshall, 2014). There may also be culturally responsive evaluation gems from evaluators' work in indigenous communities that have not been fully described in peer-reviewed articles. Some of these gems potentially remain accessible in evaluation reports, while other approaches may not be worth describing at all.

REVIEW AND INTEGRATION OF SELECTED STUDIES

Descriptive Analysis

Studies were selected because they explicitly described culturally responsive evaluation approaches to the evaluation of programs that targeted indigenous peoples. This is not to say that the approaches were always successful. A number of authors describe constraints limiting the success of their approaches. These constraints most often concerned time and resources but also included evaluator and community disposition (e.g., evaluation team disagreements, community dissent) as well as funder inflexibility.

The evaluators selected used a range of evaluation practices. While many refer to their evaluation approaches as participatory, collaborative, community driven, both-ways model, and/or empowerment—including community-based participatory research (CBPR) and tribal participatory research model (TPR)—some bypass a methodological discussion and describe their evaluations as employing qualitative (including narrative and phenomenological methods), quantitative (including pre- and postintervention measurements), or mixed methods, applied to formative, process, or outcomes evaluations. Regardless of what they called their methodology, the authors often described their rationale for culturally responsive approaches. Many expressed a commitment to being culturally appropriate, culturally competent, culturally grounded, and the like. In other words, they were cognizant of, and responsive to, the indigenous cultural context in which they worked.

Integration and Synthesis

Our reading and subsequent analysis of the empirical literature were guided by our nine locations of culture in research and evaluation practice described earlier. We also used the "key questions guiding analysis" to focus our analysis on the key cultural dimensions of evaluation practice. Our reading and analysis of these studies also informed our conceptual framework, which we discuss comparatively across our three contexts in Chapter 7. The analysis of the 31 studies is described by seven major themes: context, local programming, a kinship world, insiders and outsiders, coproduction, methodology, and accountabilities. These themes are not mutually exclusive but overlap and intertwine. Their use in this chapter will help guide readers culturally responsive evaluation in indigenous contexts. Each of the themes is explored below.

An Ecological View of Program Context

The ecology of programs within indigenous settings is often multilayered, from specific issues[2] facing people (e.g., diabetes, intimate partner violence, poverty) and how people live their lives (e.g., "living arrangements, family relationships, and constructions and enactments of [indigenous] identity" [Willging, Helitzer, & Thompson, 2006, p. 131]), to how issues play out in indigenous communities (e.g., capacity of social and community to respond), to the causal determinants of issues for indigenous peoples (e.g., education, [un]employment, housing), all the way to the macro societal context (e.g., government, legislation) of colonization and its accompanying legacy of historical trauma, mistreatment, and oppression, and the disruption of traditional family life and the transmission of traditional knowledge (Fisher & Ball, 2002; Reid & Robson, 2007; Smith, 2012; Thurman, Allen, & Deters, 2004). Jordan, Stocek, Mark, and Matches (2009, p. 74) also list here "genocide, racism, expropriation of their traditional lands, and forcible migration, as well as the kidnapping of native children and their placement in residential schools." At this macro level, indigenous contexts are still largely dominated by colonial discourses, politics, and power (Cavino, 2013).

It is incumbent upon evaluators to fully understand the ecology within which the indigenous initiative is being evaluated, so that they are capable of protecting participants' welfare and respecting their rights (Kawakami, Aton, Cram, Lai, & Porima, 2007). Otherwise evaluators are at risk of endorsing culture solely as a vehicle for individual change. Labonte (2004, p. 117) describes this as a "remedial" strategy that ignores structural barriers to social inclusion. Indigenous communities experience these remedial strategies as "imposed, alien and generally oppressive"; as perpetuating

---

[2] *Issues* is used here as most evaluations were about assessing programs designed to address indigenous peoples' issues rather than, say, supporting indigenous peoples to exploit opportunities. This reflects an overemphasis on problems and disparities versus the potential and strengths in indigenous communities, with the former possibly more likely to attract funding.

colonialism by pathologizing and individualizing the issues indigenous communities are facing (Jordan, Stocek, Mark, & Matches, 2009, p. 74). Culturally responsive evaluation approaches eschew such culturally deficit approaches whereby indigenous peoples are seen as having to change (LaFrance & Nichols, 2010). Rather, structural analyses are often undertaken with the goal of organizational or system transformation that will better support indigenous well-being and aspirations. These aspirations include scholarship that "preserves, maintains, and restores our traditions and cultural practices . . . [restores] our homelands . . . [and helps] us maintain our sovereignty and preserve our nationhood" (Crazy Bull, 1997, p. 23).

Some evaluators demonstrate awareness of these issues related to the colonization of indigenous peoples and position their evaluations within a broader self-determination or decolonization agenda (Carlson, Moewaka Barnes, & McCreanor, 2017). This agenda includes the decolonizing not only of methodology but also of indigenous lives (Cram, 2018; Smith, 2012). Similarly, Grover (2010) describes the importance of evaluators and evaluation honoring an indigenous community's goals and respecting its rights to self-determination. The lens evaluators bring to culturally responsive evaluation approaches may help them understand that the program being evaluated includes, for example, the disruption of dominant paradigms (e.g., education paradigms) (Bishop, Berryman, Wearmouth, Peter, & Clapham, 2012; Curtis, Townsend, & Airini, 2012; Santamaría, Webber, Santamaría, Dam, & Jayavant, 2016), the strengthening of nation building and self-governance (Carlson et al., 2017; Robertson et al., 2004), or revitalization of indigenous family wellness (Baker, Pipi, & Cassidy, 2015; Fisher & Ball, 2002). Indigenous knowledge may also be central to how program providers work with participants and to what they see as a program's desired outcomes (Baker et al., 2015) (see below).

When issues that affect indigenous communities play out across a complex ecology, responses to support indigenous well-being should likewise be multilayered (Hopson & Cram, 2018). Blignault, Haswell, and Jackson Pulver (2016), for example, describe the need to acknowledge the Stolen Generations of Aboriginal Australians as a determinant of young people's well-being and mental health. At the same time, they describe how responsiveness to young people's mental health issues must be addressed at the individual, cultural, and community levels. At an individual participant, family, or community level, evaluators acknowledge the entangled determinants of indigenous lives. Curtis, Townsend, and Airini (2012), for example, draw on local and international factors to describe how health workforce ethnic disparities in the health workforce are the result of "a complex mix of social, demographic, cultural, academic and financial barriers" (p. 590).

Bishop, Berryman, Wearmouth, Peter, and Clapham (2012, p. 695) describe how "a range of solutions is needed to address the ongoing issues of [Māori] educational disparities." Grey and colleagues (Grey, Putt, Baxter, & Sutton, 2016; Sutton, Baxter, Grey, & Putt, 2016) acknowledge that the policy context of protecting indigenous children and making communities safer within the Northern Territory Emergency Response in

Australia required "bundles" of initiatives, including resetting relationships between Northern Territory indigenous communities and the Australian government. Their conceptual framework (see Figure 4.2) presents a complex-systems approach to supporting the safety, health, and well-being of children. Grey and colleagues (2016) write that, "rather than examine program-specific effects, the study attempted to gather information about perceptions of changes in the social, economic and psychological factors related to safety and wellbeing of Indigenous people living in remote Northern Territory locations" (p. 17).

LaFrance and Nichols (2009) write, "Evaluation must be responsive to the history, needs, and dreams of the people participating in and being affected by the program being evaluated" (p. 9). The knowledge and perspectives evaluators have about history, colonization, intergenerational trauma, and racism, for example, influence the lens they bring to their evaluation (Grover, 2010). This lens needs to be multilayered, ecological, and sourced from the worldview of the indigenous peoples (Jones, 2008), if evaluation in indigenous contexts is to be culturally responsive.

FIGURE 4.2 ■ Conceptual Framework for the Northern Territories Emergency Response Program Logic

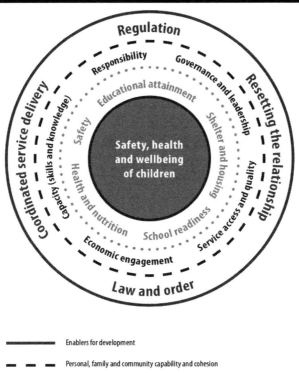

————————	Enablers for development
– – –	Personal, family and community capability and cohesion
• • • • • •	Conditions for children

Understanding the Importance of Local Programming

Evaluators need to be aware of the origins of any program they evaluate within an indigenous context, asking whether or not the program is informed by evidence of what works for indigenous peoples (Kirkhart, 2005). It is not unusual for "solutions" to be sought to indigenous "problems" by nonindigenous peoples (Janke, 1998) or, as Letiecq and Bailey (2004, p. 346) write, for programs in indigenous communities to be designed using "university-down" processes, rather than indigenous "community-up" engagement, traditions, and innovative thinking. This is especially likely when program funders restrict funding to "evidence-based" programs, since these programs have invariably been developed and evaluated within nonindigenous contexts. In the face of these funder understandings of the problems faced by indigenous communities, it is not unusual for indigenous peoples to have a completely different understanding of what their "problems" and opportunities are and of how they might be supported and helped using cultural and traditional approaches (LaFrance, 2004; Potvin et al., 2003; Smith, 2012).

> In keeping with the rhetoric of citizen participation (individuals and organisations) and capacity building, programmes can no longer be applied as universal technical solutions to local problems without being transformed by the context. (Potvin et al., 2003, p. 1296)

There is a growing body of evidence about what contributes to the success of programs in indigenous contexts that communities and evaluators can call upon to inform program development and program evaluation   (see, e.g., Noe, Fleming, & Manson, 2003; Williams & Cram, 2012). Evaluators have found that indigenous communities are committed to finding local, indigenous, self-determined solutions to meet their needs, priorities, and aspirations (e.g., Berends & Roberts, 2003; Bishop et al., 2012; Blignault, Haswell, & Jackson Pulver, 2016; Boulton & Kingi, 2011; Rowley et al., 2000). Local, in the context of indigenous programs, means that solutions are tailored for a particular community so that any particular program can fit only the community that developed it (Hamerton, Mercer, Riini, McPherson, & Morrison, 2012; Thurman et al. 2004). Fisher and Ball (2002) stress the need for even pan-tribal programs to be re-made for local indigenous contexts so that they are "based on the values and traditions of the participating tribe, thus articulating the tribe's vision" (p. 238) for its members. This vision looks inwards and touches the tribe's own development (LaFrance, 2004). There are no "generic" programs for indigenous peoples because of their intense kinship connection to the land and their sense of place (Cajete, 2000).

The meaning of *local* is reinforced by Chong, Hassin, Young, and Joe (2011), who report that a tribal substance abuse prevention and intervention program was operating differently in the two tribal communities and call for meaningful evaluations to be funded and supported in tribal contexts. A key source of the differences they noted was the stakeholders involved in each community. Similarly, Letiecq and Bailey (2004) describe how each of the 11 tribes in their state is unique, "which should exclude evaluators from aggregating data on tribal nations or generalizing from one nation to another" (p. 343). This emphasizes the performative nature of indigenous knowledge, with the knowledge gained being local and contextual knowledge, rather than universal knowledge (Turnbull, 2000). Such contextual knowledge is related to the development and growth of its community of origin and the dismantling of local systems of oppression (Carlson et al., 2017; Richmond et al., 2008).

This is not to say that the development of culturally responsive programs is necessarily straightforward, even for those used to living in indigenous communities. Difficulties arise in making existing programs culturally responsive as well as in developing new culturally responsive programs (Willging et al., 2006). Like evaluation, program development should be done in close collaboration with intended program recipients so that 'culture' does not become reified and set adrift from the day-to-day realities of people's life-world (Potvin et al., 2003; Willging et al., 2006).[3] Such an approach is described by Blignault et al., (2016). The program model comprised a community development approach based on culturally respectful ways of working with Aboriginal people and communities, involving a range of culturally appropriate early-intervention, prevention, and education initiatives driven and owned by community members and tailored to community needs.

Programs that have been developed with indigenous communities to reflect their needs, values, and aspirations make the need for culturally responsive evaluation explicit (LaFrance, 2004). Jordan and colleagues (2009, 2013), for example, write about the Cree Nation in Wemindji developing a project known as "Revitalising and Strengthening Our Traditional Philosophies and Principles Towards Building Strong Governance, Administration and Accountability Systems." The project's aim was to involve as many community members as possible in consultations about transparent, local, and culturally responsive governance. This project led to the development of core values (e.g., respect) to guide local initiatives responding to the needs of children and young people in the community. As a consequence, initiatives are "deeply connected to asserting the primacy of Cree culture within a political process of self-determination" (Jordan et al., 2009, p. 76). Robertson, Jorgensen, and Garrow (2004) agree that such initiatives are part of nation building, with evaluation providing empirical knowledge that supports this agenda.

Indigenous programs "are more likely to succeed if they are fundamentally ontological in nature" (Bishop et al., 2012, p. 696). Such programs are invariably "an integral part of an ongoing governance process that is deeply connected to asserting the primacy of [Indigenous] culture within a political process of self-determination"

---

[3] Willging, Helitzer, and Thompson (2006, p. 131) describe their program as being "built upon a biomedical model of disease risk and causation." The inclusion of their paper in this review should not be seen as an endorsement of a health model that is much criticized by indigenous peoples and does not reflect indigenous understandings of health as holistic.

(Jordan et al., 2009, p. 74). The fourth principle of the tribal participatory research model (Fisher & Ball, 2002) explicitly calls upon evaluators to pay attention to whether traditional concepts and practices have been integrated into a program (Richmond et al., 2008). Carlson, Moewaka Barnes, and McCreanor (2017) describe Kaupapa Māori evaluation "as seeking, exposing and highlighting the practiced and lived realities of Māori using Māori forms of enquiry and accountability measures and criteria" (p. 72). Similarly, Santamaíra and colleagues (2016) report in their findings that a program was "culturally situated [and] culturally appropriate" (p. 99) and had the potential to benefit the communities involved. These evaluators have acknowledged, upheld, and advocated on behalf of indigenous sovereignty and indigenous peoples' right to self-determination and liberation. Their evaluations are more valid and relevant for indigenous peoples as a result (Smith, 2006; Thurman et al. 2004). As LaFrance (2004) notes, "Evaluation can make an important contribution to developing responsive and effective programs in tribal communities" (p. 41)

The Indigenous World Is a Kinship World

The indigenous world is the spiritual kinship we have with one another, with the environment, and with the cosmos (Hart, 2007; Kennedy et al., 2015). Henry and Pene (2012) describe this world as supporting an "economy of affection" for Māori. As Chilisa points out, "the philosophical worldview of the Bantu of southern Africa is that a being is because of others. "I am we; I am because we are; we are because I am; a person is through others" (p. 276).

Culturally responsive indigenous evaluation requires evaluators to have a stake in the community with which they are working. When approaches are made in the right way and by the right people, indigenous communities can be "very keen to participate" in evaluation (Sutton et al., 2016, p. 32). Alternatively, evaluators who just swoop in and out of a community often leave it with little to gain from the evaluation experience (Robertson et al., 2004). An evaluation is an opportunity to build and strengthen connectedness, often through those who have existing relationships within the community. Connectedness is about cultivating personal as well as professional relationships and about being seen in a community (Carlson et al., 2017; Letiecq & Bailey, 2004). LaFrance (2004) describes the importance of engaging in community activities and attending special events so that community people can build relationships with evaluators that are "based on friendliness and respectful interest, rather than defined by strict roles and outside 'expertise'" (p. 48). In this way, an indigenous community can see that evaluators are building an understanding of their community.

> The value of being present—showing your face in the community, helping, touching, gifting time and presence, where people can engage with your mauri (energy) and wairua (spirit)—is more powerful than words on paper, an email communication or a phone call. (Carlson et al., 2017, p. 80)

The importance of pre-existing relationships, or taking the time to build trusting relationships with indigenous peoples, sits at the heart of many of the evaluations reviewed (e.g., Mackey, 2012; Richmond et al., 2008; Sutton et al., 2016). These relationships are foundational to the building of knowledge and to understanding of what works for a community (Carlson et al., 2017). LaFrance (2004), cited by five of the 11 North American papers in this review, described relationship building, an appreciation of tribal sovereignty, an understanding of the community, and methodological responsiveness as four priority goals for an evaluator who wants to be considered culturally competent in working with American Indian populations. By naming these aspects of a culturally responsive indigenous evaluation, LaFrance (2004) reinforces the need for evaluation teams to be willing and able to fully engage and learn from indigenous peoples. This may not always be easy, as evaluators and the community need to negotiate the nature of their collaboration as well as regularly assess their respective expectations and address differences in these (Chong et al., 2011; Potvin et al., 2003). Credibility is earned when communities experience evaluators as trustworthy, consistent, respectful, and committed to collaboration (Thurman et al., 2004). Similarly, evaluators' relationships with community stakeholders can "enhance the relevancy, ownership, and usefulness of the evaluation" (Chong et al., 2011, p. 544).

Developing relationships means acknowledging the broader contextual characteristics that impact indigenous communities. These include geography, how dispersed the population is, and the community's political organization (e.g., urban, village, reservation) (Thurman et al., 2004). Different indigenous communities have different levels of resources. Evaluators also need to be aware of happenings within indigenous communities so that they can tailor their evaluations around important events (e.g., the death of a community member, conflict, dissent, political crisis), familial and community demands, and possibly even seasonal weather that disrupts access to the community (Chong et al., 2011; Letiecq & Bailey, 2004; Sutton et al., 2016). Blignault et al., (2016, p. 55), for example, describe how they were unable to meet with participants or their parents when one of their evaluation site visits "coincided with funerals and sorry business."

Bond, Foley, and Askew's (2016) found that "not being spoken 'down to' was the basis of respectful engagement and empowering encounters" (p. S92) between themselves and indigenous community members. In order for respectful talk to happen, the researchers had to hone their translational skills and appreciate that community members would often respond to them with stories to convey indigenous experiences and lived realities.

> These were sad stories, amusing stories, and stories that had been recounted more than once. At times, the stories shared related specifically to a jury member's experience of the health research issue, while other times, the stories shared revealed the broader historical, social, cultural and political context of Indigenous health (Bond et al., 2016, p. S92).

As an evaluator who was also a member of the tribe with which she was doing evaluation, Carlson describes her use of local language and local customary practices as central to her evaluation (Carlson et al., 2017). These also come to the fore in the Māori evaluation inquiry models described by Cavino (2013). Interestingly, discussion of the role or importance of local language use within an indigenous evaluation context is largely absent from the papers included in this review. When it is mentioned, it is to acknowledge that language—as well as customs and culture—encompasses programs and their evaluation (Jordan et al., 2009). Little mention is made of evaluators' language skills—their ability to talk to indigenous peoples in their own language—or of the need for and use of interpreters in their evaluation work in indigenous contexts. In contrast, language, especially its use in protocol (e.g., prayer), is highlighted as important in LaFrance and Nichols' (2009, 2010) indigenous evaluation framework.

Hamerton and her colleagues (2012) describe their face-to-face interactions with participants as being required in order for relationships of trust to be built so that they, in turn, could "report their conceptions, responses and experiences of the programmes in a fashion appropriate to them" (p. 63). Chong et al., (2011) describe maximizing "face time" between evaluators and the community through the careful planning of site visits that had everyone's input into their agendas. This "prevented surprises, encouraged preparedness . . . and enabled a smooth and productive progression of the evaluation" (p. 530). They considered participants to be program experts who needed to be listened to respectfully. While Letiecq and Bailey (2004) also tried to have site visits as often as they could, they found that their regular trips to an indigenous community 300 miles from their university were not enough to build the professional and personal relationships they felt were needed. The evaluation team was not visible enough in the community. When communities are remote, local evaluators may stay on site and spend more time with local people who are assisting in the evaluation, eating with them, and providing fuller support and involving them in problem solving and planning (Sutton et al., 2016).

Evaluators can also bridge the gap between themselves and the indigenous community by working with local community members who have a "thorough knowledge of the community and its culture" and who can facilitate respectful engagement (Richmond et al., 2008, p. 370). It is easier to instill evaluation knowledge in such community members (Fisher & Ball, 2002) than it is to add knowledge of the "community" to evaluators (Pipi et al., 2002). The involvement of local evaluators not only supports and builds community evaluation capacity; it enables the nuances of what an indigenous community understands as "safety" to be negotiated so that sensitive (and not-so-sensitive) topics can be explored in depth (Grey et al., 2016; Letiecq & Bailey, 2004). Sensitivity can arise because the topic is deeply private to those participating in the evaluation (e.g., because of the personal, deviant, or sacred nature of the topic), or because it impinges on the vested interests of those in positions of power. Lee and Renzetti (1993) sum these up in a typology as sensitivities related to intrusion, sanction, or power. For example, the tribal community that Chong et al., (2011) were working with asked for "assurances that there would be counselors in case a topic should raise an emotional or troubled responses in a participant" (p. 531). This would represent an intrusion. The development of a shared Code of Research Ethics can also minimize "harms such as stigmatization of individuals and/or the community" (Potvin et al., 2003, p. 1299) and explicitly spell out how those negatively impacted by an evaluation experience will be cared for, how confidentiality will be ensured, and how intellectual property will be protected (Fisher & Ball, 2002). In Australia, this is done through the "principles of respect, reciprocity, responsibility, equality, survival and protection as well as spirit and integrity" that are explicitly spelled out in the code of ethics for health research with indigenous peoples (Bond et al., 2016, p. 589).

Indigenous evaluators do not take it for granted that they will be granted access to an indigenous community, even when that community is their own. Carlson, for example, described herself as both an insider and an outsider for her work in her own tribal community, maintaining that her genealogical connection with and knowledge of her people were critical to her decision to join the evaluation team (Carlson et al., 2017). Bond and her colleagues (2016) also acknowledged the multiple layers of being both insiders and outsiders to the indigenous communities they were evaluating and sought to reduce any potential bias this brought to their data collection. An age and gender mix of evaluators or local researchers may also be important in observing cultural protocols, for example, when women interview women (Sutton et al., 2016) or when young people participate in evaluating youth programs (Jainullabudeen et al., 2015). If a small community has concerns about the confidentiality of the information that will be shared, it may be necessary to bring in other, nonlocal indigenous peoples as evaluation staff (Letiecq & Bailey, 2004). These mix-and-match, insider-outsider decisions about evaluation staff may best be made in consultation with the community as it will know who is well suited to sit down with community members. In addition, all indigenous peoples involved in evaluation activities must be able to move through indigenous communities as indigenous peoples; in other words, their work for an evaluation should not compromise their relationships or standing within their communities. This could mean, for example, embedding flexibility into evaluation protocols, so they can be tailored by local evaluators (e.g., allowing subtle word changes in survey questions to reflect local meanings) (Sutton et al., 2016), or allowing time and resources for local protocols to be observed.

Lastly, in this section we will describe the importance of local engagement practices and food to relationship formation and strengthening. In many indigenous contexts, both are very important. Hamerton and colleagues (2012), for example, reciprocated participants' time and sharing during their evaluation with gifts of food. Engagement protocols may allow people to introduce themselves (e.g., who their parents are, where their home place is, which tribes they connect with) and find kinship and connections with others in a gathering (Santamaría et al., 2016). Food often plays an important role in gatherings, as part of welcoming people and demonstrating the host people's hospitality and generosity (Potvin et al., 2003; Watts et al., 2005). The sharing of food and a hot drink may also move a gathering out of a formal or sacred place to an ordinary place where evaluation business is able to be discussed (Mead, 2003). In addition to helping evaluators understand how they should respectfully engage people in indigenous contexts, this awareness may also assist them in structuring queries about participants' satisfaction with place, space (e.g., physical layout of a room), practice (e.g., prayer, offerings of tobacco), and food when they attend program gatherings (LaFrance & Nichols, 2010).

Evaluators as Both Insiders and Outsiders

The advice given to evaluators working in indigenous contexts includes a warning that they should tread carefully because of the negative experiences indigenous peoples have often had with research and evaluation that was done to or *on* them, rather than *with* and *for* them (LaFrance, 2004), and because indigenous communities have often not been listened to or received follow-up when they have identified issues of importance (Watts et al., 2005). Outsiders have also appropriated the voice of indigenous peoples—presuming to know them and to speak on their behalf (Brant Castellano, 2000). Letiecq and Bailey (2004) describe how "tribal nations have been exploited by academics who have ignored protocols, documented secret traditions without tribal permission, distorted facts, misrepresented the community, and failed to give back in meaningful ways" (p. 344). Richmond, Peterson, and Betts (2008) describe the distrust of researchers by those on Indian reservations as "common and well deserved" (p. 372), while Bond et al. (2016) describe the exploitation of Indigenous Australians by researchers and evaluators as part of Australia's "inglorious history" (p. 589).

> At worst, [health] research acted as an overt tool of colonial control espousing and enacting pseudoscientific theory and, at best, Aboriginal and Torres Strait Islander peoples, communities, aspirations and realities were ignored. (Bond et al., 2016, p. 589)

> Many times researchers exclude tribes from active involvement in the research process, make assumptions about cultural appropriateness, and do not provide active protection of tribal anonymity or confidentiality. (Richmond et al., 2008, p. 372)

> In the past much research had been conducted 'on' Māori in ways that perpetuated colonial values, and consequently misrepresented Māori understandings and ways of knowing and denied Māori ownership of their own knowledge. (Hamerton et al., 2012, p. 63)

According to Thurman, Jumper, and Deters (2004), this mistrust of evaluators and researchers also encompasses government officials and health practitioners and services, with indigenous peoples only too well aware of breaches of confidentiality, poor quality of health care, and discrimination. The rumors and innuendo these authors describe in small, tight-knit indigenous communities can also impact the credibility of evaluators and is one of the many reasons evaluators have to "be careful" when they are engaging in evaluation in these communities (Cram, 2016).

> Native people do not want to be "guinea pigs" or part of studies that focus solely on the community's problems and not their strengths or studies that do not share results with the community. (Watts et al., 2005, p. 70)

Part of taking care and being in a position to build relationships is about nonindigenous evaluators knowing where they are from and having a commitment to work in authentic ways with indigenous peoples. This is about nonindigenous evaluators developing a response to Cavino's (2013) inquiry about the conditions that support ethical evaluation practice across cultural borders. Rather than prohibit nonindigenous evaluators, Cavino interrogates whether their evaluation practice strengthens indigenous self-determination and sovereignty in contexts where indigenous peoples are unable to meet their evaluation needs themselves.

Some evaluators are very clear about their own standpoint as "outsiders" to the indigenous context in which they are working. For example, Letiecq and Bailey's (2004) purpose for writing about their evaluation is explicitly to "explore our place and perspective as 'outsider' White female researchers conducting an evaluation with American Indian families" (p. 344). These evaluators are responsive to indigenous culture and understand that indigenous people have a worldview different from a Western worldview (Chilisa, 2012). They actively strategized to build their own competence to understand the worldview of the indigenous people they were working with, so they were able to foster culturally responsive evaluation approaches (Berends & Roberts, 2003). This competence includes being able to enact formal and informal engagement and relationship protocols, respecting a community's readiness for change, and honoring self-determination within evaluation practice (Thurman et al., 2004). Evaluators can gain advice on how to be responsive through different avenues, including indigenous team members or evaluation colleagues, indigenous leaders (who act as guides or brokers for evaluators' engagement with a community), or a community-based steering group formed to support an evaluation (Letiecq & Bailey, 2004). Some evaluators are in longer-term relationships with the communities they work in, either by virtue of being related or by living or working there. These relationships may lead to invitations from community members to assist in the development of programs and in evaluation (Rowley et al., 2000).

Although a number of nonindigenous authors identified themselves as such and predicated the discussion of their evaluation on this, a number of other authors did not identify their ethnicity. Not revealing this allows important considerations to go unsaid. For example, what made the evaluator feel that he or she was the right person to be doing this evaluative work? How did the evaluator identify him or herself to the indigenous community? Did the evaluators explicitly negotiate the meaning and relevance of the ethnic/racial/cultural differences between themselves and the indigenous community? By leaving their ethnicity unstated, evaluators are implicitly reinforcing the normalcy of their "whiteness." Spencer (2006) describes how "whiteness is constructed as natural, innocent and omnipresent . . . in our common-sense reality" (p. 16). Much like the bourgeoisie that led Roland Barthes to coin the term *ex-nomination*, white people often remain anonymous because their privilege goes unnamed and unnoticed and the status quo of their society remains unchallenged (Lakoff, 2000). In this way, whiteness has become a nonideological, apolitical "normality" that does not require people to name themselves as having a race or ethnicity. This might mean, for example, examining white privilege because "whites inherit the legacy of white supremacy, from which they continue to benefit (Winant, 1997, p. 41).

> Ex-nomination is the means by which whiteness avoids being named and thus keeps itself out of the field of interrogation and therefore off the agenda for change . . . One practice of Ex-nomination is the avoidance of self-recognition and self-definition. (Fiske, 1994, p. 42).

When evaluators do not say they are indigenous, we have assumed they are nonindigenous. We have also assumed that nonindigenous evaluators "are beholden to the Indigenous laws and epistemologies of the lands" and territories in which they work (Tuck & Yang, 2012, p. 6). This underscores the necessity for evaluators to reflect upon and negotiate their insider-outsider statuses honestly with indigenous communities.

Co-Production of Evaluation Design and Implementation

Responsiveness to indigenous culture is an essential component of evaluation undertaken *with*, as opposed to *on*, indigenous peoples for the purpose of supporting transformative change in their circumstances (Cram & Mertens, 2016; Mertens, 2009). This responsiveness includes acknowledgment of indigenous peoples' right to self-determination (LaFrance, 2004; United Nations, 2007) and an accompanying shift away from Western evaluation hegemony and its disempowering implications for indigenous peoples (Sinclair, cited in Jordan et al., 2009). Linda Smith (2012) writes that indigenous peoples "constantly collide with dominant views while we're attempting to transform our lives" (p. 41). Culturally responsive evaluation with indigenous peoples moves evaluation away from a collision course as evaluators and indigenous peoples become collaborators on evaluations, generating inquiry paradigms that draw upon indigenous values, knowledge, experiences, and understandings (Jordan et al., 2009; Robertson, et al., 2004). Indigenous communities have expectations that evaluation will contribute to indigenous knowledge and to program improvement (Grover, 2010; Jordan et al., 2009, 2013), to the protection and restoration of culture (LaFrance & Nichols, 2010), to community health, to improved social and economic standing, and to sustainable development (Novins, King, & Stone, 2004; Robertson et al., 2004). It is possible to meet these expectations only if indigenous peoples are intimately involved in an evaluation. This includes the involvement of indigenous elders who are often the knowledge holders within communities (LaFrance & Nichols, 2010).

Collaboration is about co-producing "reciprocal, mutually invested and beneficial approach[es]" to evaluation in indigenous contexts (Carlson et al., 2017, p. 71). Such collaboration can be formalized through partnership agreements (e.g., memorandums of understanding), in which the values and ethics of the indigenous people involved are privileged. Or the evaluation itself may need to be approved by tribal governance structures or undergo tribal ethical review (Bond et al., 2016). The research and evaluation policy of the tribe that Carlson and colleagues (2017) worked with required projects to benefit the tribe, use methods aligned with tribal customs, involve or develop local evaluators, and engage with the community throughout the evaluation.

Consultation with a community before an evaluation begins can help clarify the evaluation's terms of reference and enable evaluators to hear the community's views, including any concerns they might have about the evaluation (e.g., Berends & Roberts, 2003; Moewaka Barnes, 2000). For example, the methodology of Chesterton's (2003) evaluation of options for indigenous children placed into care was specifically designed to be flexible enough to enable negotiation with stakeholders, including Aboriginal communities (although the funder was not necessarily open to the more ecological analysis that arose from this negotiation). Initial consultation also gives the evaluators and the community time to consider the compatibility of the evaluation with tribal governance, policies (e.g., employment of local interviewers, sharing of traditional knowledge), legal codes, and other governance aspects (Fisher & Ball, 2002). The involvement of indigenous peoples in the early stages of an evaluation should also prompt consideration of the suitability of evaluation methods and the potential of recruiting evaluation staff (e.g., interviewers) who are respected by and have relationships with the community.

Involving local evaluators brings their knowledge and expertise to evaluation design as well as to the reporting and dissemination of evaluation findings and supports evaluation credibility and validity (Chilisa, 2012; Cram, 2018). If they are not already part of the evaluation team (and even if they are), local people can be engaged as interviewers, guides, facilitators, and brokers, with the evaluation team supporting them by providing opportunities for review and professional development. Involving and working in partnership with local people provides all those involved with opportunities to share knowledge and to learn from one another (Potvin et al., 2003; Thurman et al., 2004). As Richmond et al. (2008,) stress, there should be "equal weight and respect for diverse expertise and knowledge" (p. 375), as there would be in any transdisciplinary evaluation team (Cram & Hopson, 2018). When true collaboration occurs between evaluators and indigenous peoples there are opportunities for synergies and new learnings (Santamaría et al., 2016).

Ensuring the inclusion of multiple voices means being conscientious about gender, age, sexuality, and other issues of intersectionality within a community, and working to overcome perceived or actual barriers to people's participation in and support of programs and evaluations (Willging et al., 2006). Bond et al. (2016) note that urban indigenous peoples who are often dispersed and diverse can be engaged as "community" through indigenous urban organizations and support services.

> Although no formal entities analogous to a tribal government may exist in nontribal (e.g., urban) communities, other community organizations can enter into agreement to provide oversight, to guide decisions, and to establish ground rules similar to those contained in tribal research codes. What remains is for researchers to engage with communities in ways that ensure such safeguards are established. (Fisher & Ball, 2002, p. 239)

Successfully engaging and involving indigenous peoples in evaluation supports program sustainability, as indigenous communities become adept at inclusive program design, implementation, development, and evaluation aligned with their own worldviews, traditions, and aspirations (Rowley et al., 2000).

Community ownership of an evaluation can also be facilitated by community members being involved in report drafting and codeveloping or reviewing draft recommendations (Berends & Roberts, 2003). Presenting evaluation findings back to a community can also support this, and local researchers may be well placed to do this as a report back demonstrates not only that the evaluation has taken a community's views seriously (Sutton et al., 2016) but also that the community can trust the local researcher to tell them how it all turned out (LaFrance, 2004). Feeding back evaluation findings can also happen through presentations to stakeholder groups and decision makers, and more broadly to community members through community media outlets (e.g., newspapers, radio shows, social media). Moewaka Barnes (2000) describes how this utilization focus, achieved through providing feedback to the communities that were involved, was embedded in agreement problem evaluation approach from the beginning. Using feedback loops enables evaluations to gain a sense of validity in the eyes of indigenous community members (Bond et al., 2016).

> Community stakeholders do not dispute the findings of this study and indicated, during presentation of study results, that the reported changes [in young people's drinking] are possibly true and that they had observed positive changes amongst youths. (Jainullabudeen et al., 2015, p. 6)

In addition to feedback to the community, Potvin and colleagues (2003,) report that

> community members have presented findings and organized workshops at Aboriginal health conferences. They have reviewed, and contributed to, all scientific communications, collaborated with researchers for joint presentations at scientific conferences, participated as co-investigators in research grant applications, and taken active roles in policy development meetings at national, regional, and local levels. (p. 1298)

While this was seen as a necessary dissemination schedule in order to build community capacity as well as secure both program funding and transformative outcomes, it created additional demands and challenges (Potvin et al., 2003). Taking these into account in evaluation planning and funding will help ensure that a community can participate. Rowley and colleagues (2000), for example, acknowledge the sponsorship they received for community members to travel and present their work at conferences.

Finally, in this section, co-production of evaluation by evaluators and indigenous communities means a broader network of people is engaged in evaluation work that may take unanticipated time and resources and require courage merely because stepping into and being responsive to indigenous culture and contexts is about system transformation. This is an inherently political enterprise because it involves institutions acknowledging the effects of colonization and seeking to decolonize themselves, and it is about the liberation of indigenous peoples and the societal level power-sharing that this entails. This becomes more possible if many people are mobilized to upend evaluation and try and achieve it (Robertson et al., 2004; Smith, 2012). Having said this, however, it is acknowledged that evaluation is also political because evaluations are commissioned by agencies that have the power to discontinue contracting evaluators their does not think are working for their greater good (Stake, 1998), so there may well be pressure on evaluators to "toe a party line" in which the continued colonization and oppression of indigenous peoples is the desired status quo.

A Power-Sharing Evaluation Methodology

At a roundtable discussion at the 2006 AEA Conference in Portland, OR, Kawakami, Aton, Rawlins-Crivelo, and Napeahi reminded us that methodology should support community empowerment through the collaborative design of evaluation. Their project in a Native Hawaiian community "uses methods that operate within the cultural milieu and empower the community through collaborative design of methods, data collection, analysis, and use" (Kawakami, Aton, Rawlins-Crivelo, & Napeahi, 2006, p. 3). Both Bagele Chilisa (2012) and Linda Smith (2012) write about indigenous methodologies that honor indigenous control over the whole of the research process and that actively seek out traditional methods and tools that can be used to provide insight into the lives of indigenous peoples and the initiatives that are responding to their needs and supporting their aspirations.

> Indigenous methodologies are those ones which permit and enable Indigenous researchers to be who they are while they are actively engaged as participants in the research processes. This way of being not only creates new knowledge but transforms who researchers are and where they are located. (Weber-Pillwax, cited in Hart, 2007, p.78)

At the heart of many evaluators' engagement with indigenous communities is a commitment to power sharing in order to support indigenous voices being heard in their evaluation (Letiecq & Bailey, 2004). Carlson, however, challenges the term *power sharing* and expresses her preference for the phrase "power acknowledgement and shift: I had certain powers and other stakeholders had power . . . While input may not have been equal, I hoped it was equitable" (Carlson et al., 2017, p. 91). Jordan and colleagues (2009) describe this approach as integral to participatory action research, whereby evaluators "set their expertise alongside the lay knowledge, skills and experiences of people who are the focus of their investigations" (p. 78) and share how to prevent the oppression and exploitation of indigenous peoples. This approach to power—where people come to share the power that they have within an evaluation context—helps ensure the validity of their evaluation work and the usefulness of that work to supporting indigenous well-being, self-determination, or nationhood. Improving the responsiveness of learning environments for indigenous students is an example here (Curtis et al., 2012).

> [S]tudents emphasised teaching and learning approaches that were holistic, supporting both the academic and affective, cultural and pastoral aspects of being a learner . . . [Provision of a study room] helped to remove academic barriers whilst fostering a sense of worthiness associated with students having their own space. (p. 595)

Evaluators who are committed to being culturally responsive find that participatory methodologies are good vehicles for engaging with and working alongside indigenous communities (Thurman et al., 2004) and being open to the possibility that Western methodologies are not appropriate ways of knowing for indigenous peoples (Letiecq & Bailey, 2004). Participatory methodologies tend to be non-positivist and hence amenable to qualitative methods and evaluator reflexivity and are seen as localized and therefore less susceptible to colonization, openly political (e.g., committed to working with and for rather than on marginalized peoples), and explicitly committed to shifting responsibility for the process of evaluation away from the academy and into the community (Jordan et al., 2009, 2013). The participatory methodologies included: Action Research (Santamaría et al., 2016), Community Action Research (Moewaka Barnes, 2000), Community Based Participatory Research (Watts et al., 2005), Empowerment Evaluation (Robertson et al., 2004), Participatory Evaluation (Chong et al., 2011; Grey et al., 2016; Jordan et al., 2013; Potvin et al., 2003; Sutton et al., 2016; Thurman et al., 2004; Willging et al., 2006), Participatory Action Research (Robertson et al., 2004), Tribal Participatory Evaluation/Research (Fisher & Ball, 2002; Letiecq & Bailey, 2004; Richmond et al., 2008), Kaupapa Māori (or other Māori) evaluation (Baker et al., 2015; Boulton & Kingi, 2011; Carlson et al., 2017; Curtis et al., 2012; Hamerton et al., 2012; Santamaría et al., 2016), and utilization-focused evaluation (Moewaka Barnes, 2000). Kaupapa Māori evaluation (Cram et al., 2018) and the tribal participatory research model (TPRM) are the most explicit about how culturally responsive evaluation can occur in indigenous contexts. TPRM, for example, has four mechanisms: tribal oversight, an intermediary, community workers, and culturally responsive intervention and assessment (Richmond et al., 2008).

Evaluators working in participatory ways may take on various roles during an evaluation, including facilitator, teacher, collaborator, sounding board, and advocate (Jordan et al., 2009). Such work is not always a priority for program and evaluation funders, with evaluators sometimes left feeling as if they are the cultural go-betweens, bridging community and funder expectations of an evaluation and trying to satisfy both parties.

> The evaluator . . . can become an advocate for the community by respecting and honouring community values and concerns, explaining these to the mainstream grantor to help alleviate frustration with a grantee whose ways of working and knowing are sometimes different from mainstream grantees. Such a role calls upon qualities of respect, honesty, and tact on the part of the evaluator toward both cultures. (Grover, 2010, p. 39)

Even when a particular participatory method was not named, evaluators worked in participatory or collaborative ways within their indigenous contexts, often being guided by a community-based advisory group, using mixed-methods designs to gather community voices, and hiring local people to facilitate engagement and data collection. Grey and colleagues (Grey et al., 2016; Sutton et al., 2016) describe their "both ways" evaluation methodology, whereby nonindigenous and indigenous knowledges is integrated, with the result that the evidence gathered is relevant for both indigenous communities and decision makers. This is intended to make their evaluation work "safer" (Sherwood, 2013) and more relevant (Curtis et al., 2012) for indigenous communities. Working in participatory ways to undertake an evaluation in indigenous contexts means that evaluation methods become tailored and responsive to these contexts. The establishment of a community-based evaluation advisory group can support this. Carlson, for example, wanted her advisory group to confidently "build enthusiasm, ownership, commitment and a sense of purpose to enable the intervention to be evaluated on their terms" (Carlson et al., 2017, p. 83).

However, it cannot be taken for granted that indigenous intermediaries or a community advisory or steering group will build culturally responsive methods as these require a strong bridge between evaluators and community. Working in an evaluation team with junior and senior indigenous evaluators did not prevent what Willging, Helitzer, and Thompson (2006) describe as "naïve interpretation . . . and inability to ask the right questions or document with confidence the social complexities in which . . . urban American Indian women were enmeshed" (p. 137). These evaluators now conduct cognitive interviews with participants to check the validity of the terminology they employ in their evaluation tools, and they recommend that formative research be used to check the helpfulness of any cultural examples and imagery. Other evaluators go through multiple revisions of tools (e.g., surveys) with their indigenous advisors to ensure that what they are asking is culturally responsive (Chong et al., 2011).

Community participatory methods, where community members come together to discuss the issues affecting them, can promote more community ownership of evaluation findings as what is said is more transparent than findings based on the analysis of, for example, survey findings. Grey and colleagues (2016) also note that "being involved in collecting and interpreting the evidence meant that local people could see how the evaluation process works, what it produces, and the uses made of the findings" (p. 22). The use of visual methods can support program providers to feel more comfortable with and own a program logic and can help families feel more comfortable in evaluation interviews (Baker et al., 2015). Grover (2010), however, describes a paradox from her evaluation work when she engages community people in the sorting and analysis of information (e.g., school-collected survey data). On the one hand, buy-in is facilitated by having community members in this process from the very beginning. On the other hand, community members often find this arduous and then call for the evaluator to do initial sorting and sifting of the information and present it back to them. If she had done this second step first, she is certain that the community members would have queried her work and asked to see the raw information themselves. Letiecq and Bailey (2004) also raise the issue of program staff feeling inundated by evaluators' demands for their participation in an evaluation. Their solution has been to implement research methods training so that program staff can make informed decisions of when and how they would like to participate in and add their voice to evaluation design and decision making.

One of the questions Linda Smith (2012) recommends indigenous communities ask researchers and evaluators is "Who owns the data?" This is about more than the physical output from the use of evaluation methods or tools; rather it is about extending the discussion about indigenous data sovereignty (Kukutai & Taylor, 2016) to encompass all indigenous data gathered for the purpose of making representations or judgement calls about things indigenous (LaFrance, 2004). Robertson and colleagues (2004) describe their efforts to collate data on tribal justice issues within a Lakota evaluation process. They attributed people's willingness to help them to people observing and understanding the evaluation process, "that the data would be used responsibly, would be shared with the public, and were being gathered as part of a process aimed at changing the system" (p. 513).

Evaluator Accountabilities to Community

Kawakami and colleagues (2006) ask after the purpose of evaluative knowing: Is it to inform funders or to inform grantee communities? While a funder may want to know whether it is doing good grant-making, a community wants to have the right agenda in place to support the well-being of its members. This means that evaluators have accountabilities to the indigenous peoples with whom they are working, as well as any additional accountabilities they may have to program or evaluation funders. This is not an either-or—either the community or the funder—although this bifurcation of stakeholder interests is not unusual as program funders may be narrowly focused on individual outcomes such as students' academic achievement while tribal communities seek this and other family and community outcomes aligned with their values (e.g., respectful family environments) (Chesterton, 2003; Mackey, 2012). Good evaluation is able to cope with the complexities of these expectations (LaFrance & Nichols, 2010). Curtis et al., (2012), for example, enquire after indigenous tertiary students' "sense of accomplishment and [them] fulfilling personally important goals" (p. 590). Competing outcomes—funder versus indigenous—are relatively easily resolved by "balancing competing principles" (Stake, 1998, p. 207) or, better yet, broadening the scope of an evaluation so that all stakeholders are recognized, and their evaluative needs responded to (W. K. Kellogg Foundation, 2017). Thurman et al. (2004) report that each community involved in the development and evaluation of its local mental health service model for children ended up with a body of knowledge that was also relevant to other stakeholders.

> This body of knowledge will continue to assist tribes, villages, and other policy-makers and program planners of child-serving systems in improving systems of care for AI/AN populations. Moreover, these tribal communities now possess an evaluative product and accompanying knowledge base from which they can draw in the exercise of self-determination. (Thurman et al., 2004, p. 145)

Some evaluators were only too well aware that their indigenous evaluation practices are at risk of being impacted by colonization and compromised by funders whose accountability requirements and understanding of programs do not align with those of local indigenous communities who are the intended program participants (Carlson et al., 2017). For other evaluators, an aha moment of what evaluators' roles and responsibilities really are comes after the negotiation of an evaluation contract. For example, Richmond et al., (2008) describe how they made an "easy" choice between a funder's desire for a quasi-experimental evaluation design and the evaluators' commitment to the indigenous communities where such a design would not work for both practical and ethical reasons. An ethically appropriate approach won out. In Phase 1 of a two-phase evaluation, Chesterton (2003) and his colleagues were commissioned by a government department to provide a detailed description of care placement practices when indigenous children deemed at risk of maltreatment were removed from their families. Their literature review and stakeholder interviews highlighted structural and cultural factors that created the need for care placement and led them to ponder their obligations as evaluators.

> Were we in fact helping to perpetuate the placement into [the] care system by seeking to identify its strengths and weaknesses and then making recommendations for its improvement? Should we not have been more focused on the causal factors and ways of tackling these rather than coping with the effects?

Were we really serving the interests of Aboriginal children and young people, their families, and their communities by adopting this particular evaluation focus? (Chesterton, 2003, p. 54)

They decided to include a description of structural and cultural factors in their first phase evaluation report, alongside information about proactive programs seeking to prevent child removal. Chesterton (2003) also signals that the team's ability to do this should have been negotiated as being within the scope of the project when it was first commissioned. The decision of the funder not to proceed past this first phase of the evaluation may have been because of its stated shift in funding priorities, but there is a lingering suspicion that the funder was not exactly thrilled to have a broader ecological picture of indigenous peoples within its society. Such an ecology requires multilayered and often structural change that is about acknowledging the wrongs of colonization and seeking redress that is not solely about programs that support indigenous peoples to change. Accountability within indigenous evaluation contexts therefore brings us full circle to the opening theme in this chapter of evaluators fully understanding, respecting, and responding to the rich ecological context of indigenous needs, priority and aspirations. As LaFrance and Nichols (2010) note, "There is always a subtext about self-determination in Indian Country that must be heard by evaluators" (p. 18).

CRITICAL DISCUSSION AND IMPLICATIONS FOR PRACTICE

Determining which sort of evaluation is culturally responsive and best serves indigenous communities is not about what we call the evaluation. Rather it is the responsiveness of that evaluation that is central. Is it good evaluation practice for that indigenous group? Does it reflect their values, culture, experience, and history? Is there a structural analysis of the societal context (often a colonial context) that the indigenous peoples live their day-to-day lives in? Does it recognize and work within their worldview, ways of knowing, and aspirations for future generations? In other words, does indigenous culture infuse all aspects of the evaluation and define the methodology (LaFrance, Nichols, & Kirkhart, 2012)? Does the evaluation have catalytic validity (Lather, 1988)? Is the evaluation culturally meaningful for indigenous peoples (Cavino, 2013)? If so, indigenous peoples will recognize themselves in the evaluation and be informed by it about how to create positive change and a sustainable future as self-determining, sovereign peoples. When this happens, evaluation becomes "a vehicle for sustaining cultural knowledges that have otherwise been targeted for extinction" (Tuck & Yang, 2019, p. xvi).

LaFrance (2004) and other indigenous evaluators learned these lessons from their own evaluation work with their own tribes in the 1990s, so it should be no surprise that indigenous peoples are impatient for evaluation that meets their needs

(Cram, 2018; Smith, 2018). This chapter extends the work of the American Indian Higher Education Consortium (AIHEC), where 34 tribally controlled colleges and universities integrated indigenous and Western inquiry paradigms to develop an "Indigenous Framework for Evaluation" (LaFrance & Nichols, 2009, 2010). Like that framework, this chapter posits that local programming as well as local evaluation need to be co-produced with local people to address the community's needs, to honor their priorities, and to help facilitate their aspirations. LaFrance, Nichols, and Kirkhart (2012) describe how this often implicit process is "brought to life through language, protocols for behaving, deeply held relationships with the community and with the land, and the people's lived experiences" (p. 65).

Culturally responsive indigenous evaluation is therefore the opposite of what is sometimes referred to as "helicopter" or "seagull" evaluation, where evaluators swoop into a community to collect data that they then take back to their homeplace to analyze and manufacture into evaluation reports, conference presentations, and journal articles (LaFrance, 2004). Such practice makes evaluation a tool of scientific colonialism (Nobles, 1991). As Linda Smith notes, "There are still more scholars working with deficit approaches who are trying to either 'save' us from ourselves or fix us up, sort us out, and, in some cases, still, convince us that they 'know best'" (Smith, Tuck, & Yang, 2019, p. 6). The consideration of indigenous culture in these types of evaluations, if it is considered at all, is as a clip-on that adds flavor to the evaluation context but does not challenge Western epistemology or undermine the Western definition of what and whose knowledge is legitimate (LaFrance et al., 2012).To help us understand the difference between "helicopter" evaluation and culturally responsive indigenous evaluation, Boyer (2006) retells the story of a fifth grader, Kyle Swimmer (Laguna Pueblo), who asked a question about the best way to grind corn. If the amount of ground corn is considered to be the key performance indicator, then mechanical grinding is the best answer to this question. However, if a stronger community is the key performance indicator, then the social and cultural activity of traditional hand grinding is the best answer.

> At the end of the day, both methods make cornmeal. But which method also creates a stronger community? To put the question another way, where would you rather be: Working in a mill, or sitting alongside the women as they grind the corn and the men as they sing their songs? (Boyer, 2006, p. 13)

Understanding the importance of this kind of difference can determine whether or not evaluators "get" what is of value and merit to indigenous peoples, and whether the work evaluators undertake will be useful to an indigenous community (Jordan et al., 2009). The culturally responsive indigenous evaluation practice canvassed here has demonstrated the importance of evaluators having or being committed to developing an understanding of the complex ecology of indigenous contexts and then engaging in evaluation practices that are respectful and responsive to that ecology. This work is best done in close collaboration with indigenous peoples: as evaluation team leaders, members, and community workers; as cultural liaisons and advisors; and as audiences who are actively engaged in meaning making, dissemination, and transformation informed by evaluative evidence. There are mainstream evaluation approaches that advocate for such participatory and partnership practices throughout an evaluation cycle. What sets culturally responsive indigenous evaluation practice apart is its commitment to indigenous self-determination and sovereignty. This includes evaluators attending to "processes of marginalization, structures of oppression, histories of struggle, and the contemporary and tangible impoverishments many indigenous communities face" (Cavino, 2013, p. 350).

The colonization of indigenous peoples—the theft of land and children, the silencing of language, the threat to life from warfare, disease, and systemic neglect—is possible only if indigenous peoples are seen as less than human (Smith, 2012) and "made into ghosts" (Tuck & Yang, 2012, p. 6). We cannot ignore the role of evaluation within this context as a tool that either supports or challenges colonization. If the choice is to challenge lingering colonial perspectives, the task for evaluation is to support a view of indigenous people as fully human and as living with the legacy of power and deprivation brought about through colonization (Cram, 2018). As Kawakami et al. (2007) write, "By decolonizing *evaluation* methodologies, we aim to re-center ourselves within our own lands" (p. 222). It is from this sovereign position that indigenous peoples can identify and challenge the preconceptions and stereotypes evident in other worldviews that work to maintain their marginalization.

CHAPTER SUMMARY

Culturally responsive evaluation in indigenous contexts recognizes the sovereign rights of indigenous peoples to live cultural, self-determining lives that strengthen their vitality and sustainability. In order for evaluation to serve this broader agenda and be useful for indigenous peoples, evaluators need to build their own understanding of the indigenous context they are working in by being in relationship with the indigenous people of that context. By having indigenous people involved as members of the evaluation team and building respectful relationships with local liaisons, elders, advisors, and fieldworkers, evaluators can improve their chances of understanding the ecology of the programs they are evaluating. The co-production of the evaluation with local people begins and ends with these relationships, which in turn can be strengthened by evaluators being present both formally and informally in the community. The creation of methodological opportunities to involve and include local people in the evaluation journey then helps ensure the validity of the evaluation as well as its use in supporting indigenous peoples' nation building and self-determination.

Bibliography of Further Readings

Cram, F., & Mertens, D. (2016). Negotiating solidarity between indigenous and transformative paradigms in evaluation. *Evaluation Matters: He Take Tō Te Aromatawai, 2*, 161–189.

Cram, F., Tibbetts, K. A., & LaFrance, J. (Eds.). (2018). *Indigenous evaluation. New Directions for Evaluation, 159*, 33–46.

Kawakami, A., Aton, K., Cram, F., Lai, M., & Porima, L. (2007). Improving the practice of evaluation through indigenous values and methods: Decolonizing evaluation practice—returning the gaze from Hawai'i and Aotearoa. In P. Brandon & P. Smith (Eds.), *Fundamental issues in evaluation* (pp. 219–242). New York, NY: Guilford Press.

LaFrance, J. (2004). Culturally competent evaluation in Indian Country. *New Directions for Evaluation, 102*(Summer), 39–50.

LaFrance, J., Nelson-Barber, S., Rechebei, E. D., & Gordon, J. (2015). Partnering in Pacific communities to ground evaluation in local culture and context: Promises and challenges. In S. Hood, R. K. Hopson, & H. T. Frierson (Eds.), *The role of culture and cultural context: A mandate for inclusion, the discovery of truth, and understanding in evaluative theory and practice* (pp. 361–378). Greenwich, CT: Information Age.

LaFrance, J., Nichols, R., & Kirkhart, K. E. (2012). Culture writes the script: On the centrality of context in indigenous evaluation. In D. J. Rog, J. L. Fitzpatrick, & R. F. Conner (Eds.), *Context: A framework for its influence on evaluation practice. New Directions for Evaluation, 135*, 59–74.

Smith, L. T. (2018). Indigenous insights on valuing complexity, sustaining relationships, being accountable. In R. Hopson, & F. Cram (Eds.), *Tackling wicked problems in complex ecologies: The role of evaluation* (pp. 45–66). Redwood City, CA: Stanford University Press.

Exercises Based on Case Examples

1. Select one of the case examples at the beginning of this chapter and specify what about the example demonstrates understanding by the evaluation team of the indigenous context in which they were working. How do you think they gained this understanding? Is there more about the context you feel they should have known or learned about? Use your own research skills (e.g., Internet searches) to locate other knowledge about the indigenous context (history, land, people, circumstances) that may have informed the evaluators' understanding.

2. Select one of the case examples at the beginning of this chapter. What informed the evaluation team's choice of evaluation methodology and methods? Do you feel there is other information that could have been used by the evaluators to inform their decision making about methodology and method? If you were entering this community, would you have followed a similar process, or are there other things you would have done to help you decide about the evaluation methodology and methods?

3. How do you think the findings of the evaluations described in the three case examples could best be made available to community participants and agencies? To external funders and decision makers? To the evaluation profession? Are there other stakeholders you think would be interested in the findings or the methodology used?

Discussion Questions

1. What part should evaluation play in the aims and aspirations of indigenous peoples for nation building and self-determination?

2. List four challenges to evaluators contributing to indigenous people's aspirations. Describe how you would work to resolve or overcome these challenges.

3. What responsibility should evaluators take for resolving tensions or conflicts between indigenous communities and evaluation funders (e.g., about evaluation methodology)? Should evaluation be culturally responsive to funders and other external stakeholders as well as to communities?

4. If you were part of an evaluation team working in an indigenous community, how would you reflect upon and describe your insider and outsider status? Do you think your insider/outsider status would help or hinder you in building relationships of trust with evaluation stakeholders? How would you seek to either moderate or overcome any hinderance?

5 THE WESTERN/NORTH AMERICAN CONTEXT

OVERVIEW OF CHAPTER

In this chapter, we explore culturally responsive approaches across Western jurisdictions, including STEM, Latin American, immigrant, and minoritized populations. In total, we located, reviewed, and analyzed 24 published studies, the majority of which are reflective case narratives based on prior evaluation experiences with programs situated in culturally diverse communities, spanning 17 years (from 2000 to 2017). To provide a sense of the range of programs and contexts included in this chapter, we begin with three case descriptions drawn from the literature. We then provide a brief description of the 24 studies, focusing on the rationales for the adoption and use of cultural responsiveness, and a description of approaches and combinations of approaches used to address culture in evaluation practice. The main focus of the chapter is our review and integration of the 24 studies, focusing on implications for culturally responsive practice as it relates to experiences in the field and relevance to our understanding of culture. We conclude the chapter with a recommended bibliography and questions for discussion, some of which relate to the case examples provided below.

CASE EXAMPLE 1: "Breaking the Silence" is a family violence prevention project designed to produce critical knowledge about family violence in immigrant and refugee communities. Working with a group of 18 members from nine immigrant and refugee communities and participating agencies (called the Legacy Team), the purpose of the project was to develop knowledge about family violence and develop and pilot a curriculum. Specific objectives of the project were (1) to build capacity in the community to better support families impacted by violence, (2) to develop culturally and linguistically relevant information about the initiative, and (3) to create the opportunity for discussion of family violence within the community—"break the silence." As a member of the Legacy Team, the evaluator, who also served as a project coordinator, intended to facilitate a participatory evaluation from a culturally competent perspective. The overall purpose of the evaluation was to document project activities and provide opportunities for group reflection, leading to the formative use of findings throughout the duration of the project. A project-coordinating group (three members of the Legacy Team) met biweekly to discuss the project and evaluation. The Legacy Team itself provided reflective comments and participated in evaluation activities throughout the project. The primary data collected for this evaluation was a synthesis of monthly discussions (focus groups) with the Legacy Team, all of which informed the written reports. The evaluator provided three interconnected lessons: (1) the need to build sufficient time in the project to enable collaboration among participants and to build cultural competence; (2) the importance of incorporating learning in the evaluation process and of an open, adaptable willingness to "go with the low"; and (3) the need for evaluators to understand and develop cultural competence and fluency, especially if they do not share the same cultural ethnicity and history as program participants (Anderson-Draper, 2006).

CASE EXAMPLE 2: The Family, School, and Community Partnership Program (FSCPP), a school-based family, school, and community partnership program for Black students in a low-income urban high school sought to improve student academic achievement and social competence in secondary schools. The goal of the program was to improve stakeholders' knowledge, attitudes, and participation in activities designed to improve students' academic achievement and social competence. The evaluation was informed by the Talent Development Model (a whole school, evidence-based practice model), participatory action research, and practical participatory evaluation to ensure the active involvement of participants throughout the process. The Talent Development framework encourages early and ongoing engagement of key school and community stakeholders and includes strategies for engagement, co-construction, responsiveness, triangulation, and cultural context. Stakeholders became "assistant evaluators" and received ongoing training and were able to provide ongoing input on design, implementation, data collection, and analysis. Evaluators made an effort to match evaluators and participant characteristics (in terms of racial, ethnic, gender, age, and social class affiliation). The evaluators provided four key lessons: (1) To reduce social distance between evaluators and participants, it is necessary to recruit, train, and actively engage participants throughout the process, wear casual business dress, and avoid technical language; (2) ensure evaluators and participants share similar ethnicity; (3) get to know the program site well, build relationships, create feasible action plans, and select and reward participants; and (4) cultural responsiveness requires an asset-based rather than a deficit-based approach (LaPoint & Jackson, 2004).

CASE EXAMPLE 3: The Cambodian youth dance program, described jointly by the evaluator and participants, was designed to increase awareness and pride in Cambodian culture, promote healthy behaviors, and create linkages with the community. Evaluators created an advisory committee that included troupe members and collaborating agencies. From the start, the evaluation team struggled with balancing the needs of all stakeholders, as the program funder required the use of standardized procedures and measures that were not culturally commensurate with the local Cambodian culture (e.g., the survey, a condition of the funding, described self-esteem measures that espoused American values). While students were involved in data collection and analysis, which consisted of interviews, questionnaires, focus groups, surveys, and reflections and feedback from audience members, they could not alter the specific instruments provided by the funder. Upon reflection, they felt they should have taken a stronger stance with the funder, as it may have hindered the level of acceptance and trust with the youth dance program, ultimately hindering community ownership of the process. They also note that the collection of data that is not culturally appropriate or relevant may actually interfere with the evaluation process and outcomes. Chief among the lessons learned, the dynamics of diversity and context strongly influence the evaluation. They attempted to understand the cultural context of their research through collaboration and through questioning the assumptions of methodological equivalence, relying on qualitative methods to incorporate local voices and perspectives (Coppens, Page, & Chan Thou, 2006).

DESCRIPTION OF SAMPLE

Selection

Our primary consideration in selecting these studies was that they in some way and to some extent consider culture a historically, methodologically, and epistemologically relevant and important construct to consider in designing and conducting evaluations no matter their program context. While we noted some commonality across studies, especially in the widespread use of collaborative practice, such as participatory evaluation, transformative evaluation participatory action research, empowerment evaluation, and community research, we nonetheless identified over 29 different approaches designed to address culture:

culturally sensitive approach	multicultural validity
cultural competence	responsive
values engaged	anthropological
educative	integrated empowerment model
social justice	ethnographic
context sensitive lens	postmodern
critical theory	talent development
constructivist	transformative
ecological theory	critical race theory
culturally responsive	culturally relevant democratic
cross-cultural	inquiry

Numerous studies also cited a combination of approaches, including randomized control trial and culturally sensitive approach, social justice and empowerment models, critical theory and constructivist, ecological theory and cultural responsiveness, with a mix of either quantitative or qualitative methods, or both. We also identified a number of approaches that identified culture more specifically in the approaches used, such as culturally sensitive approach, cultural competence, culturally responsive evaluation, cross cultural evaluation, multicultural evaluation, anthropological evaluation, ethnographic evaluation, critical race theory, and culturally relevant evaluation.

Characteristics

The 24 studies selected were published between 2000 and 2017, with the majority published between 2004 and 2006 (62.5%). Of note is the volume *New Directions in Evaluation* volume edited by SenGupta, Hopson, Thompson-Robinson in 2004, which inspired the empirical research on culturally responsive evaluation practice. As Figure 5.1 illustrates, no studies were identified in 2003, 2008, 2009, 2012, 2013, or 2015. Moreover, 79% (n=19) of the studies were published in the first 8 years (2000–2008), with only 21% (n=5) published in the final 8 years (2009–2017), representing a significant drop in the total number of published studies.

The vast majority of the studies were located in the United States (n=22), with only two situated in a Canadian context. Target populations included African Americans (n=9), Latina/o (n=6), underrepresented populations (n=6), immigrant and refugee populations (n=3), "at risk" populations (n=2), Asians (n=1), and veterans (n=1).

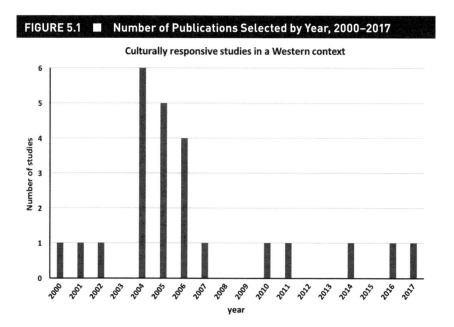

FIGURE 5.1 ■ Number of Publications Selected by Year, 2000–2017

Culturally responsive studies in a Western context

The domains of practice range over a violence prevention for childcare staff, a student program involving a National Science Foundation Science and Technology Center, a school-to-career intervention program for at-risk students, an outreach program to increase admission of underrepresented groups, a parent education program for low-income mothers, a summer college readiness program, a violence prevention program in an immigrant community, a veteran treatment program, a Cambodian youth dance program, a community revitalization project, and a variety of health programs, including HIV prevention and smoking prevention.

REVIEW AND INTEGRATION OF SELECTED STUDIES

Descriptive Analysis

Our primary consideration in selecting these studies was that they in some way and to some extent consider culture a historically, methodologically and epistemologically relevant and important construct to consider in designing and conducting evaluation no matter its program context. While we noted some commonality across studies, especially in the widespread use of collaborative practice, we nonetheless identified over 29 different approaches designed to address culture, as noted earlier. Numerous studies also cited a combination of approaches, such as randomized control trial and culturally sensitive approach, social justice and empowerment models, critical theory and constructivist, and ecological theory and cultural responsiveness.

We have also noted a broad range of rationales for the adoption of culturally responsive approaches: increased understanding, reflexivity, responsiveness to stakeholder needs, validity, learning, relevance, and empowerment, with a number of studies citing numerous, intersecting rationales. We have also noted evidence of the more aspirational aims of culturally responsive approaches related specifically to the amelioration of past injustices and the promotion of social change, greater equity, enhanced community well-being, and greater social justice, as indicated in their stated methodological orientations, which are inspired by naturalistic, emancipatory, critical theory, constructivist, ethnographic, and anthropological approaches and rationales. Despite the broad range of approaches to cultural responsiveness, the studies predominantly employ qualitative or mixed methods, with most being based on reflective case narratives.

Despite significant variation in practice across cultural contexts, the vast majority of studies included in this review adopted a participatory or collaborative approach to evaluation, with a focus on knowledge creation within the community as a way to mitigate potential contextual, political, and cultural complexities; tensions; and misunderstandings. At the same time, all of the studies adopted participatory approaches in combination with other culturally-framed approaches, often including a mix of approaches at various points during the evaluation, representing significant variation in practice across program communities. While we identified over 29 different approaches used to address culture, these approaches were combined with one or more of the following:

randomized control trials	anthropological evaluation
quasi-experimental methods	postmodernist approaches
social cognitive theory	participatory action research
responsive evaluation	transformative methods
democratic evaluation	critical race theory
social justice and empowerment	values based approaches
critical theory	grounded theory
constructivist models	systems-oriented evaluation
ecological theory	utilization-focused evaluation
case study	

Integration and Synthesis

Our analysis of the 24 empirical studies yielded seven key areas of thematic interest: the interpretation of cultural, the manifestation of power, the complexities of language, the variety of identities, the dimensionality of time, the cultural appropriateness of evaluative measurements, and the use and influence of evaluative findings. While we acknowledge the intersection of many of these themes, they each highlight a particular cultural focus and merit individual attention and discussion.

Interpretation of Culture

Our conceptualization of culture (see Chapter 2) provides a comprehensive and fairly inclusive definition intended to position culture as both an epistemologically and methodologically vibrant construct in evaluation. Because it is an "ineradicably imprecise" (Geertz, 2000, p. 11) term, our conception of culture is intended to provide for its richness and depth, as well as its inherent tensions, historical equivocity, and illusiveness. It is also intended to highlight the fundamental aspects that will ensure its continued relevance in methodological work. Across our studies, we were struck by the sheer variety in the definitions of culture, from those that consider culture primarily as a demographic marker of a specific community requiring cultural awareness and "situational responsiveness" (Patton, 1985) to those that move beyond the localized program context to include the broader social, political, and historical contexts that define, shape, and constrain local practices. Some see culture as something that circumscribes their understanding, ultimately shaping how they see the world. Others consider the influence of culture in developing their research methodologies, noting that social inquiry is not culture free, and the production of knowledge is historically, culturally, economically, and politically mediated and bound.

Many of the studies considered culture from an *emic* perspective, drawing on the cultural history of program participants to frame the evaluation methodology and inform the interpretation of findings (e.g., Alkon, Tschann, Ruanne, Wolff, & Hittner, 2001; Jay, Eatmon, & Frierson, 2005). For some, this led to detailed discussions about the local culture, based on a detailed description of the population and its cultural characteristics, origins, and language. The description of culture provided a vivid backdrop to help situate the evaluation within the local cultural milieu, with links to methodological design choices and principles of inclusion.

In other studies, culture was interpreted *self-reflectively*, leading to questions about bias, values, and cultural competence within the program context (e.g., Copeland-Carson, 2005; King, Nielsen, & Colby, 2004). As Anderson-Draper (2006) reflects, "In search for my own cultural competence, I too asked myself, a White Mainstream Canadian woman, how my experiences, evaluation training, and assumptions influenced the way I approached a cross-cultural evaluation" (pp. 61–62). For King, Nielson, and Colby (2004), cultural competence comes from "a deliberate and continuous process of self and organizational introspection" (p. 68), a process that positions evaluators as "informed not-knowers" (p. 69). For Small, Tiwari, and Huser (2006), the process of writing led to an awareness of privileged status, leading to further reflection about how these differences might have influenced practice.

Other studies in our sample positioned culture as a *sociopolitical and historical* construct that influences the local community and program context (e.g., Butty, Reid, LaPoint, 2004; Copeland-Carson, 2005). Within these studies, the cultural context of the program is broadened to include the "totality of the environment" (Butty et al., 2004, p. 38), which encompasses geographic location, political and social climate, history, and economic conditions. Local cultural dynamics are seen as embedded within a larger, fundamentally interconnected social system composed of a "hierarchy of social forces" (Guzman, 2003, p. 174), all of which interweave throughout the evaluation, highlighting the multilevel and interactive social, political, historical and cultural influences at play within the evaluation context.

For others, culture was thought to actively inform the traditional processes and practices of *academic knowledge*, as seen from the perspective of a White, Western and male worldview (Small, Tiwari, & Huser, 2006). This led to the recognition that evaluators bring a professional culture that contains certain cultural assumptions, values and beliefs (Anderson-Draper, 2006). In many of these studies, we could see a clear link between evaluation as a form of cultural authority, and the design and use of culturally appropriate measurement instruments within the local culture.

The various conceptions of culture found across the 24 studies illustrates the continued contestability of culture as a concept in our society, as well as the immense difficulty in defining what remains a stubbornly ambiguous, contradictory, and elastic term (Barth, 1994; Williams, 1981). Along with the range of definitions and constructs used to describe culture, the 24 studies provided incredible variation in examples of cultural adaptation and methodological accommodation. While the studies highlight the "push-and-pull" (Boyce, 2017) between funder priorities and local community needs, they also highlight the creativity and ingenuity of evaluators in devising ways to circumvent the use of culturally incongruent methods in their evaluation work. At the same time, the studies highlight the need for evaluators to possess a deep cultural understanding of the community, its language, traditions and history, in order to be able to refine methods to fit the community's cultural context, and to identify issues of multicultural validity that potentially threaten the accuracy, soundness, and appropriateness of data and analysis (Kirkhart, 1995).

While we would expect to see methodological diversity in culturally responsive practice, such eclecticism may make it challenging to distinguish amongst approaches and methodologies and their possible links to practice, potentially obfuscating our understanding of the relationship between theory and practice in evaluation (Christie, 2003; Donaldson & Lipsey, 2008). As culturally responsive practice in evaluation is a relatively new field of study, such methodological eclecticism makes it difficult to identify which approaches, and which types of adaptations and connections among these approaches, can best support culturally responsive practice. Moreover, with so few empirical studies published over the past 18 years (only 24 identified, with 63% between the years 2004 and 2006), there are even fewer examples of practice for evaluators to draw from in their work. In fact, over the past 10 years, we located only five published studies that were based on a discussion of empirical work, a troublingly low number if, as others have stated, such research is essential to the development of evaluation theory and to the development of current practice (Smith, 1993).

Manifestations of Power

Power and culture are inextricably linked together (Rosaldo, 1989; Seidman, 2004), as issues of power, inequity and privilege continue to influence and shape evaluative practice (Chouinard, 2014; Haugen & Chouinard, 2018). While the concept of power resists simple characterization and description, in evaluation work it can be portrayed in terms of who participates, under which conditions they participate, to what extent they participate, and whose knowledge frames the evaluation and is ultimately considered most valuable. Across our 24 studies, we noted multiple, interconnected examples of power, relational, political, and discursive.

A number of studies identified *relational* manifestations of power in terms of the processes of negotiation, alliances among stakeholders, competing and conflicting interests, rules of inclusion and exclusion, and the dynamics of the evaluator role (Clayson, Castaneda, Sanchez, & Brindis, 2002). For some, this level of power was influenced by social class, education level, race, gender, status and needs (Thomas, 2004). Others noted that stakeholders themselves often have competing agendas and interests, which play a role in defining relations of power (Copeland-Carson, 2005; Harklau & Norwood, 2005). Some saw power as evident in forms of resistance, as students questioned the role of the evaluator and attempts to control the agenda, and what evaluators wrote about them (Harklau & Norwood, 2005). Others saw evidence of power in the tensions that arose among Latin American members of the evaluation committee about the writing of the final report (Prilleltensky, Nelson, & Valdes, 2000). For the majority of the studies, power was also inherent in the role of the evaluator, especially evident in the relationship between evaluators and participants (e.g., Anderson-Draper, 2006; LaPoint & Jackson, 2004; Small et al., 2006). Despite attempts at inclusion, the evaluator nonetheless continued to play a larger role in designing the evaluation and in shaping decision-making processes (Cooper & Christie, 2005).

Across studies we also identified *political* power at the level of the process and planning of evaluations and at the more general level of the organizational and societal application of evaluation results, often operating simultaneously. For most studies in our sample, evaluation was seen as intrinsically political, and the perspectives and agendas of certain stakeholder groups were considered more valued than others (e.g., Butty et al., 2004; Harklau & Norwood, 2005; Ryan, Chandler, & Samuels, 2007). For Anderson-Draper (2006), this led to further reflection on whose agenda evaluators were trying to advance, since their timelines and group consultations were not consistent across program team members. Other studies situated evaluation within a complex and politically charged environment, both locally and at the macro level (Christie & Barela, 2005; Cooper & Christie, 2005), which for some also influenced power at the relational level (Clayson et al., 2005). Beyond these local manifestations, we also note instances of political power at a societal level, where it influences and shapes evaluation design, methods, process, and planning (e.g., Alkon et al., 2001; Boyce, 2017; Clayson et al., 2002; Coppens et al., 2006). As Boyce (2017) notes, evaluators had only limited success persuading program managers to include diversity as a criterion for recruitment and selection, resulting in a push-pull between the two groups each year.

We also observe power operating at a *discursive* level, in terms of the internalized values, beliefs, and norms that govern practice and that inherently influence and position evaluation designs, objectives, and outcomes. For some evaluators, the evaluations had predetermined metrics about what is considered valid, with prefigured outcomes and values (Cooper & Christie, 2005; Copeland-Carson, 2005; Thomas, 2004), most often driven by funder priorities rather than by participant or stakeholder perspectives and needs (Alkon et al., 2001; Coppens et al., 2006). As such, evaluation strategies were aligned with funder requirements, as were definitions of what is considered valid knowledge, while evaluators struggled with balancing participant and funder needs (Clayson et al., 2002; Harklau & Norwood, 2005).

As our findings indicate, the co-construction of knowledge and meaning between diverse stakeholders and evaluators is not uncontested, particularly given that one of the most difficult and vexing issues, as well as one of the biggest threats to genuine community inclusion, is precisely the imbalance of power (House & Howe, 2000), particularly in communities with a history of exploitation and marginalization. While collaborative approaches may mitigate some power differentials, merely inviting everyone to the table is not enough. The use of collaborative methodologies and culturally responsive methods cannot mask the inherent cultural authority of evaluation (House, 1993), or obscure its power to define what constitutes legitimate discourse and knowledge in the social sciences (Reagan, 1996). Reliance on methodology through the use of stakeholder agreements or terms of reference is insufficient in light of the broader social, cultural, and political conditions within which programs are embedded. As Schick (2002) points out, "It is naïve to think that a history of exclusion can be overcome by 'including' individuals already identified and selected because they are disempowered by those very structures" (p. 647). As such, it becomes essential for evaluators to develop cultural fluency, not only about themselves and about the program and the people involved, but about the wider cultural system within which they (and we) are all enmeshed.

Complexities of Language

Language is considered a critical issue in culturally responsive practice (Dahler-Larsen et al., 2017; Hood, Hopson, & Kirkhart, 2016; Mertens, 2009). Concerns about race, culture, power, and gender saturate the relationship between language and evaluation (Hopson, 2000a, 2000b). Seen or unseen, spoken or unspoken, there are codes or rules that relate to communication, to language use, defined by what Delpit (1988) refers to as a "culture of power" (p. 280), shaping the implicit and explicit rules of dialogue, beyond the spoken word itself. Who speaks, who writes, who puts pen to paper, who names, who translates from one language to another, who constructs the narrative text—all of these considerations are critical in culturally responsive practice. As Madison (2000) points out,

> Power to coin a language, to describe social phenomena is variably distributed among the intellectual elite, policymakers, evaluators, and service providers. From a sociopolitical perspective, one social class has almost exclusive power to decide the contextual meaning of terms and concepts that describe social problems. (p. 26)

The studies in our sample provide numerous examples highlighting the dynamics of communication, language and meaning as it surfaces among evaluators, stakeholders and funders, not to mention underlining issues of power, politics and cultural difference (Mertens & Hopson, 2006; Small et al., 2006).

While Samuels and Ryan (2011) encouraged dialogue about culture between evaluators and stakeholders as a way to stimulate self-reflection, others considered these discussions controversial, leading to issues of power, conflict and tension between evaluators and stakeholders (e.g., Boyce, 2017; King et al., 2004; Noblit & Jay, 2010; Ryan et al., 2007). Some saw these discussions as surfacing differences in language and communication styles (Coppens et al., 2006; Small et al., 2006), highlighting the need for excellent communication and rapport-building skills (Alkon et al., 2001), cultural and linguistic competency (Clayson et al., 2002), the creation of formal and informal opportunities to foster open communication (Boyce, 2017), and the need to understand the nuances of language to ensure cultural responsiveness (Butty et al., 2004). As Copeland-Carson (2005) points out, communication styles among authors were strongly influenced by cultural worldviews and life experiences. As they describe it, "We learned that context is critical to our communication . . . we needed to actively listen to ourselves and each other, and to clarify verbal and nonverbal messages" (p. 324).

For other studies in our sample, language was seen as a manifestation of cultural complexity, especially in contexts where people spoke several different languages. For Conner (2004), communication included using the literal language of participants, which as he explains, has "degrees of language use to attend to, both in speaking and in writing" (p. 60). For Clayson et al. (2002) this led to the deconstruction and reconstruction of words and concepts during interpretation or translation were needed to ensure cultural relevance to the community. While some studies noted the importance of making every effort to derive valid meaning from the language used to ensure correct interpretation (Butty et al., 2004), others saw this effort as going beyond simple word-by-word translation to a deliberate effort to consider context and meanings (Mertens & Hopson, 2006).

Some of the studies in our sample altered the words in the evaluation to accommodate perceived differences in stakeholder and funder perspectives. For instance, according to Hong et al. (2005), program coordinators called the goal "harm reduction," whereas participants called it "getting clean." To address these differences in perception, the coordinators altered the language to portray harm reduction as a gradual process of getting clean. In another study, LaPoint and Jackson (2004) reduced the jargon in their evaluation to reduce the social distance between evaluators and stakeholders. To ensure culturally responsive practice, some of the studies in our sample revised their language to accommodate funders primarily focused on more reductive indicators, opting to use language the funder (or other stakeholders) would not question. Copeland-Carson (2005) never explicitly stated that she was using an anthropological model. Instead she translated the concepts of sociocultural systems to institutional and organizational culture and comprehensive community development, all in an effort to provide terms people would find more familiar and palatable. Noblit and Jay (2010), for their part, avoided the terminology of critical race theory altogether, since funders were looking for assessments of effectiveness and an instrumentalist critique. This allowed the evaluators to challenge the White narrative by positioning race theory namelessly within the broader majoritarian discourse.

In culturally complex contexts, translation is not a simple verbal reconstruction, a mere re-telling, because language itself has different interpretive frames, comes from somewhere, and possesses different implicit meanings (Agar, 2000). As Guzman (2003) points out, "While translating a measurement tool or having someone who speaks the language of the target population is a step in the direction of cultural sensitivity, these two steps do not constitute cultural competency" (p. 177). Dahler-Larsen et al., (2017) point to "untranslatables," words that simply have no equivalent meaning in another language. These can be understood only in relation to larger systems of meaning. When we use language as evaluators, our notion of translation thus needs to consider power, specifically the power of the Western tradition to shape, frame, and define the words we use to describe, represent, and understand. As Dahler-Larsen et al. (2017) state, "Some meaning systems are put in better institutionalized positions than others. Some vocabularies are mandatory" (p. 117). Translating the "untranslatable" thus shifts the focus away from the words themselves to the meanings that influence, shape, and frame our understanding, all before we have even uttered a single word.

The Variety of Identities

A significant challenge in conducting culturally responsive approaches to evaluation is ensuring evaluators have sufficient knowledge of the culture, language, and history of the community. For some of the studies in our sample, this concern led to an internal dialogue about identity and self. The evaluators were brought to wonder whether they were the right people for the task. For others, it led to a search for the right cultural informants, or to the selection of evaluators with similar ethnicities as program participants. As our studies highlight, questions and assumptions made about cultural identity influence the evaluation in numerous ways, shaping the relationships that we build and the knowledge that we co-construct with stakeholders.

A number of studies in our sample questioned the need for evaluators to share cultural characteristics with the communities in which they were working (Alkon et al., 2001; Harklau & Norwood, 2005). Some pondered the feasibility of matching cultural traits between evaluators and stakeholders (Anderson-Draper, 2006) and the relevance of insider-outsider status (Clayson et al., 2002). For others, the notion of cultural matching led to questions about personal identity and subject positions, as women, local or nonlocal, or as insiders or outsiders (Harklau & Norwood, 2005). To facilitate cultural understanding and increase cultural sensitivity, some of the studies created bridging roles between external evaluators and the community (Copeland-Carson, 2005; Prilleltensky et al., 2000). We note that these bridging roles included any group or person who played an intermediary function, including cultural facilitators or advisory committees. Copeland-Carson (2005) equates the use of cultural facilitators to the adoption of key informants in anthropology, who provide field workers with valuable information about the local culture.

For a number of studies in our sample, cultural or ethnic matching was considered essential. Matching of this kind meant that evaluators provided a shared life experience and awareness of the reality of community members (Butty et al., 2004), minimized insider-outsider status (LaPoint & Jackson, 2004), and fostered a common language, cultural experiences, and values (Prilleltensky et al., 2000), all of which would supported program success (Zulli & Frierson, 2004). According to Prilleltensky et al. (2000),

A person from outside of this community would need to go through a much more prolonged period of entry to gain the trust of this community.

The principal investigator was able to serve an important bridging function between the Latin American community, a federal granting agency, and academic resources for evaluation. (p. 110)

According to Zulli and Frierson (2004), "The similarity of backgrounds ensures cultural competency and enables the staff to relate to the students in a way that others may not have the capacity to do" (p. 88). For Butty et al., (2004), shared racial background between the evaluator and the community ensured that "team members went into the urban school context with an increased level of sensitivity and awareness to the plight and lived experiences of the various stakeholder groups" (p. 44).

Other studies in our sample hired and trained local community members in evaluation and data gathering techniques (e.g., LaPoint & Jackson, 2004; Prilleltensky et al., 2000; Uhl, Robinson, Westover, Bockting, & Cherry-Porter, 2004). They believed it would increase acceptance of evaluation findings, improve the quality and the practical value of the research, build community capacity and development, and help with understanding cultural norms. Still others created advisory or steering committees composed of diverse stakeholder groups to increase cultural relevancy and build an active partnership based on joint construction of findings (Coppens et al., 2006; King et al., 2004; Noblit & Jay, 2010).

The search for the right cultural informants and the use of evaluators from similar ethnic backgrounds as program participants underscore the challenge of endorsing fixed notions of identity, particularly if we consider the difficulty of determining what is salient within a specific context. It is rarely obvious who is in or out, or which markers of identity—ethnicity, gender, class, for example—matter most in a particular context. The notion of matching cultural traits among evaluators and program participants thus raises important questions about the construction of identity, not to speak of the intersecting identities that abound in evaluation contexts. Before deciding how to bridge the cultural chasm, we need to question what we mean by a social category and the related concept of inclusion (Rogoff, 2003; Schick, 2002).

The Dimensionality of Time

The dimensionality of time brings focus to the emergent, fluid nature of programs and evaluation, conceptualized as processes and practices that unfold and evolve over time, becoming all the more complex in culturally diverse community contexts. For many of the studies in our sample (e.g., Alkon et al., 2001; Anderson-Draper, 2006; Harklau & Norwood, 2005; Uhl et al., 2004), time is a critical dimension of culturally responsive practice. The ongoing influence of past histories, the legacy of past experiences and prior relationships, the evolving nature of personal and cultural growth, and the role and methodological understanding of the evaluator all matter here.

A number of studies noted the need to understand the influence of time, in the sense just explained, on individuals, groups and communities. They believed it could help shape the evaluation (e.g., Anderson-Draper, 2006; LaPoint & Jackson, 2004).

For some, gaining a deep understanding of a community's history, was essential in helping evaluators understand a community's political culture and history, and thus the power dynamics that might influence the evaluation (Small et al., 2006). Others described the importance of understanding the influence of history on the roles and beliefs of participants (Anderson-Draper, 2006). Alkon et al. (2001) also reflected on the within-group differences of particular cultural groups based on the differences in their historical experiences. For others, the historical context of the programs them-selves could provide an enhanced understanding of the success or failure of program outcomes (Copeland-Carson, 2005).

Time is important for another reason. While a number of studies identified time as a significant challenge, particularly in terms of the length of time required to be culturally responsive and the consequent lack of time to do the work (e.g., Alkon et al., 2001; Anderson-Draper, 2006; Copeland-Carson, 2005; Uhl et al., 2004), time also provided the opportunity for growth, change, and learning. Over time Ander-son-Draper (2006) came to understand more about her own cultural positioning, and thus became more flexible in facilitating discussions and gathering data. Ryan, Chan-dler, and Samuels (2007) moved from a superficial understanding of culture to a more nuanced understanding, ultimately leading them to look at their data differently. As they became more familiar with the needs of the community, Cooper and Christie (2005), switched from a responsive evaluation approach to a social justice approach so that they could capture the voices of the underrepresented stakeholders. Accord-ing to Cooper and Christie (2005), "Our approach become more closely aligned with the program's goal of serving local district parents and providing parents educational opportunities for their children" (p. 2249). Copeland-Carson (2005) modified the methodology throughout the evaluation process to capture new findings and issues as they emerged and to accommodate the social dynamics of the community and budget-ary constraints.

In other studies from our sample, the role of evaluator was constantly being reshaped and transformed throughout the evaluation process, with the role being characterized as multifaceted, fluid, and shifting (Clayson et al., 2002), not stable but highly dynamic (Harklau & Norwood, 2005), negotiated over time (Anderson-Draper, 2006), and flexible (Butty et al., 2004). The role of evaluator was also shaped by a par-ticular historical and cultural context (Clayson et al., 2002) and intertwined with rela-tions of power involving societal and political discourses (Harklau & Norwood, 2005). For others, the element of time provided the opportunity to develop relationships with stakeholders (Boyce, 2017), become more familiar with the program and participants (Conner, 2004), and develop trust with participants (Coppens et al., 2006).

We were struck by the construction of time as an emergent, evolving, influential, and potentially transformational force throughout the evaluations we examined. The dimension of time underscores the importance of looking at programs and the evalua-tion process, not as fixed entities in time and space, but as sets of relations connected to larger sociopolitical systems that act in myriad ways on the local setting, the program, the people, and the relationships (Chouinard & Milley, 2016). The dynamic and highly interactive context of culturally responsive practice presents tremendous opportunities of growth and transformation for evaluators working in these settings, an aspiration motivating all culturally responsive approaches to evaluation. The dimension of time means that our evaluation contexts are socially constructed through a complex history that shapes the knowledge co-created between and among evaluators and program stakeholders. Thus, although these contexts may hold tremendous potential for understanding, they are not neutral, ahistorical settings.

The Cultural Appropriateness of Evaluative Measurements

The use of culturally appropriate methods, or more specifically their "methodological validity" (Kirkhart, 1995), remains an ongoing concern in culturally responsive evaluation practice (Hood et al., 2016). A number of studies in our sample describe the challenges experienced in developing culturally and contextually appropriate approaches to accommodate diverse values, beliefs, and practices (e.g., Clayson et al., 2002; Coppens et al., 2006; Small et al., 2006). For many of the studies, this challenge was intensified by the use of predetermined or standardized measures, outcome indicators and measurement techniques. Such predetermined measures may not have conceptual or metrical equivalence, making it difficult to interpret the data for a specific population (e.g., Alkon et al., 2001; Butty et al., 2004; Coppens et al., 2006; Small et al., 2006).

For many of the studies in our sample, despite extensive community engagement in the evaluation process through the use of collaborative approaches, designing culturally valid instruments remained an ongoing challenge, especially if the funder required predefined metrics (Clayson et al., 2002; Coppens et al., 2006; Novins, King, & Stone, 2004; Small et al., 2006). As Clayson et al., (2002) explain, "Often funders were locked into particular concepts that they regarded as relevant for all contexts and communities; and it was difficult to convince them otherwise" (p. 39). In the study by Coppens et al. (2006), the funder insisted on using a measure of self-esteem, reflecting a preference for instilling internal motivation and individualism, both of which were culturally inappropriate for the study population. To address this cultural incommensurability, the evaluators revised the instrument to emphasize interdependency and certain relational aspects of self-esteem. Small et al. (2006) describe a similar situation in which they were required to adopt a culturally inappropriate instrument. Although negotiations with the funder ultimately led to modifications of the instrument, it nonetheless failed to meet the standards of multicultural validity (Kirkhart, 1995).

To address these challenges, a number of studies in our sample developed creative approaches to accommodate funder requirements and achieve standards of methodological validity. Some studies devised means to engage diverse stakeholders (Alkon et al., 2001; Prilleltensky et al., 2000), collecting multiple forms of data and triangulating the findings (Butty et al, 2004; Coppens et al., 2006; Prilleltensky et al.,

2000; Small et al., 2006), modifying instruments through stakeholder feedback (Coppens et al., 2006), working with stakeholders and community members to inter-pret the meaning of challenging terms (Clayson et al., 2004; Coppens et al., 2006), using established methods in new ways to create a safe space for marginalized voices (Christie & Barela, 2005), using survey instruments as interviews to cultivate better understanding and conceptual equivalence (Coppens et al., 2006), and broadening the stakeholder group to meet established cultural norms (Clayson et al, 2002). In their work with Chinese and Chinese-American children, Alkon et al. (2001) transformed the interview content into a puppet show in order to improve children's responses. For their part, Christie and Barela (2005) used the Delphi technique in a new way to create opportunities for stakeholders to share their voices anonymously. Others used mixed methods to ensure valid and reliable findings (Prilleltensky et al., 2000), navigate funder requests with culturally appropriate methods (Butty et al., 2004; Prilleltensky et al., 2000), and mitigate power dynamics (Christie & Barela, 2005). Meanwhile, some used multiple methods to provide a comprehensive overview of the positive and negative aspects of the program (Prilleltensky et al., 2000). In reflecting on their work with diverse parents and children, Alkon et al. (2001) recommended mixed methods, noting that "integrating qualitative and quantitative methods would have helped estab-lish conceptual equivalence of the instruments across diverse ethnic groups" (p. 54).

Despite the use of collaborative approaches and the opportunity for community input on instrument development, the studies in our sample continued to struggle to ensure the development and use of culturally validated measures. This challenge was particularly burdensome when funders insisted on using predetermined or stan-dardized measures, outcome indicators, and metrical instruments. Although nego-tiations with funders led to some modifications, what is striking is that despite these methodological adaptations, there was still a sense that these modifications failed to meet the standards of multicultural validity (Kirkhart, 1995), considered a hallmark of culturally responsive practice. As stated in the American Evaluation Association Public Statement on Cultural Competence in Evaluation (2011), "validity is central to evaluation. It marks the extent to which an evaluation 'got it right' regardless of approach or paradigm" (p. 5). Considerations of validity in evaluation, particularly in culturally complex evaluations, brings focus to key aspects of culturally responsive practice: the salience of cultural context, the need to develop measures and instru-ments that have established validity and reliability in a cultural context (Frierson, Hood & Hughes, 2002), the crucial importance of becoming familiar with cultural context and of building relationships with participants (Chouinard & Cousins, 2009), the understanding that our methodologies are themselves cultural prod-ucts (Smith, 1999; Stanfield, 1999), the methodological indispensability of pilot-ing metrical instruments and vetting them with community members (American Evaluation Association, 2011; Mertens, 2009), and the utility of mixed methods that more fully address complexity of context (Frierson, Hood, Hughes, and Thomas, 2010; Hood et al., 2016).

The Use and Influence of Evaluative Findings

The studies in our sample provide numerous rationales for their use of culturally responsive approaches, including social justice, advocacy, empowerment, voice, understanding, validity, complexity, and responsiveness. They all aspire to ameliorate social inequities and past injustices. While our findings are not explicitly connected to evaluation use, we do note connections to more distal outcomes and influences, as found in similar transformative and collaborative approaches (Cousins & Chouinard, 2012; Mertens, 2009), bringing the focus to underexplored aspects of evaluation use and influence in culturally responsive evaluation contexts.

While we were able to identify a few instances of justificatory or symbolic use, either to satisfy funder demands (Coppens et al., 2006), increase the perception that evaluation results may be useful (Butty et al., 2004), or inflate the prestige of the evaluation (Harklau & Norwood, 2005), we were also able to identify evidence of instrumental and conceptual use. For some, instrumental use was represented by the formative use of data to improve the program (Butty et al., 2004), make changes to program mandates (Clayson et al., 2002), support program decisions that affect the day-to-day operations of the program (Coppens et al., 2006), advance the evaluation of reform models using critical race theory (Noblit & Jay, 2010), and create additional program materials for clients (Conner, 2004). As Coppens et al. (2006) explain, the instrumental uses of the evaluation "demonstrated the importance of evaluation being specifically tailored and that the process can bring about concrete and positive results" (p. 326). For others, the conceptual use of findings led to a more complete understanding of how and why the program worked (Butty et al., 2004), to an enhanced understanding of other stakeholder perceptions and needs (Prilleltensky et al., 2000), and to the use of findings to create a "counter narrative" (Noblit & Jay, 2010).

The studies we reviewed also provided multiple instances of process use (e.g., Conner, 2004; King et al., 2004; Samuels & Ryan, 2011), which we were able to discern at the individual and interpersonal levels, an observation that was not surprising given the use of participatory or collaborative approaches in culturally responsive practice (Cousins & Chouinard, 2012). Studies in our sample identify change at the individual level in terms of a sense of personal importance from having participated in the study and a willingness to participate further (Conner, 2004), a new understanding about conducting and designing evaluation (Prilleltensky et al., 2010), a way of thinking evaluatively (Coppens et al., 2006; Ryan et al., 2007), an approach to capacity building (LaPoint & Jackson, 2004; Ryan et al., 2007), an avenue for developing trust in administrative decision making (Christie & Barela, 2005), and a means of fostering empowerment (Conner, 2004) and of increasing project ownership (Small et al., 2006).

We also note multiple shifts in perspectives about culture, leading to further reflections on cultural positionality or to reconceptualizations of data and of the research process itself. Our findings indicate that culturally responsive approaches ultimately lead evaluators, stakeholders, or clients to reflect on themselves, on their roles and values, and on the impact of culture on evaluation processes and practices. We refer to this as a form of "cultural process use," which can touch on the evaluator (e.g., Anderson-Draper, 2006), the stakeholders (Coppens et al., 2006) or the clients (Clayson et al., 2002). As Ryan et al. (2007) explain, while schools struggled with the meaning of culture, initially relying on more traditional definitions, "as schools began to define culture and recognize contextual factors and their importance for culturally responsive evaluation, they began to recognize that culture moved far beyond ethnic festivals and events" (p. 204). In so doing, they moved from a superficial to a more nuanced understanding, ultimately prompting them to look at data differently. For Samuels and Ryan (2011), the exploration of cultural positionality with the evaluation team moved them beyond single loop learning to some evidence of double loop learning, as they questioned assumptions about current practices, values, and beliefs in applied contexts.

We also identified instances where cultural responsiveness encouraged evaluator reflexivity and an awareness of positionality, a process use that refers to a shift in the *evaluator's* thinking about culture and its influence on the evaluation process. As Anderson-Draper (2006) describes, over time, she came to understand more about her own cultural positioning, which she then used to facilitate discussions about data collection processes. For others, cultural awareness and personal growth led to revised decisions and shifts in direction and in their role during the course of the evaluation (Butty et al., 2004; Cooper & Christie, 2005; LaPoint & Jackson, 2004). For King et al. (2004), who adopted a starting position as "informed not-knowers, cultural competence arises through a deliberate and continuous process of self and organizational introspection" (p. 68).

The studies in our sample provide a number of justifications for their use of culturally responsive approaches, primary among them are aspirations of social justice, empowerment, voice, and responsiveness, since they ultimately seek to ameliorate social inequities and past injustices through their evaluation practice. While culture has received little attention in studies of evaluation influence (Kirkhart, 2011), and our own studies indicate little direct linkages between cultural responsiveness and results-based outcomes, we do observe more distal outcomes and influences, as found in similar transformative and collaborative approaches (Cousins & Chouinard, 2012). Kirkhart's (2010) alternative to "evaluation use," framed as "evaluation influence," provides an important shift in perspective from an instrumental, outcome-based focus to distal, multidirectional, indirect, and often unexpected influences. While we did note instances of findings use, as well as combinations of findings use and process use, our analysis identified what we termed *cultural process use*, a type of use and influence that exemplifies double loop learning (Argyris & Schön, 1978), as cultural self-awareness leads to changes in direction, decision making, evaluation outcomes and future findings. Kirkhart's (2011) focus on evaluation influence, defined in terms of source, intention and time, enables a reconceptualization of use and influence in culturally responsive practice as a more fluid and dynamic process linked to local, immediate and potentially distal influences and consequences. An understanding of culture, located along on a continuum from a more local to a broader understanding, significantly led to further reflection on the cultural community and context and to an enhanced understanding of evaluation as a cultural product and to the self as cultural being, not to mention the evaluation process itself, leading to the potential for more distal outcomes and influences in the future. At the same time, we note very little evidence of influence in terms of the aspiration related to social justice and equity, especially in terms of distal consequences.

CRITICAL DISCUSSION AND IMPLICATIONS FOR PRACTICE

Our analysis of the 24 studies led us to identify seven broad, interconnected themes we believe capture the dynamic tensions and complexities of culturally responsive approaches to evaluation in the Western context. While all seven themes (broad understanding of culture, multiple manifestations of power, cultural complexities of language, identity as multifaceted and fluid, temporal dimensions of practice, developing culturally valid measurement instruments, and use and influence as expressed across cultural contexts) describe quite distinct implications and experiences of cultural practice across diverse community sectors, populations, and programs, there is also significant interplay among them that collectively shapes and defines the unique experience and practice of cultural responsiveness in the West. As we look across the 24 studies, we perceive the identified themes and their interconnections as relational, dynamic, and emergent, shaped and configured by local interactions and experiences and by historical and global influences and practices.

Across cultural and program contexts, such as violence prevention programs in immigrant communities, HIV prevention programs in Latino communities in the USA, and outward bound programs for African Americans, studies describe an inherent tension between the local and broader dimensions of place, as evaluators attempt to learn, relearn, reflect, integrate, accommodate, and adapt to multiple and often conflicting needs and priorities throughout the evaluation process. From this perspective, the practice of evaluation is envisioned as an interweaving of connections (Gherardi, 2009), an iterative social and discursive practice (Schwandt, 1997), and an "institutionalized doing" (Bourdieu, 1972, p. 117) that is culturally and historically constituted (Smeyers & Burbles, 2006), as well as shaped and informed locally by forces that originate outside the immediate setting (Smith, 1987). As Kemmis, Edwards-Groves, Wilkinson, and Hardy (2012) explain,

> Practices are always *situated* in time and space, and unfold in site ontologies . . . always already shaped by, the particular historically given conditions that exist in particular localities or sites at particular moments. Specifically, practices are always constituted in and through the particular cultural-discursive, material-economic and social-political conditions that exist in the site. (emphasis in original, p. 35)

Understood as a practice that occurs within "site ontologies," evaluation thus emerges as deeply implicated in the sociopolitical relations and dynamics of context, where identity, language, power, and culture shift and tussle with the norms, standards, and often predefined metrics of evaluative practice.

In a number of studies, we noted an ongoing dialogue about identity, location, and positioning, whether referring to a shift from outsider to insider, or from identifying self as insider or outsider, to locating cultural insiders from within the community. Whether considered as in or out, as insider or outsider, identity is conceptualized as a spatial property, framed as a "production" and a "positioning," always in process and never complete (Goffman, 1959; Hall, 1990), opening up a multidimensional understanding of identity that is created and recreated through discursive practice (Hall, 1996a, 1996b). As Hall (1990) describes,

> Cultural identities come from somewhere, have histories. But like everything which is historical, they [identities] undergo constant transformation, Far from being eternally fixed in some essentialized past, they are subject to the continuous "play" of history, culture and power. Far from being grounded in a mere "recovery" of the past, which is waiting to be found, and which, when found, will secure our sense of ourselves into eternity, identities are the name we give to the different ways we are positioned by, and position ourselves within, the narratives of the past. (p. 70)

Interconnected notions of identity occur across cultural, class, gender, and racial divides, and across political, economic, and social histories. As Cockburn (1998) points out, "The social formation and the moment certainly shape the range of identities at play" (p. 213). The many points of inclusion and exclusion, the coming and going, and the in and out underscores the very complexity of place, location, and self as we move from points of connection to disconnection and from unity to discord within the contexts of practice. Identities are thus created discursively, constructed in and through specific historical and political contexts (Hall, 1996b) in relation to others both near and far, and are defined by ethnicity, gender, race, age, history, and experience.

While the complexity of identity and its associated philosophical concerns remain challenging in culturally diverse communities, we also note challenges between the local culture and the normative demands of professional practice. As professionals, evaluators have been socialized and trained in a set of historically and normatively produced practices that influence and define their professional identities (Bauder, 2006) and that shape the parameters of local evaluation. Based on earlier empirical research on institutions, Foucault (1991) identified "regimes of practices" as

> not just governed by institutions, prescribed by ideologies, guided by pragmatic circumstances—whatever role these elements may actually play—but possess up to a point their own specific regularities, logic, strategy, self-evidence and

"reason" [as such these "regimes of practice"] have both prescriptive effects regarding what is to be done (effects of "jurisdiction"), and codifying effects regarding what is to be known (effects of "veridiction"). (p. 75)

These influences are not slight. In the majority of studies we note ongoing tensions between the local context and the disciplinary constraints of evaluation, tensions concerning language, power, methods, culture, or identity. There was a disconnection between local frames of meaning (who speaks, whose voice in included, what matters, and to whom) and prescriptive approaches, guidelines, and practices of the discipline, an issue that extends beyond the incommensurability of prescribed instruments in local cultural contexts.

Long considered a type of "assisted sense making" (Mark, Henry, & Julnes, 2000), evaluation provides judgments of value that are defined, analyzed, and ascribed based on what are often predefined measures of quality. The methods, tools, and approaches used thus reflect certain values, beliefs, and assumptions, shaping our interpretations and practices in certain ways and in certain directions (Dahler-Larsen, 2012). These prescribed measures have a regulatory power, let alone what Dahler-Larsen (2012) refers to as "constitutive effects," insofar as they frame "values, orientations, interpretations and practices in the direction of a particular construction of social reality" (p. 199). Thus, while culturally responsive approaches are intended to liberate the perspectives and voices of the local community, the mandatory use of prescribed and standardized measures not suited to the local culture remains an ongoing and serious challenge. The issue is not simply about the mandatory use of a measurement instrument not suited to the local population, or about the technical merits of one methodological approach over another, but rather about what Schwandt (2007) has termed "epistemological politics," that is, the privileging of some knowledge and some knowers over others. In contexts of practice where issues of diversity are profound, the obligation to use standardized measures must also be regarded as a form of "epistemological ethnocentrism" (Reagan, 1996), a practice that frames and legitimizes the parameters of the local evaluation context (Chouinard, 2013). As Kushner (2000) points out,

> Forms of investigation have to be understood as forms of social organization—they do not happen outside of our institutions, our social relations, our politics and economics . . . research is cast in the image of the institutions which bear it and which husband it. (p. 16)

The power to establish legitimate forms of knowledge is validated by the profession outside of the local community, an issue that draws attention to the ongoing politicized nature of knowledge construction in the social sciences, not to mention the ongoing challenge of designing culturally responsive approaches to evaluation in local communities.

CHAPTER SUMMARY

Culturally responsive practice in the evaluation of programs in a Western context provides a broad and varied backdrop against which to understand the application of culture in our methodological practices. Overall, the diversity in conceptual and methodological approaches to culture—what we would call "methodological eclecticism"—makes it particularly challenging to distinguish among approaches and contexts, and to extend our understanding of theory and practice. Power in its many guises continues to define and redefine the boundaries of culturally responsive practice, particularly in instances where funders require predefined measures. Evaluators working in the Western context nonetheless demonstrate incredible resilience and creativity as they continue to forge new methodologies grounded in the cultural context of community.

EXTENDING INQUIRY

Bibliography of Further Readings

Agar, M. (2000). Border lessons: Linguistic "rich points" and evaluative understanding. In R. K. Hopson (Ed.), How and why language matters in valuation. *New Directions for Evaluation, 86*, 93–109.

Chouinard, J. A. (2013). The case for participatory evaluation in an era of accountability. *American Journal of Evaluation, 34*(2), 237–253.

Chouinard, J. A., & Cousins, J. B. (2009). A review and synthesis of current research on cross-cultural evaluation. *American Journal of Evaluation, 30*(4), 457–494.

Hopson, R. K. (2000). How and why language matters in evaluation. *New Directions for Evaluation, 86*. San Francisco, CA: Jossey-Bass.

Stanfield, J. H., Jr. (1999). Slipping through the front door: Relevant social scientific evaluation in the people of color century. *American Journal of Evaluation, 20*(3), 415–431.

Exercises Based on Case Examples

1. Select one of the three cases at the beginning of this chapter and design a culturally responsive approach to evaluation based on your understanding of the program and its context. How are you positioned in your evaluation? Where does culture fit into your design? Where does culture fit in data collection and analysis? Once you have thought through some of these questions, download the study (see bibliographic references) and read how the author(s) designed their evaluation.

2. Select one of the cases in the beginning of this chapter. How would you ensure that the history, culture, and background of the community inform your

evaluation design? Which stakeholders will you include in your evaluation? Which would you exclude? And why?

3. In each of the three cases highlighted, how would you ensure that you meet the information needs of the funders and stakeholders?

Discussion Questions

1. Identify and describe the concerns touching on language in culturally responsive approaches to evaluation? How might you address some of these issues?

2. List four of the key challenges in conducting culturally responsive approaches. Describe these issues and state how you would address them.

3. If a funder provides you with predefined instruments (e.g., survey questions, measures), how would you deal with the possible lack of cultural relevance? How might you address it with the funder? With the community?

4. From a methodological perspective, what is the point of reflecting upon your own cultural position? How does your positioning influence the evaluation?

6

THE INTERNATIONAL DEVELOPMENT CONTEXT

"Culture is not simply the folkloric or exotic surface of peoples 'not like us,' but is the underlying fabric of their whole society." (Eversole, 2005, p. 300)

OVERVIEW OF CHAPTER

The focus in this chapter is on the shifting and increasingly globalized international development context, a place where boundaries and borderlands become spaces of cultural interaction and contestation, particularly as multiple and diverse communities now share this historically controverted terrain. Our review turned up 25 published articles, the majority of which are reflective case narratives based on prior evaluation experiences with programs situated in culturally diverse communities, spanning 17 years (from 2000 to 2017).

We begin with a brief discussion of the context in which international development evaluations take place, focusing on the issues and tensions surrounding international aid and "development" in addition to the cultural implications of current practices. We then turn to a brief description of our sample of 25 studies, followed by a review and integration of this literature, addressing implications for culturally responsive practice as it relates to experiences in the field and to our conceptual framework (see Chapter 2). Our goal is to locate culturally responsive practice in evaluation, from the initial stage of planning all the way to the later stages of dissemination and use of results. To further our understanding of cultural influences in the international development context, we then look to our conceptual framework to see *where* and *how* culture is located in our programs and evaluations. We conclude the chapter with a summary discussion of the findings.

CASE EXAMPLE 1: This study concerns an applied drama and theatre project in Africa based on a participatory evaluation approach using the "language" of drama and theatre. In this approach, indicators are linked to the transformative nature of "play" as participants take on new roles and engage in an immersive, artistic style of learning. The author of the study challenges the "modernist framework" that imposes a methodology on local communities based on the assumption that change in Africa can occur only as a result of outsider strategies aimed at modernizing the culture to international norms and standards. This impelled them to devise a more culturally inclusive approach to participatory monitoring and evaluation that privileges local knowledge for planning, implementation, and appraisal. He places an emphasis on public dialogue to create space for community members to negotiate with external experts and evaluators as a way to generate local knowledge. He questions how evaluators can align indicators with local knowledge systems, especially since the cultural relevance of indicators determines the extent to which they become meaningful and valid for local communities. He also questions the extent to which knowledge production in evaluation reflects communication within the program and community. He also discusses what he calls "outsider syndrome," a condition in which evaluators, practitioners, change agents, and activists fail to move beyond a conception of themselves as "experts." Overall, he notes the cultural incommensurability of Western-based social science models in an African setting, making a link between these models and approaches to evaluation, whether participatory or not (Chinyowa, 2011).

CASE EXAMPLE 2: This study takes up a sustainable agriculture biodiversity management project in China that educates rural farmers on agricultural biodiversity. The evaluation team consisted of three Chinese national consultants and one international consultant. While all spoke basic Mandarin, farmers spoke a local dialect, requiring translation throughout. A participatory rural appraisal approach was used to reflect local knowledge and to enable the poor and marginalized to discuss their concerns. The terms of reference for the evaluation were written with little to no input from the community. As such, many of the instruments were predefined by the funder and found to be culturally incommensurate. The evaluators note that it took villagers a long time to complete the standardized questionnaire, and during interviews the villagers could not relate to many of the predefined questions that were asked. To create a more culturally responsive approach, the evaluators switched to a participatory visualization and diagramming approach (called an "H" diagram) to facilitate local dialogue among farmers. Reflecting on the process, the evaluators identified the need to seek early advice on the cultural appropriateness of methods to ensure that the evaluation design was rooted in the cultural context. While evaluators point out that speaking the language of the community helps improve communication and build rapport throughout the evaluation process, it alone is no guarantee that the cultural nuances essential to constructing culturally responsive evaluations are understood. (Luo & Liu, 2014).

CASE EXAMPLE 3: The authors designed three culturally responsive surveys to assess the land rights and livelihoods of Brazil's *quilombos*, or former fugitive slave communities. Their goal is to combat the negative stereotypes of this population and provide them with data they can use to advocate for themselves. They used a mixed methods approach that included qualitative historical and background information about the communities, detailed questionnaires, semistructured interviews, focus groups, observation, and surveys. Throughout the process, community members were involved in providing feedback on the design, process, and implementation of the evaluation. The evaluators also participated in the daily activities of the community to enrich their understanding of the cultural context of the community. They sought feedback on their survey questions regarding the relevance and appropriateness of certain questions and on the length of the survey and input on which communities should be included in the survey and how best to disseminate the results. They hired local university students and students from the community to administer the household and agricultural surveys. Despite all of the input they solicited at the front end, they nonetheless faced challenges: finding suitable phrases for the survey items, cultivating an understanding of the survey purpose, and establishing a proper grounding for the survey in the cultural context of the community. In the end, they note that there is continued tension between cultural responsiveness and conventional methods of survey development, data collection, and analysis (Bowen & Tillman, 2015).

THE INTERNATIONAL DEVELOPMENT CONTEXT IN EVALUATION

In this section, we depict very broadly the context in which international development evaluation takes place. Even though we recognize that our characterization of the international setting will not do justice to the breadth of the field and the complexity of the issues and challenges that prevail, our goal is to depict the international context in order to set the stage for an understanding of evaluation in this highly challenging context. In the current period of globalization, with its increasing cleavages between the Global North and Global South, the goals of international development remain elusive. Despite decades of "development" and the flow of international and humanitarian aid to the Global South, disparities between high- and low-income countries continue to grow at an accelerating pace, nearly doubling in the past 20 years (United Nations, 2013). Against this backdrop lies a history of colonialism, violent intervention, and poverty, not to mention civic, religious and tribal tensions, postwar conflict, deadly epidemics, and natural disasters. Addressing these challenges is imperative but extremely difficult.

Since the end of colonial rule, there have been numerous shifts in international theories of development, from a focus on donor designed economic policies to an emphasis on strategies that focus on partnerships and local ownership (Conlin & Stirrat, 2008; Slater & Bell, 2002). More recent policy trends have imposed conditions of austerity; favored public-private partnerships (the merging of aid and business); redirected focus on frontline states such as Afghanistan, Pakistan, Iraq and other zones of ongoing conflict; and witnessed the rise of new donor nations (e.g., China, India, Russia) (Mosse, 2013). At the same time, the focus for many international and bilateral aid agencies over the past 20 years has shifted from the UN-sponsored Millennium Development

Goals (MDGs), designed to address issues of extreme poverty and hunger across the Global South, to, more recently, the Sustainable Development Goals (SDGs), part of the 2030 Agenda for Sustainable Development. The SDGs represent a global call to action on 17 interconnected goals, many of which focus on ending poverty, improving health and education, reducing inequality, spurring economic growth, and dealing with climate change.

DESCRIPTION OF SAMPLE

Selection

As noted previously, we selected these studies because they consider culture a construct historically, methodologically, and epistemologically relevant to designing and conducting evaluations in the international development context. While we noted commonality in the approaches, particularly in the use of participatory or collaborative approaches—participatory monitoring and evaluation (n=5), participatory evaluation (n=4), feminist evaluation (n=2), developmental evaluation (n=2)—we were also able to identify over 28 different approaches to evaluation across 25 studies, with multiple studies citing two or more approaches in various combinations. At the same time, we identified only a handful of studies specifically focused on culture. Examples include culturally competent evaluation, culturally responsive evaluation, emancipatory action research, ethnography, gender equity evaluation, and culturally sensitive evaluation. A number of studies also combined approaches. Some addressed the cultural contingencies of the local context (e.g., *Sistematization*, SISDEL), and others sought a balance between local needs and funder needs. Examples here included community-based monitoring and evaluation, outcome mapping, realistic evaluation, results-oriented and impact approaches. A significant number of studies employed a participatory or collaborative approach to evaluation, without however ever considering a methodologically or epistemologically relevant construct (see Chouinard & Hopson, 2016). We therefore discarded these studies.

Characteristics

In the international context, we identified 25 studies published between 2000 and 2017, with no studies conducted in 2002, 2004, 2007, 2013, and 2017 (see Figure 6.1). The studies were located in Africa (n=10), South/East Asia (n=8), Central/South America (n=7), and in the Middle East (n=4). Target populations included students, at-risk students, teachers, youth, young violent offenders, infants, women, girls, sex workers, conservationists, and agricultural workers. The domains of practice included teacher training in a Bedouin community, including a leadership training program; international education; educational programs aimed at youth who have been convicted of violent crimes; community and social services, including children's clubs, women's

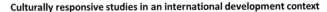

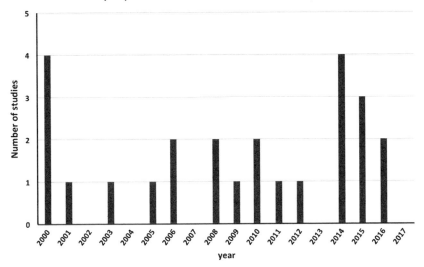

FIGURE 6.1 ■ **Number of Publications Selected by Year**

Culturally responsive studies in an international development context

rights and gender equity, and a program empowering girls and young women; a program to reduce educational gaps for at-risk students; a curriculum project; a program to effect social and community change; health and mental health, including HIV/AIDS education, HIV prevention program for sex workers; an infant feeding program; a health and nutrition program; and agriculture and the environment programs, including women working in agriculture, impacts of new conservation technology, sustainable agricultural biodiversity management project, and rural development programs.

REVIEW AND INTEGRATION OF SELECTED STUDIES

Descriptive Analysis

We also observed a number of reasons for the adoption of culturally responsive approaches. A number of studies offered several reasons: building capacity, building a theoretical framework, aligning with the cultural context, developing culturally valid instruments and data, creating authentic data, fostering learning and decision making, facilitating stakeholder involvement, cultivating cultural sensitivity, localizing monitoring and evaluation strategies, capturing transformative aspect of program, producing a more robust picture of the evaluation context, balancing impact with local context, integrating the organizational mission with evaluation approach, and collaborating with stakeholders to develop a project sensitive to cultural dynamics.

In other cases, we noted aspirational aims related to social justice and the amelioration of past injustices: to popularize and further develop local indigenous methods;

advance empowerment and learning; combat reductionist portrayals of historically marginalized communities; improve the lives of marginalized people; address issues of social justice, considering power, gender, and ethics; build community capacity to evaluate needs and take action; acknowledge local knowledge that has been buried; allow others to represent their own concerns; improve practice through dialogue and understanding; stimulate reflection and debate in the broader society; and construct local cultural knowledge instead of imposing Western knowledge.

At the same time, the majority of studies used participatory or collaborative approaches to advance their aims, such as participatory impact evaluation, participatory evaluation, participatory monitoring and evaluation, democratic deliberative evaluation, developmental evaluation, utilization-focused evaluation, and participatory action research. Only one study did not use a collaborative approach, and this study was based primarily on a results-oriented or impact-based understanding of evaluation (Elkins, 2010).

Integration and Synthesis

Our reading and subsequent analysis of the empirical literature was guided by our conceptual framework for inquiry that identified the nine locations of culture in research and evaluation practice. We also used the "key questions guiding analysis" to focus our analysis on the more salient cultural dimensions of evaluation practice. Our reading and analysis of these studies also informed our conceptual framework, which we discuss comparatively across the three contexts in Chapter 7.

Whereas some of our specific observations relate directly to the specific dimensions themselves, others point to considerations within dimensions, opening up further questions and implications for exploring culture in evaluation practice. Through this process, we bring a critical focus to seven key areas of thematic interest: contextual complexity, temporal dimensionality, participatory strategies, methodological dissonance, going beyond the spoken word, cultural translation, and the ethical imperative. While many of the themes intersect, they each highlight a particular cultural focus, and as such merit individual attention and discussion.

Contextual Complexity

The evaluation literature characterizes context as a complex, multifaceted, highly relational, and interactive phenomenon composed of social, historical, political, economic, institutional, ecological, and cultural dimensions, which together influence program and evaluation characteristics, possibilities, and outcomes (Mathison, 2005; Vo, 2013). Context is considered not a static, predefined entity but a social construction with a performative and highly interactive quality (Dilley, 2002). As Dahler-Larsen and Schwandt (2012) explain, "evaluators (and evaluations) do not simply identify and respond to contextual factors, but by virtue of their actions are always constructing, relating to, engaging in, and taking part in some construction of the context in which they operate" (p. 84). This observation provides a sense of the multidimensional and multifaceted nature of a program's context, which in culturally responsive approaches becomes all the more significant (SenGupta et al., 2004), since context itself becomes the site of confluence where program, culture, and community interconnect. Context, according to LaFrance, Nichols, and Kirkhart (2012), "defines the entire evaluation landscape, including how it is viewed, understood, designed, performed, and used" (p. 73).

For many of the studies in our sample, keen awareness of these complexities of the program and community context was considered essential to good evaluation practice, as contextual factors were found to significantly challenge evaluation planning and implementation (Donaldson, Azzam, & Connor, 2013; Kelly, 2006). Some of the studies focused specifically on the relational aspects of evaluation, coupled with an understanding of gender inequality, power imbalances, and local inequities (e.g., Brandon, Smith, Ofir, & Noordeloos, 2014; Buskens & Earl, 2008; Lustig, Ben-Baruch-Koskas, Makhani-Belkin, & Hirsch, 2015). As Pouw et al. (2017) explain,

> The quality of thinking and practice on local development interventions can be improved by engaging in a continuous discussion with the intended beneficiaries and broader group of stakeholders (program administrators, funding agencies, local leaders, ministries) about the formulated goals of the development intervention, the process itself, and outcomes realized. (p. 3)

Although taking the time to develop relationships is considered essential to good evaluation practice, others noted that the use of culturally responsive approaches can surface underlying issues and tensions between stakeholder groups, causing a host of methodological challenges as tensions arise between diverse groups (Brandon et al., 2014; Buskens & Earl, 2008; Nandi, Nanda, & Jugran, 2015). As Hart and Rajbhandary (2003) describe, in Nepali culture, children often waited to voice their responses until after they had heard their "leaders" speak, making it a challenge to adapt collaborative approaches and gather authentic qualitative responses. Problematic relationships between program staff and participants ultimately led Buskens and Earl (2008) to revise their counseling and training formats. For Brandon, Smith, Ofir, and Noordeloos (2014), power dynamics between male supervisors and female participants had methodological implications, necessitating a review of data aggregation strategies and a reconsideration of both data collection and analytical strategies. Similarly, Haylock and Miller (2016) noted that their feminist approach led to a reflection on evaluator–partner power dynamics, ultimately leading to the creation of additional ways for partners to design and steer evaluation processes.

We will take up the theme of methodological preferences later; it is important to note here that for many of the studies in our sample, a focus on understanding the cultural complexities and challenges of international development contexts was linked to methodology, balancing Patton's notion of "situational responsiveness" and the "best fit" between methods and context (e.g., Abes, 2000; Botcheva, Shih, & Huffman, 2009; Elkins, 2010; Sidersky & Guijt, 2000). In their work evaluating health policies in southern Africa, Buskens and Earl (2008) used outcome mapping to facilitate greater project clarity by mapping the boundaries of the program, partnerships, and processes. As a result of this process, they adopted appreciative inquiry to promote positive outcomes focused on transformation, rather than utilizing an approach that might have increased the negative perception of public health. In an evaluation of children's clubs in Nepal, Hart and Rajbhandary (2003) used social mapping as an introductory activity to help them better understand the physical distances and locations of children in relation to the program.

Working within the peace-precarious context of war-torn Iraq and Afghanistan, Elkins (2010) describes a revised framework for monitoring and evaluation that is profoundly shaped by implementation elasticity, cost elasticity, situational interests, stakeholder complexity, and political sensitivity, leaving aside the pervasive risk of violence. As she states, the risk of violence impacts the willingness of funders, evaluators, and program coordinators to participate. It can lead to uncertainty and instability within the program, significantly modifying expectations about outcomes. In her description of a prevention program for sex workers in a remote region of northern Brazil, Laperrière (2007) underscores the importance of local cultural and social contexts, since they can influence analysis and discussion, limit outcomes, and hinder researcher control. In response to a challenging evaluation they conducted in rural China, Luo and Liu (2014) conclude "grounding an evaluation design in its particular national and cultural context is a precondition to the success of any evaluation" (p. 6).

Context matters a great deal in these studies. The need to consider context becomes all the more pressing, we believe, when societies and institutions are subject to instability of various kinds. For many of the studies in our sample, adopting a culturally responsive approach was not straightforward. It was often necessary to contend with multiple challenges, constraints, and trade-offs, an experience that highlights the dynamic and complex relationship between evaluators and their contexts of practice.

As many have noted, the challenge is not in finding an ideal match between evaluation approach and context, but of acknowledging the difficulty of translating a Western-based methodology in appropriate contextual terms across the Global South (Chouinard & Hopson, 2016; Ginsberg, 1988). The other themes in this chapter—methodological tensions, participatory strategies, crossing borders—provide further examples of this ongoing historical, political, and cultural struggle.

Temporal Dimensionality

The temporal dimension has both a real and a metaphorical quality. Rooted within notions of connection, possibility, and change, time can either impede or facilitate the evaluation process. While studies in the international domain were temporally bounded, time also offered the opportunity for growth and learning, relationships with stakeholders, understanding the cultural context of the program and community, and adapting the evaluative methodology to better fit the circumstances and conditions of practice. The temporal dimensional also signifies a past history of colonial rule, as well as relationships based on the donor–recipient dynamic. Time also signifies a continual construction and reconstruction of self and identity, as evaluators and stakeholders together construct the evaluative narrative.

A number of studies described the transformational potential of culturally responsive practice, with learning depicted as a continuum along which evaluators and stakeholders progressed throughout the process (e.g., Bi Niba & Green, 2005; Brandon et al., 2014; Lustig et al., 2015). In a description of a school-based educational program for Black South African youth, Bi Niba and Green (2005) highlight a mutual learning experience as stakeholders shifted from learners to facilitators of knowledge through a process of reflective dialogue focused on preparation, training, and implementation. For Botcheva, Shih, and Huffman (2009), cultural responsiveness is a learning process which they picture as a continuum based on learning from stakeholders, recognizing individual subjectivities, and recognizing and understanding the cultural context. Working in a South African context, Buskens and Earl (2008) describe their focus on cultural responsiveness as a transformational process, focused on self-awareness in terms of race, gender, sexuality, and class.

In other studies, the temporal dimension was understood at a relational level, focused on mutual reflection and learning, spending time in the community, and getting to know people and cultural norms and meanings (e.g., Brandão, Braga, Renato Silva, & Codas, 2012; Holte-McKenzie Forde, & Theobald, 2006; Lustig et al., 2015). In their description of a culturally responsive evaluation in former fugitive slave communities in Brazil, Bowen and Tillman (2015) reflect on the importance of relationship building: "[I]n the development phase, considerable preliminary fieldwork is critical to carefully contextualize marginalized communities and to increase the researchers sensitivity to cultural norms and nuances" (p. 13). For Nagai (2001), an expatriate now considered an "outsider" in the community, living in the Maiwala community in Papua New Guinea and being re-immersed in the culture slowly shifted community perspectives about her. As she describes, "Through the sharing of my data . . . parents and teachers began to rethink the supportive role and symmetrical status of me, an outsider" (p. 84). Describing his experience in Filipino culture, Abes (2000) similarly notes the need for evaluators to spend time becoming what he describes as "insiders," which allows them to learn and acquire respect for community norms and values.

All told, we can identify some degree of methodological adaptation across all 25 studies. However, modifications and revisions occur as evaluators become more familiar with the program, cultural context, and stakeholder community over time. As a result, some of the studies portrayed time as an enabler, creating an opportunity to adapt the methodology to better fit the cultural context of the community (e.g., Abes, 2000; Sidersky & Guijt, 2000). As Hart and Rajbhandary (2003) point out, modifying participatory methods in line with Nepalese children's culture took considerable time and required "significant experimentation" (p. 64). For others, collaboration led to greater familiarity, which in turn led to "fundamental changes in every step of the evaluation process" (Botcheva et al., 2009, p. 177). For their part, Durham and Tan (2010) noted a shift in methodology and cultural responsiveness as the evaluation progressed and they gained familiarity with the culture and cultural context of the program community.

As the evaluations in our sample suggest, evaluations are bound, shaped, and framed by time and space, by the context and culture of the program community; meanwhile, the rituals of our practice are played out and "performed" in measured and sequential parts. The temporal dimension, as these studies make clear, provides a sense of change, unfolding and transformation, a learning and a becoming, denoting emergent possibilities in shifting the typically linear rituals of our practice. There is a "happenstance" quality of play and performance in culturally responsive practice; evaluators and stakeholders come together and, through a process of reflection and learning, create new methodological possibilities. The temporal dimension is essentially fluid, with people transitioning from one transformational possibility to another. The temporal dimension elucidates research as a process that unfolds in time. A crucial part of this unfolding comes in the often gradual development of relationships among researchers and participants. As we shall see, this process becomes all the more complex in international development contexts because the range of stakeholders and stakeholder interests is often so variegated.

Participatory Strategies

Prior research (see Chouinard & Cousins, 2009; Chouinard & Hopson, 2016; Hood, Hopson, & Kirkhart, 2016) suggests that culturally responsive evaluation is seen as a form of collaboration and partnership between evaluators and community members, leading to increased understanding of unique sociocultural characteristics, processes, and perspectives. In our sample of studies, we note the widespread use of collaborative approaches to advance culturally responsive evaluation practice and capture local realities, what Ofir and Kumar (2013) refer to as a "developing country lens" (p. 12). While the motivation for inclusion varied widely across all studies, for instance, the motivation of mitigating contextual and cultural complexity or of ensuring valid and reliable instruments, we also note significant variation in practice across studies based on the level and nature of stakeholder involvement, the diversity of stakeholders, and the level of evaluator control over the evaluation process (Cousins & Whitmore, 1998). Despite rationales cited for inclusion, we note that participation can be understood, interpreted, and practiced in myriad ways depending upon the program, the complexity of the community context, the range of stakeholder involvement, the evaluation purpose and clients' information needs and goals, and the evaluator's own value stance.

The majority of studies in our review adopted participatory approaches, either alone or in combination with other approaches, to wit, monitoring and evaluation, developmental, empowerment, realistic, and contribution analysis (Brandon et al., 2014), ethnographic and goal-free evaluation (Laperrière, 2007), participatory and appreciative approaches (Nandi et al., 2015), and systematization and multistakeholder evaluation (Tapella & Rodríguez-Bilella, 2014). Evaluators are sometimes called "creative pluralists" (Chambers, 2007, p. 23) on account of these eclectic combinations, often the product of improvisation in participatory methods and techniques to better address the cultural and political dynamics of the program context. This creativity is seen throughout our studies: Evaluators adapt collaborative strategies to address the cultural complexity of the program context, including the diversity of stakeholders, the broad range of stakeholder interests and needs, and program funder requirements. Our findings suggest that this issue becomes all the more demanding in the international development context, since there are numerous stakeholders representing widely diverse roles and constituencies (e.g., multiple agencies, donors, beneficiaries, politicians, evaluators, community program managers) (Bamberger, Vaessen, & Raimondo, 2016), very often with competing and contrasting issues, interests, and voices. In a survey of international development evaluators, Cullen, Coryn, and Rugh (2011) found that 77% of evaluators noted that stakeholder selection was often too challenging. While we note complex and intricate arrangements concerning who is selected for inclusion and what form their inclusion might take in practice, we also note a range of techniques used by evaluators to create spaces for stakeholder involvement.

Our findings suggest that the matter of whom to include (or exclude) ranged significantly across the studies in our sample. In his evaluation of a drama and theatre program in Africa, Chinyowa (2011) describes his formal effort at recruiting participants across multiple levels in the social context, focusing on whom he believed could potentially share control over the form and content of the program. Brandon et al. (2014) included selection criteria based on geographic representation, with different stakeholder groups identified at different phases of the evaluation, and for different purposes. Others authors identified different levels of involvement depending upon the stakeholder group (Abes, 2000), whereas others involved key stakeholder groups and farmers in the entire process, using annual seminars to bring together about 40 farmers to review progress and reassess priorities (Sidersky & Guijt, 2000). In other studies, whom to include in the process was focused on issues of gender equity, aiming to recruit women or girls in the process to ensure the equality of their voices and perspectives (Brandon et al., 2014; Nandi et al., 2015).

We were also struck by the innovative ways in which evaluators created spaces for active stakeholder involvement and representation in the evaluation process, especially given the broad and incredibly diverse range of stakeholders and program sponsors involved. Brandon et al. (2014) established a 13-member project steering committee based on geographic representation of "key partners" that included an M&E subcommittee to provide advice and guidance on evaluation planning discussions about empowering African stakeholders. This approach resulted in the selection and development of 22 African trainers to lead more than two dozen training, monitoring and learning events per year. Sidersky and Guijt (2000), for their part, integrated stakeholders from three key groups into a permanent participatory planning process that included annual seminars bringing together 40 local actors to review progress and reassess priorities.

A number of studies also reported multiple gatherings with different purposes, often including different audiences. In an evaluation of a federal education program in Brazil for youth convicted of violent crimes, Brandão Braga, Renato Silva, and Codas (2012) described how marginalized youth who shared the same language and life experiences were trained to conduct peer-based interviews with other youths, resulting in what they describe as "an authenticity that might be difficult to achieve otherwise" (p. 52). Nandi, Nanda, and Jugran (2015) recruited girls from different regions of the country, and they, along with religious and linguistic minorities, worked together to draft evaluation plans and reports, identify issues and questions, foster ownership, build active engagement, and develop common understanding of evaluation purposes and activities. For Torres (2000), training sessions were used to build facilitation skills for local management teams who had been nominated by village authorities to be responsible for the project plan, implementation, monitoring, and evaluation, with workshops taking place in the context of large-scale community assemblies in which participants from different stakeholder groups analyzed evaluation findings to help inform public action mandates. In his description of a project in Zimbabwe, Chinyowa (2011) described a process that began with a "mammoth" community engagement event, leading to youth-led theatre performances with post-performance public policy discussions held with stakeholders (grouped by age and gender categories), eventually leading to an advocacy phase.

While extensive stakeholder inclusion at various points in the process may have mitigated some of the cultural and political challenges, for many (e.g., Haylock & Miller, 2016; Nandi et al., 2015; Tapella & Rodríguez-Bilella, 2014) the breadth and diversity of stakeholder inclusion merely increased complexity and created ongoing conflict. As Tapella and Rodríguez-Bilella (2014) observe, there is a definite risk in complicating and overburdening the evaluation by including too many stakeholders, or in trying to include as many stakeholders as possible to ensure a plurality of perspectives. As they describe, "There is a risk of creating a sort of 'boxing ring' where people can fight for what they believe is the truth" (p. 129). For Brandon et al. (2014), the power dynamics between supervisors (men) and participants (women) created ongoing issues, as did cultural differences among participants included from countries across sub-Saharan Africa especially given the diversity of issues and histories present at the table. For others (e.g., Chinyowa, 2011; Tapella & Rodríguez-Bilella, 2014), evaluation itself represents a form of cultural authority, deeply implicated in, and influenced by, a "modernist agenda," underscoring the need to look critically at the methodologies we use, despite good intentions to collaborate and create greater social justice intent.

Although the literature on participatory evaluation literature has always remained vague (Hall, 1992) regarding methods, our 25 studies provide multiple examples of evaluators as "creative pluralists" who together invent and improvise participatory methods and techniques to meet particular contextual, cultural, community, and sectoral needs. We were struck by the sheer number of program sponsors and stakeholders, not to speak of the highly creative and innovative approaches and techniques evaluators adapted to ensure that anyone can have a voice, regardless of location, language, gender, age, or culture. Even though it was often difficult to determine whether participants were collaborating as true collaborators or as "data sources" or "informants," evaluators spent considerable time focused on the architecture of collaboration and the inclusion of all participants.

Methodological Dissonance

Across the 25 studies selected for review, we are able to identify a broad range of approaches, orientations, and outcomes, highlighting the incredible diversity of programs, stakeholders, communities, and cultures across the Global South. While we note the majority of studies adopted a participatory or collaborative approach to address the contextual, cultural, and political complexities of practice, many adopted this approach in combination with other impact-oriented approaches. A dominant theme throughout our selected studies was dissonance between two conflicting constructs or narratives at the level of either politics, epistemology, culture, or methodology, a tension Chinyowa (2011) describes as "walking on a tightrope" (p. 353). For some evaluators, the struggle between cultural responsiveness and incommensurate methodological demands led to a focus on finding technical solutions to provide the "right" combination of methods, techniques, and approaches. For others, this tension was positioned as part of a much larger development discourse framed by the social, historical, political, and cultural relations prevailing between donor and recipient nations (Crush, 1995; Ebbutt, 1998).

A number of the studies included in our review observed an explicit and on-going methodological tension between participatory/culturally responsive approaches and accountability-focused monitoring and reporting (e.g., Bowen & Tillman, 2015; Brandon et al., 2014; Chinyowa, 2011; Newman, 2008). Some saw this tension manifest itself in the contradiction between predetermined outcomes and the principles of development intervention and evaluation (Haylock & Miller, 2016; Tapella & Rodríguez-Bilella, 2014), a focus on reporting and audit rather than on learning (Newman, 2008), donor interests over local interests (Chinyowa, 2011), standardized measures over a community focus (Elkins, 2010; Luo & Liu, 2014), grassroots development frameworks over donor requirements (Torres, 2000), a quantitative focus over the desire to be culturally responsive (Bowen & Tillman, 2015), direct outcomes and impacts over local contexts (Durham & Tan, 2010), and cultural sensitivity over external imposition (Brandon et al., 2014).

For others, resolution of these tensions was focused on finding technical solutions to provide the "right" combination of methods, techniques, and approaches. In their discussion of a 22-site evaluation of children's clubs in Nepal, Hart and Rajbhandary (2003) describe a process involving "considerable experimentation" (p. 64) to find a culturally appropriate approach for the program context. Other studies provide combinations of approaches between what are historically, politically, and culturally discordant narratives (see Chilisa, 2012). For example, we note combinations of outcome mapping and participatory approaches (Buskens & Earl, 2008), instrumental and transformative approaches (Chinyowa, 2011), monitoring and evaluation and developmental and empowerment approaches (Brandon et al., 2014), and feminist evaluation and monitoring and evaluation approaches (Haylock & Miller, 2016). Although it was sometimes difficult to determine which approaches were used, we also see multiple combinations of approaches, such as monitoring and evaluation; developmental, empowerment, realistic and contribution analysis (Brandon et al., 2014); outcome mapping, emancipatory action research, utilization focused and appreciative inquiry (Buskens & Earl, 2008); theory-based, mixed methods and realistic evaluation (Durham & Tan, 2010); democratic deliberative, participatory and empowerment evaluation (Hart & Rajbhandary, 2003); and developmental evaluation, cultural sensitivity, and feminist methodology (Zamir & Abu Jaber, 2015).

Other evaluations positioned the tensions between approaches as part of a much larger development discourse framed by the social, historical, political, and cultural relations that prevail between donor and recipient nations (Brandon et al., 2014; Laperrière, 2007; Luo & Liu, 2014; Tapella & Rodríguez-Bilella, 2014). Chinyowa (2011) focused his critique on the challenges posed by conventional monitoring and evaluation strategies in African countries, or more specifically the cultural incommensurability of the principles that motivate these approaches. To be culturally relevant in these communities requires significant sensitivity to other ways of knowing and a concomitant awareness of the cultural implications of our own methodological practices. Tapella and Rodríguez-Bilella (2014), for their part, critiqued technocratic and instrumental forms of participation, arguing that "the tendency to view an approach that fosters local involvement as the only alternative to local economic decline means that empowerment is defined in a way that is complicit with dominant neoliberal narratives of globalization and technological change" (p. 129).

The issue of methodological dissonance, as it emerges in the studies, seems reduced to one of method choice, related to locating the "right" combination of approaches, what Leal (2010) refers to as "technification of social and political problems" (p. 95). The underlying motivation seems to be that the right methodological approach, however Western in historical and epistemological origin, will address the complexities of culture and cultural context. We return to Carden and Alkin's (2012) distinction between "adopted" and "adapted" methodologies, and to the cultural differences and cultural incommensurabilities of knowledge systems, practices, and histories between the West and the rest (Hall, 1992). Given the history of colonialism, we in the West need to be particularly critical of our methodological approaches, of our evaluator's toolkit, since we wield power by virtue of a historically powerful narrative that amounts to a kind of regulatory paradigm. The cultural continuum reflects the complexity of evaluation practice in international development contexts and the challenges of modifying Western methodologies in non-Western cultural contexts (Smith, 2008).

Going Beyond the Spoken Word

Language is central to understanding culture, and therefore remains an ongoing concern in international evaluation (Hopson, 2000a, 2000b; Hopson, Kirkhart, & Bledsoe, 2012; Lee, 2007; Merryfield, 1985; Smith, 1991), as evaluators, most often from the West, work in culturally and linguistically distinct and diverse communities across the Global South. Language is a key part of our social interactions, and is considered by poststructuralists and structural linguists to be a highly contextualized and culturally situated construct that shapes our understanding of the world (Bonvillain, 1997; Weedon, 1987). Meaning, in other words, is constituted in language (Weedon, 1987), and is never separate from the society that produces it (Bonvillain, 1997). Turning to our findings, we recall that while some of the studies in the international domain positioned language within this broader sociocultural context (see Bowen & Tillman, 2015; Chinyowa, 2011; Laperrière, 2007; Luo & Liu, 2014), and others considered it primarily as a technical concern.

For some of the studies, the number of different languages within one project site was viewed as a serious limitation to effective evaluation (Bi Niba & Green, 2005; Nandi et al., 2015). Some studies involved up to 16 different indigenous languages, signaling the need for multiple translators (Buskens & Earl, 2008). Other studies remarked on challenges with understanding and translating local dialects (Luo & Liu, 2014), let alone challenges developing meaningful measures and means of inclusion with illiterate populations (Nandi et al., 2015). Some studies noted challenges working in communities with oral cultures (Brandon et al., 2014), whereas others highlighted their inability to speak the language of the community (Elkins, 2010; Luo & Liu, 2014). Others experienced challenges with translating the language of evaluation, whether written from the evaluator or funder's perspective or framed in the language of the field itself, into something locally meaningful and culturally appropriate (Brandão et al., 2012; Laperrière, 2007). No matter how concerns with language were framed, most of the studies in our sample identified alternative strategies for data collection, including hiring translators who could speak the language of participants and help with interpretation.

For Bi Niba and Green (2005), this meant hiring internal people who could communicate in the language of participants, and when that was not possible, hiring field assistants with requisite language skills. Buskens and Earl (2008) used ethnographic data recorders to help out with the first data collection phase of their evaluation. For their work with youth in Brazil, Brandão et al. (2012) hired peer interviewers with shared experience. As they explain, "Marked by shared language and stories potentially developed through complicity, the dialogue presented in the interview allowed the sharing of memories, information, and feelings, with an authenticity that might be difficult to achieve otherwise" (p. 52). Durham and Tan (2010), in an evaluation of an unexploded ordinance clearance program in Laos, hired "cultural brokers" who assisted with verbatim translation. For Nandi et al. (2015), interpreters facilitated focus groups and translated audio recordings so participants could speak in their preferred language.

A concern with language, for instance, with levels of literacy, led other studies to develop innovative methodological approaches to ensure broad inclusion and participation in the evaluation. In reaction to traditional monitoring and evaluation, Chinyowa (2011) created an approach to participatory evaluation drawing on the "language" of drama and theatre, where indicators were linked to the transformative nature of "play" as participants took on new roles and engaged in immersive approaches and styles to learning. After recognizing that questionnaires and interviews failed to elicit responses from local farmers in China, Luo and Liu (2014) created what they referred to as an "H" diagram, a dialogic process of sorting group responses immediately into benefits or pitfalls. In their work on an HIV/AIDS education project with youth in Zimbabwe, Botcheva et al. (2009) realized that language referred to more than the spoken word, so they emphasized art and storytelling to collect narrative data, together with videos, poems and vignettes. To accommodate language differences, Haylock and Miller (2016) used video to record interviews rather than relying on note taking. Hart and Rajbhandary (2003) for their part, created hands-on activities to address the low levels of literacy among their participants. To move outside of the language of evaluation, Brandão et al. (2012) used images as conversation starters with youth, hoping to better capture a more complex picture of their experiences.

Language is a significant issue in the international domain, since evaluators rarely speak the same language as the community. While this does create linguistic challenges to basic understanding, it also presents methodological challenges in data collection and analysis, especially given the emphasis on collaborative approaches. At the same time, the relevance of language in evaluation in these contexts concerns much more than understanding utterances, syntax, and grammar. Language is a crossroads of culture, meaning, power, politics, and history. Agar (2000) uses the term *languaculture* to highlight the difference between the surface utterances and meaning of words and their implicit or intended meanings. For Agar (2000), "language is linked seamlessly with background knowledge that is a product of biology, history, and culture. To interpret and use a language, then, this background knowledge is as critical as mastery of the surface linguistic details" (p. 94). The term *languaculture* draws attention to language as a multitiered and highly impactful concept that we need to consider in our work as evaluators, especially in our work with non-Western cultures.

Cultural Translation

The theme of cultural translation was initially about gaining access to a culture, with evaluators hiring people from within the community to act as bridges between the community and the evaluation team. Even though access to the community remains an ongoing issue in international evaluation, the challenges are much more significant than we had initially conceptualized. In fact, however "invisible" the issue of translation may seem (Dahler-Larsen, 2017), it has significant epistemological consequences (Freeman, 2009; Temple, 1997), especially for the practice of cultural responsiveness. Translation is an active, productive process of interpretation (Dahler-Larsen, 2017), where meaning is constructed, reproduced and rewritten through the process of communication (Freeman, 2009). Translation involves not only the interpretation of words, but of ideas, concepts, meanings, and perspectives. The position of interpreters or translators must thus be rethought, since they play an active interpretive and ethnographically significant role in the evaluation and in the construction of knowledge.

In the studies selected, translation and cultural brokering were treated primarily as technical or methodological issues. The boundary person played an intermediary bridging role and was hired to help the evaluation team gain access to the community and help out with language and cultural translation (see Buskens & Earl, 2008; Laperrière, 2007; Nandi et al., 2015). To help with the evaluation of an infant-feeding research project in Southern Africa, Buskens and Earl (2008) hired what they termed "boundary partners" to help facilitate the evaluation and better meet the needs of the various stakeholder groups. Durham and Tan (2010), for their part, hired "cultural brokers" who assisted evaluators in translation and the conduct of interviews. Nandi et al. (2015) hired interpreters to facilitate focus groups and translate audio so participants could respond in their preferred languages. For Bi Niba and Green (2005), 80% of the evaluators could not speak the local language, so they hired interpreters to help them complete the evaluation. Others adapted their methodology to address issues of illiteracy (Hart & Rajbhandary, 2003; Luo & Liu, 2014).

Despite the need for translation and cultural brokering in our sample of studies, the cultural and political implications of translation were never considered. To translate something, as Freeman (2009) explains, means to carry over or transfer meaning from one place to another, from one context to context to another, to transform something and "make something go where it was not" (Sontag, as cited in Freeman, 2009, p. 433). Multiple layers of meaning emerge here. Epistemologically, data is being translated from one language to another, and from one person to another. The translator is not a machine, but a cultural, social, political, and historical being, someone who interprets the world through and from a particular perspective and worldview. This perspective shapes what they hear, how they hear, and how they interpret. Given translators' power to establish meaning, they are often considered the principle actors (Freeman, 2009) or real authors (Agar, 2000) of the text. The translated text is then relayed back to the evaluator, who reformulates and reconstructs the text once again, but this time through the language of evaluation, which, as Patton (2000) points out, is rarely neutral, and is in fact embedded within the language of the dominant culture (Madison, 2000). Indeed, the process of translation (Freeman, 2009; Temple, 1997) is epistemologically layered. Meaning is created and recreated at multiple ethnographic moments and by multiple people throughout the process. The process of translation thus raises questions of authorship, authority, power, status, relationship, and voice, all immensely relevant and powerful concerns in culturally responsive practice.

Ethical Imperative

Evaluation and ethics are interconnected. Evaluators initiate and navigate questions of design, inclusion, perspectives, power, approach, positionality, and method, made even more complex in international contexts, known for their multiple cultural, political, and historical interconnections. Questions of ethics and morality are thus inseparable from cultural ones (Fleischaker, 1999). How we define what it means to do "good" evaluation, or how we define "social betterment" (Mark, Henry, & Julnes, 2000), is a normative rather than a descriptive question. Schwandt (2015) refers to a "thick" interpretation of ethics, essentially a requirement that evaluators reflect critically on their own practice and positionality, the influences that shape and inform their methodological choices, and the understanding they bring to context and approach. At the level of principle, they evince an appreciation for inclusion and the privileging of voice. In our selected sample, we note portrayals of an "ethic of engagement" (Schwandt, 1996, p. 34) and of advocacy (Greene, 1997), as rationales for engagement shift from developing required outcome-focused quantitative measures of program success to the inclusion of voices and perspectives often excluded from the evaluation conversation.

For many of the studies in our sample, adapting evaluation approaches to the cultural context of the community had ethical implications, touching mainly on issues of social justice—a responsibility to ameliorate past (and ongoing) injustices and inequities, a recognition of diverse others and their unique cultural perspectives, and a responsibility to ensure that the voices and perspectives are heard and included in the evaluation process. Although in practice these issues are interconnected, as the studies make clear, we also note connections to role of the evaluator in relation to method selection, approach, inclusion criteria, process design, and dissemination.

Some studies focused on overcoming political obstacles to participation and creating instead a space to allow the voices and perspectives of others to be heard. For instance, Buskens and Earl (2008) focused on using a strength-based focus to help address issues of social justice and "ecological well-being." Nandi et al. (2015) also used a strength-based approach to create a gender- and equity-based process to ensure the inclusion of women. Haylock and Miller (2016), for their part, integrated women's rights and gender equality into their evaluation approach and created reflective spaces for partner organizations to discuss capacity for gender and justice work. In an effort to be sensitive to the cultural dynamics of the Bedouin society, particularly in terms of the intersection of gender, social status, and power, Zamir and Abu Jaber (2015) used mixed teams (male and female) to avoid "falling into the trap of the patriarchal ways of creating knowledge" (Reinharz, as cited in Zamir & Jaber, 2015, p. 77). Hart and Rajbhandary (2003) used a collaborative approach to empower children to look critically at their own organizations and provide meaningful feedback to the evaluation team.

In other studies, ethical rationales were related to issues of empowerment and shared responsibility, focused on efforts to promote self-determination and ameliorate ongoing issues of injustice and inequity. For many, cultural responsiveness and collaborative approaches were intended to counterbalance the imposition of external measures of accountability (e.g., Brandon et al., 2014; Chinyowa, 2011; Newman, 2008), support an ethic of empowerment (e.g., Bi Niba & Green, 2005; Luo & Liu, 2014; Nagai, 2001), build local capacity for communities to define and evaluate their own needs (Holte-McKenzie et al., 2006), and empower communities to ensure more equitable visibility of experiences and perspectives that have historically remained hidden or erased (Laperrière, 2007).

In other studies, ethics was related to cultural competence, to learning about other cultures and about themselves and their own cultural standpoints. For Buskens and Earl (2008), this competence led to a focus on self-awareness related to issues of race, gender, and class, to an "inward looking dimension." For Chinyowa (2011), it resulted in the creation of an approach that privileged local knowledge systems and local cultural realities. Botcheva et al. (2009), for their part, acknowledged cultural differences and alternative worldviews at the outset, while recognizing their own ethnocentric biases and assumptions.

The majority of the studies in our sample frame cultural responsiveness as an ethical orientation to social inquiry, motivating a critique and reframing of evaluation as a means of disrupting or challenging the current standards of practice. Schwandt (2002) frames ethics in evaluation along three dimensions: (1) as a value-neutral, technical craft; (2) as an emancipatory, value-committed perspective linked to emancipatory politics; and (3) as a value-critical orientation that redefines not only social inquiry but also the role of the inquirer as dialogical and reflective, with an orientation to reflecting on the moral and political dimensions of practice.

These latter two stances, the emancipatory and critical stances, are very much in line with the rationales and motivations of cultural responsiveness that we observed in our sample of studies. The "ethic of engagement" thus poses fundamental questions. What is the purpose of social inquiry? What is the responsibility of the evaluator in relation to questions of aim, purpose, and role? How should the evaluator go about meeting the obligation to include the distinct perspectives of diverse others? (Fraser, 2001; Fraser & Honneth, 2003). In culturally responsive practice, understanding ethics as a dimension of social inquiry means transforming it from the neutral positioning of a narrow positivism to an aspirational meliorism inspired by values, moral principles, and a desire for social justice. Culturally responsive practice wears its values on its sleeves. It remains critical in always demonstrating a commitment to explore its own assumptions and presuppositions. And more, in its willingness to listen, to privilege every voice. It is in this sense a critical ethics.

CRITICAL DISCUSSION AND IMPLICATIONS FOR PRACTICE

Our analysis of the 25 studies selected for review provides a comprehensive understanding of the empirical literature in culturally responsive approaches to evaluation published in the international development domain over the past 17 years (2000–2017). Through our reading and analysis of these studies, we identified seven broad themes that capture the dynamic and complex experiences of culturally responsive practice in the Global South. Although all of the contexts vary significantly in terms of cultural community, population, geography, politics, history, and program, our seven interconnected themes—contextual complexity, temporal dimensionality, participatory strategies, methodological dissonance, from beyond the spoken word, cultural translation, and ethical imperative—together paint a distinct portrait of culturally responsive evaluation practice across complex ecological, social, economic, cultural, and political contexts. We have seen the diversity of program and community contexts, languages and cultures, the challenges of communication, the range of evaluation approaches and methods used, the level of methodological adaptation, the ongoing and persistent tension between community needs and institutional requirements, the range and depth of cultural understanding across studies, and the tension between evaluation as a technocratic, accountability-based mechanism and evaluation as a leverage for community change and community empowerment.

To understand these themes, we need to position and frame them against the backdrop of the development agenda, specifically in terms of the history of colonialism and donor–recipient relationships that define, drive, and determine North–South relationships. Evaluation is an intensely cultural practice founded on Western conceptions of science, rationality, and progress, and it enters the international development scene at the behest of multinational development agencies to support project delivery and evaluate the flow and impact of aid (Carden & Alkin, 2012). As Carden (2013) states, evaluation in the Global South is "borne out of the need of funding agencies" (p. 577).

As such, the international development context is not a neutral space. Struggles over meaning, identity, representation, power, and equality continue unabated (Bauman, 2000). Thus, our reading and analysis of the 25 studies in the international development domain is situated in a geopolitical context in which a top-down development agenda predominates, externally imposed and accountability driven, rather than a bottom-up agenda based on the sociocultural and economic needs of the program community. Evaluators struggled to conduct culturally responsive and collaborative evaluations designed and framed by the local community.

Evaluation is positioned as an end point, rather than as a means to understand context and develop culturally responsive interventions. Thus no matter how rigorous the evaluation, the focus on effects might very well be on evaluating something that has been imposed on communities from the outside.

While these 25 studies are shaped by the complexity of geography, place, and history, and by the inescapable realities of neoliberal ideology and globalized politics, the attempt to design culturally responsive evaluation nonetheless enabled evaluators to practice innovative methodological approaches, develop new cultural awareness and understanding of themselves and of the world around them, and sow the seeds of hope for local change. The theme of temporality thus depicts our conception of time and space within these 25 studies as potentially transformative *and* at the same time constrained by the pressures of time and place, stitched together by a politics and a history that endures. Massey (1999) points out that space, place, and time are dynamic and relational concepts that exist within a "simultaneous multiplicity of spaces" (p. 3) conceptualized in temporal terms, whereas modernist notions of development persist in shaping or "occluding" (p. 280) our understanding of transformation and change.

For many of the studies in our sample, we note two persistent polarities, between donor and recipient and between Westernized conceptions of knowledge and local values, needs, and interests. While binaries help simplify complexity, they are also based on Western ideas, depictions, and categories of progress and modernity (Hobart, 1986; Smith, 1999) and used as a way to name "others" (Slater, 1999). Binaries also assume a temporal logic and become how we order and structure our thinking (Whatmore, 1998), limiting our ontological and historical imaginations, as our understanding begins (and ends) with the binary itself (Gupta & Ferguson, 1992). As Hobart (1986) points out, the concept of "development" is a teleological concept, constructed by reference to the dominant state, denoting a predefined path from traditional to modern, from underdeveloped to developed. As such, it simplifies the connection between two polarities, distorting history and the relations of power and politics that define relations between the North and the South.

For Massey (1999), this temporal ordering (e.g., from underdeveloped to developed, from premodernist to modernist) has significant effects. For one thing, it obscures the understanding and appreciation of material differences between perspectives and "lived experiences." It is not enough to know "others," or to come to know "others," but to understand the historical and geographic constructions that have created (and continue to create) "others" to begin with. The trajectories, as Massey (1999) argues, cannot be aligned into one coherent and neat linear story, as there are a "multiplicity of narratives" (p. 281), of stories and experiences that are uniquely local. Space then, for Massey (1999), is a place of coexistence but also of potential conflict, as people, place, and geography merge and come apart, always in process, always in flux. As Eversole (2005) argues, "What is needed is to move beyond the dichotomies of insiders and outsiders, and bottom-up versus top-down development initiatives, to think clearly and constructively about cultural differences and its implications for development work" (p. 298).

Another persistent theme we noted throughout our studies was the attempt to identify the right combination of approaches, methods, and techniques as a way to address the complexities of program and community contexts and locate the best fit between methods and context. In some cases, this led to the search for the ideal combination of methods and methodological approaches, in others to the search for translators to help address cultural and language differences. Leal (2010) refers to this as a problem of "technocracy" (p. 95), a process of depoliticization that, he argues, ultimately maintains the status quo. As Smith (1999) explains, "Understanding is viewed as being akin to measuring. As the ways we try to understand the world are reduced to issues of measurement, the focus of understanding becomes more concerned with procedural problems" (p. 42). This shift to a focus on procedural and technical solutions may help evaluators address the complexities of context in the short term; however, the focus on technification (Leal,

2010) obscures the broader sociopolitical and cultural implications and questions of our practice, potentially simplifying and "normalizing" local knowledge (Kothari, 2001).

Although these tensions might appear at some level to be related to method choice, many argue that the fundamental issues have little to do with method choice and everything to do with power and politics, with who defines the problem, and with who collects and analyzes the data (Cornwall & Jewkes, 1995; McGee & Gaventa, 2011). The use of culturally responsive and participatory approaches, though perhaps valorizing local voices and perspectives, cannot disguise evaluation's inherent cultural authority (House, 1993) or obscure its power to define what constitutes legitimate discourse and knowledge in the social sciences (Reagan, 1996). The methodologies, collaborative though they be, remain social, cultural, economic, and political constructions of knowledge (Hopson, 2003; Chouinard & Cousins, 2015). In a world dominated by Western discourses of modernity, rationality, and progress, methodology itself becomes far more problematic, particularly if we consider the broader social, cultural, economic, and political context within which our methodologies are embedded and supported (Morgan, 2013; Ofir & Kumar, 2013). For some, participation has itself become a form of "tyranny" (Cooke & Kothari, 2001), reflecting little more than another form of Western cultural imperialism (Cornwall & Jewkes, 1995).

At a fundamental level, the positioning of participatory approaches alongside other, more donor-driven approaches sets up an artificial dichotomy between what are two, historically, politically, and culturally discordant narratives (see Chilisa, 2012). While the mixing of methods and approaches may indeed provide a way of embracing the plurality of perspectives and engaging with difference (Greene, 2007), the emphasis on finding a technical solution to what we consider a much broader issue continues to be problematic.

In her analysis of institutional processes and practices, Canadian feminist scholar Dorothy Smith (1987) reminds us that people's everyday world of experience is historically and politically mediated by social and institutional forces often invisible and undiscussed, that originate outside the local setting. In other words, stakeholder, evaluator, and donor relationships are socially constructed prior to the evaluation, and must thus be understood within this broader historical, cultural, political, and economic narrative. Our evaluations take place under metanarratives (Lyotard, 1979) of North and South, developed and developing world, and the like, all of which serve to create, enact, and re-invigorate colonial discourses and perpetuate ongoing sociohistorical processes and practices. A broader focus on the *how* and *why* of development, on the visions and values situated within specific cultural contexts rather than on the *who* and *what*, can reveal hidden assumptions and worldviews that critically inform participatory processes and practices (Eversole, 2005). Considerations of culture in international development evaluation must thus transport us far beyond demographic interests to epistemological and ontological concerns about who is involved in the construction of knowledge, how considered knowledge itself is defined, and which forms of knowledge are validated, valued, and taken seriously.

CHAPTER SUMMARY

Culturally responsive practice in the international development context provides a diverse range of methodological applications and adaptations across a broad canvas, providing examples of practice in complex geographical, social, and cultural contexts. Numerous scholars and practitioners have recognized that an understanding of culture and cultural context is essential to successful work in the Global South (see Eversole, 2005; Escobar, 1995; Hobart, 1986). However, to ensure that evaluation does not serve as a means of monitoring compliance with oppressive policies (Kirkhart, 2015), we must ensure that discussions about evaluation in international development contexts are framed against the broader concepts of aid and development (Ebbutt, 1998). Colonialism and development represent institutionalized discourses that originated in the West (Kothari, 2001), and that thus represent Western-based perspectives and frames of meaning. To ensure that our work as evaluators is decolonizing, we must ensure that marginalized and historically oppressed peoples are provided the opportunity to speak and communicate from their own perspectives and frames of meaning (Chilisa, 2012), for otherwise we risk recreating the colonizing past (Verhest, 1987).

EXTENDING INQUIRY

Bibliography of Further Readings

Bhola, H. S. (2003). Social and cultural contexts of educational evaluation: A global perspective. In T. Kellaghan & D. L. Stufflebeam (Eds.), *International handbook of educational evaluation* (pp. 397–416). Boston, MA: Kluwer.

Clifford, J., & Marcus, G. E. (Eds.). (1986). *Writing culture: The poetics and politics of ethnology*. Berkeley: University of California Press.

Cornwall, L. A., & Eade, D. (Eds.). (2010). *Deconstructing development discourse: Buzzwords and fuzzwords*. Warwickshire, England: Practical Action.

Estrella, M., Blauert, J., Campilian, D., Gaventa, J., Gonsalves, J., Guijt, I., & Ricafort, R. (Eds.). (2000). *Learning from change: Issues and experiences in participatory monitoring and evaluation*. Ottawa, ON, Canada: International Development Research Centre.

Eversole, R. (2005). Whose vision, whose rules? A culture and development typology. *Canadian Journal of Development Studies, 26*(2), 294–308.

Heron, J., & Reason, P. (1997). A participatory inquiry paradigm. *Qualitative Inquiry, 3*(3), 274–294.

Long, N., & Long, A. (Eds.). (1992). Battlefields of knowledge: The interlocking of theory and practice in social research and development. London, England: Routledge.

Mosse, D. (2013). The anthropology of international development. *Annual Review of Anthropology, 42*, 227–246.

Rosaldo, R. (1989). *Culture and truth: The remaking of social analysis.* Boston, MA: Beacon Press.

Verhest, T. G. (1987). *No life without roots: Culture and development* (B. Cumming, Trans.). London, England: Zed Books.

Exercises Based on Case Examples

1. Looking over the three cases at the beginning of this chapter, how would you say evaluators translate funder requirements into meaningful local application? What challenges would you anticipate in this case? What is the role of the evaluator in negotiating culture?

2. Identify any common themes in the three cases at the beginning of this chapter. Please describe them in some detail. State their implications for culturally responsive practice.

Discussion Questions

1. Suppose you are an evaluator who does not speak the language of the participants. What would you do differently as a result? What if you did speak the language, but did not come from the same community (or country) as the participants?

2. What are some of the most challenging issues identified across the 25 studies? What makes them so challenging? How would you address them in your work as an evaluator? What methodological issues would you need to consider?

3. How would you negotiate with the funder to ensure the cultural commensurability of prescribed data collection instruments? How might you adapt these methods to better fit the cultural context of the community?

7

A DISCUSSION OF THE CONCEPTUAL FRAMEWORK ACROSS DOMAINS OF PRACTICE

A key conclusion from the first two chapters of our book is that there is nowhere evaluators can go that will not require them to be culturally responsive. In other words, there is nowhere—no place, no people, no community—that is culture-free. Everywhere, whether it be a nongovernmental organization, a community, a school, a local drama group, a health care provider, a government agency—to name just a few possibilities—there are people who will be somehow connected to other people. These people may reside in old or new places; be marginalized, forced out of or stolen from their original homes, or just looking for new opportunities in new lands; or they may remain in the lands of their ancestors but now have new neighbors. All of these people practice cultural traditions that express their belongingness and connectedness to each other and to place. Culturally responsive approaches to evaluation have an important place in all of these cases. We are, however, prone to assume that these approaches are most appropriate only when a people's culture is evident because it is somehow marginal to what is considered "normal" within a society.

What people think of as normal comes fully into view only when they meet another cultural group and come to understand its ideas of "normal." If they do not meet other groups or have no cause to pay attention to another group's cultural framing of the world—perhaps thinking that their own cultural ways are *the* normal—then they may never know that there are myriad worldviews, and thus many "normals." This is one reason why the need for culturally responsive approaches in evaluation is more pressing when the focus is "downward" on communities who bear the burden of colonization, marginalization or vulnerability—as they are "marked" as "ontologically uncommon" and "politically salient" (Brekhus, 1998, p. 34).

Unsurprisingly, though not as readily acknowledged, is the need for cultural responsiveness when evaluators focus "upward" to inquire with communities whose privilege has come to be seen as "normal" or "regular" (and who often become the enforcers and benefactors of the marginalization and removal of others). We are more likely to acknowledge the culture of indigenous and minority peoples but leave the privilege and cultural context of whiteness unquestioned or "unmarked." In this final chapter, we want not only to review the chapters on culturally responsive evaluation practice in our three contexts, but we also want

to interrogate what is left marked or left unmarked when we consider our practice as culturally responsive evaluators.

In Chapter 2 we presented a conceptual framework for inquiry consisting
originally of seven interconnected dimensions: the epistemological, ecological,
methodological, political, personal, relational, and institutional. This framework
was based on the analysis of empirical literature about evaluation practice in
culturally diverse program contexts. Two additional dimensions were subsequently added to this framework (axiological, ontological), based on discussions
Fiona has had with Donna Mertens about the responsiveness of evaluation in
indigenous contexts. We then searched for culturally responsive evaluation
practice in three specific contexts: indigenous, Western/North American, and
international development.

The integration of the evaluation literature led to the emergence of several
themes in Chapters 4 through 6 that enabled an exploration of how evaluators
were thinking about and implementing culturally responsive approaches to
evaluation. In this chapter, we use our conceptual framework to highlight the
lessons drawn from these chapters in an effort to push evaluators to extend
and enrich culturally responsive approaches. In essence, we are celebrating the
efforts of evaluators while at once pushing them to try even harder. If we sound
impatient here, it is because we want evaluators to live up to the aspirational
motivations that inform culturally responsive approaches in evaluation.

THE EPISTEMOLOGICAL DIMENSION OF
CULTURAL PRACTICE

Guba and Lincoln (1994) ask the following epistemological question: "What is the
nature of the relationship between the knower or would-be knower and what can be
known?" (p. 108). We argued in Chapter 2 that responses to this question within the
context of culturally responsive approaches to evaluation must involve evaluators and
stakeholders co-constructing knowledge through this relationship. This was seen by
evaluators largely as a methodological issue, leading to participatory or collaborative
methodologies that promote the inclusion of local people and the tailoring of methods
to fit, when possible, the preferences of local people.

Evaluators implementing culturally responsive approaches in the Western context
co-constructed knowledge with community members as a way of mitigating against
misunderstandings and the consequent potential for tensions these hold. Some evaluators had a broad ecological approach, understanding that knowledge production and
social inquiry occurred within the context of culture, history, economics, and politics. Others provided a description of the cultural context to situate their evaluation.
Methodological choices were informed in different ways, from evaluators wishing to
say where they were working to those who more fully understood the nuances beneath

the surface of demographic descriptions of their locations. Often, however, their decisions were similar because they relied on technical and methodological fixes to help ensure the cultural responsiveness of their evaluation work.

Evaluators working within indigenous communities reported on the importance of building and strengthening relationships with people in those communities. These trust relationships helped give a community confidence that the evaluators "knew" them. The relationships were built over time as evaluators often spent time in the community, both formally and informally. While evaluators often saw these relationships as pivotal to gathering data, indigenous communities—whose world is relationships—see knowing as performed within the context of these relationships. Amartya Sen's (1999) distinction between the constitutive and instrumental elements of human development helps illuminate this difference further.

For indigenous peoples, relationships are constitutive; they are ends in themselves. In other words, the relationship between people is the indigenous world is how the world is known (Wilson, 2008). Nonindigenous peoples more often see the building of relationships as instrumental, as a necessary prelude to the "real" purpose for which they are in an indigenous community. Once the task is completed, the relationship may no longer be seen as needed and will thus likely come to an end. There are, however, evaluators who describe cultivating a larger, relationship-based context for the work they have undertaken with indigenous communities. Some encourage the community to become involved in evaluations, whereas others step up to advocate for the communities when they know that an evaluation will not work—nothing valid will become known—given the community's culture and worldview. When this happens, funders may grant "concessions" or they may simply have canceled evaluation contracts.

Issues between evaluation funders and indigenous communities are echoed within the international development context. Funder-community tensions that are fundamentally ontological (see below) and epistemological elicit methodological or technical fixes from evaluators who maintain they are working collaboratively with that community. These fixes obscure, rather than patch up, the tensions arising from the North funding the South, or developed countries funding developing countries. At the heart of these tensions are dichotomies that anchor a development continuum from developing countries to developed countries. The issue is that these endpoints are defined by funders, who often then also decide on the actions needed to shift nations along this continuum. Ignored in this dichotomy is any recognition of what recipient countries know about their own baseline status, especially if what they know is founded upon the beauty, strengths and potential of their people. If these broader factors were recognized, and brought into the calculations of funders, then programs would and be more about opening people's access to the resources and services of their own countries. This is what cultural responsiveness advocates. Instead, the lens is often on how to change "the people" rather than on how to change their ecology. In contrast, our chapter on evaluation in indigenous communities presented a case for understanding the full ecology of a community so that programs are about both the lived context of community well-being and the aspirations for nation-building.

Whether we are evaluating in communities that confront oppression or benefit from privilege, evaluators should be committed to addressing the issue of culture. As evaluators we often straddle both worlds—of marginalization and of privilege. And yet, an overarching theme from our analysis is that culturally responsive approaches *see* the need to be culturally responsive, which often means resisting imperatives to adapt culturally responsive evaluation approaches to the needs of funders, who often have power over both the evaluation and over the future funding of initiatives in that community. If our aspirational aim is community well-being, equity, or social justice, then it makes sense to try to get everyone on one side by speaking into the world and culture they occupy, in ways that will inform them and motivate them to act.

THE ECOLOGICAL DIMENSION OF CULTURAL PRACTICE

The question that guided the review of the ecological dimension of cultural practice across the three contexts concerned what evaluators saw as the boundaries of the program "community," together with their impressions of the layers of the ecology within those boundaries. We wanted to know how much culturally responsive evaluators felt they needed to know about the place and the people with whom they were working and whether they saw the cultural context as complex. There are overlaps here between the ecological dimension and the ontological dimension of practice, since evaluators provide insights into the worldviews of the peoples with whom they are working. The ecological dimension complements this by asking how evaluators understand the needs, priorities, and aspirations of the community. Is this understanding on a small issue-by-issue basis, or does it extend to a wider societal context where people are positioned in relation to other people in their nation, and their nation is likewise positioned in relation to other nations around the globe? There are connections between the intimate, personal context and the broad, national and global context. Our interest in this case touches on the ecology that evaluators feel they need to understand to convey the evaluation context to others.

The outer layer of evaluation ecology was documented by evaluators who explained histories of colonial terrorism, forced relocation, and migration; the drawing of maps and boundaries by outsiders; and the redistribution of resources out of the hands of their traditional owners and guardians. The explanation provided a context for evaluators to describe their work as a small part of a bigger effort at decolonizing and nation-building. In the international development context, it helped evaluators explain the power and dominance in the relationships of donor and recipient countries. This was however more of a salve—evaluators knew the bigger picture—than an impetus for evaluation to become a means of advancing national sovereignty and self-determination. While this bigger context may also have helped those working in Western contexts to situate their evaluations, like those in development and many of those in indigenous contexts, the understanding of this context informed only methodological solutions rather than allowing evaluators to see evaluation as part of something bigger, led by the vision of the very people they were working with. Perhaps it is we, then, who are naïve in thinking that evaluation can and should be actively supporting justice, equity, and self-determination through other channels. Methodological fixes may result in more collaborative approaches and the temporary appeasement of people who are held accountable for funds sent into their communities for programs they may or may not value or want.

When evaluators gain an understanding of the ecology of the place where they are working, they become more informed about both the community and the positioning of the program they are evaluating vis-à-vis that community's own aspirations for a good life. This then informs what they know are valued outcomes, with this knowledge potentially extending and possibly conflicting with what funders need to know. Time in context is the best way to build evaluators' understanding of the community. The more time evaluators spend in a community in their formal role—not to mention the informal option of hanging out in the community, attending gatherings and other community events, talking with locals and being seen in community—the more they will understand context.

Both time and distance were discussed by evaluators as barriers to this happening. They often lived at a distance from the evaluation site or the budget did not support their visiting or there was nowhere for them to stay that was close to where they were working. However, time in community demonstrates the willingness of evaluators to strengthen their own understanding of the evaluation context, and to gain more nuanced insights into the lives of people, insights that may challenge or obviate any deficit-based, individualized explanations about the changes needed. In this way, the ecological dimension intersects with the personal dimension of cultural practice—evaluators need to be open to this learning, especially when it requires them to set aside their own stereotypes and assumptions, engage in cultural practices that are not their own, and potentially challenge the politics of funders and the practices of the evaluation profession.

Across all three evaluation contexts there was acknowledgment by evaluators that being "in tune" with and understanding the local context of a program could also be enhanced through the involvement of local steering or advisory groups, local data gatherers, and the collaborative building of the evaluation design. Collaboration can also make collective sense of the information collected so that accurate and reliable assessments can be made about the community's experience of a program. A community will then be well positioned to tailor a program based on evidence of their own experiences, strengthening it if the community wishes to see it retained. Culturally responsive approaches do not end with the evaluation findings; rather, the evaluators' responsibilities extend to supporting program revision, dissemination of program findings, and possibly also informing community advocacy for continued funding. This is the domain not solely of culturally responsive evaluators but also of feminist evaluators and transformative evaluators, who have also been stressing these additional responsibilities for some time.

Some evaluators do couch their community engagement and the desire to understand the ecology of the program within the larger context of community concerns. They warn evaluators to be aware that other community events (e.g., funerals) may postpone evaluation commitments. These other events may be ones that evaluators should, through respect, attend. At times, community stakeholders may simply be overburdened by evaluator requests or may feel potentially endangered by participation in evaluation. Being in community also requires evaluators to be sensitive, patient, and kind so that they can feel the flow of the community's own concerns and be open to invitations being ignored by those who judge that evaluators cannot or should not be involved. The clear message is that the more evaluators know about the ecological context of an evaluation, the more they should recognize that a community has its own hum, its own conflicts and celebrations, and that evaluation is most likely to be part of a lower layer in its multilayered ecology: nice to have but sometimes difficult to accommodate in the midst of other, larger concerns.

THE METHODOLOGICAL DIMENSION OF CULTURAL PRACTICE

Evaluators working in Western contexts recognized the assumptions, beliefs, and values underpinning their profession and the implications of these for methodology. They authored comprehensive stories about programs, using qualitative or mixed methods, so they could respond to both community and funder requests for evaluative information. When measurement instruments did not work with the population from which they were collecting data, they created new, culturally responsive measurement tools. They were also committed to maintaining this type of methodological flexibility throughout the evaluation. Even so, they struggled with the tensions that often arose when results based on community engagement were not commensurate with funder demands. It was not unusual for evaluators working in indigenous contexts to experience similar struggles as they endeavored to be responsive to community input and concerns. Like those working in the other contexts, evaluators in indigenous contexts strove to implement evaluation methodologies that let program beneficiaries and communities be who they are.

Evaluators in international development contexts also draw upon a large toolkit of methodological approaches, rising to the challenge of modifying Western methodologies so they were a better "fit" with non-Western contexts. Participatory and collaborative evaluation approaches were often used in combination with other, impact-oriented approaches. Evaluators strove to make their evaluations culturally responsive and effective at capturing local realities in the face of methodological constraints and trade-offs.

Time was key to this. The more time evaluators had to become familiar with their context, the better able they were to adapt their evaluation methodology to fit that context. Time then informed their methodological reflections throughout the evaluation process. Even so, tensions often arose between culturally responsive approaches and accountability-focused monitoring and reporting.

Culturally responsive evaluators use a variety of names for their collaboration with communities or organizations. What they call their methodology is however no guide to their evaluation practice. Regardless of the variety in the forms of collaboration or participation, it is clear that evaluators are trying to enable program beneficiaries to "co-pilot" evaluations. This can raise the hackles of funders whose requirements are disputed by, or at odds with, what beneficiaries themselves want from an evaluation. Instead of evaluators facilitating a process whereby funders and beneficiaries co-pilot together, evaluators often find themselves as the go-betweens, trying to bridge the divide between beneficiaries and funders. In their attempts to be culturally responsive to beneficiaries, however, evaluators may neglect to apply similar culturally responsive principles to their engagement with funders. They may for instance overlook cultural brokers who can work with funders, establish a steering group, and work with locals to ensure that engagement follows cultural protocols and is conducted in local languages.

Funders often unconsciously work within the confines of Western evaluation paradigms. It should therefore be no surprise to evaluators when funders challenge co-piloting involving non-Western peoples who, in turn, recognize and often seek to challenge the cultural hegemony of these paradigms. Evaluators in turn may seek methodological or technological fixes' to the tensions that arise between beneficiaries and funders, confining their disagreements to small, evaluation moments. The alternative is a bigger dispute about whose worldview is privileged within these Western evaluation paradigms, let alone the larger history that many beneficiary communities hold of past grievances and wrongs by Western approaches that have sought to exploit their knowledge, their labor, their culture, and their resources. Indigenous peoples for instance know only too well the implications of ongoing colonization at the hands of researchers and evaluators. They have seen "neutral" evaluations prop up colonial systems that see indigenous peoples as responsible for their incarceration and psychiatric illness, lack of education, child abuse, early death, and self-harm and suicide.

THE POLITICAL DIMENSION OF CULTURAL PRACTICE

The question asked in the political dimension of cultural practice is this: "Where do power and privilege reside within an evaluation?" This query raises the more specific question: "Where are evaluators positioned within these power structures?"

Indigenous and tribal peoples are sovereign, self-determining peoples, whether they are living on their own lands and under their nation's own regulatory and governance systems, or whether they are living in minoritized spaces or in fourth-world places within first-, second-, or third-world colonial nation-states (Manuel & Posiuns, 1974). Minoritized peoples also have a right to self-determination within the context of the nation-state. Cram (2018) writes that, like indigenous communities, many nonindigenous communities long for evaluators who "get" them, who understand their history, their contemporary resources and assets, and their political landscape. Similarly, an important part of cultural responsiveness in Western contexts was making explicit the often tightly woven interplay of social, political, historical, and cultural influences within an evaluation context. It comes as no surprise therefore that partnership and power sharing are expected from those going into indigenous communities to undertake work that will subsequently impact that community. This includes evaluation. Nor is it surprising when funders who have no knowledge of, let alone motivation to recognize, indigenous sovereignty find themselves framing an evaluation that ignores sovereignty and the need for negotiated partnership.

Within the Western context, power was reflected in the tensions that could arise among stakeholders. Who gets to participate in an evaluation and under what conditions are paramount considerations. This may be described as a discursive level of power, with evaluators called upon to balance stakeholder agendas and interests. To do this, evaluators may need to name explicitly the power and privilege embedded in different meaning systems, and thereby encourage, or perhaps insist upon, shared understandings about the distribution of power within a context. In this way, evaluators are able to push stakeholders to look at the political dimension of how they are positioned in relation to one another—within a program, an evaluation, and a community—and reflect on the manifestations of power, both big and small.

This knowledge of power dynamics, together with a critique of participatory methodologies, supports stakeholder inclusion in international development contexts. Indeed, this is most critical in the context of international development, owing to violent conflict, growing income disparities, and political obstacles to the inclusion of women and children. Culturally responsive practice can be a stabilizing influence in this context.

Evaluators who want to practice in culturally responsive ways may well have to negotiate between community expectations and funder demands. The saving grace is that funder demands are often minimal, and community expectations are fully articulated and feasible rather than perceived as onerous. The most pressing threats to meeting these expectations were time, distance, and resources.

Many evaluators live at a distance from the place where they work as evaluators and, as Kumok (2017) says, "A long-distance relationship can be tough emotionally and financially." Luckily, Kumok also offers good relationship advice: make it part of your budget, discuss it with your partner, divide costs, be a cheap date, and take a bus rather than your car. While Kumok is talking about intimate relationships, many of her tips are relevant to partnering with a community to ensure the rigor, validity, and usefulness of an evaluation (Cram, 2018). Her tip about dividing the cost is useful for evaluators who think that they are the only ones who can persuade funders to support the community's participation in all stages of the evaluation. Community leaders will have contacts that they can leverage and will usually be quite accustomed to advocating for their community. Additionally, they may be more motivated to do so if they are assured that an evaluation will improve the accessibility and quality of community services and programs.

THE PERSONAL DIMENSION OF CULTURAL PRACTICE

Many evaluators actively reflected on the cultural context of the evaluation. This extended from their own self-examination—as white, say, or as privileged, or as someone from outside the tribal area—to thinking about how they might shape their practice to be culturally responsive. Frierson, Hood, Hughes, and Thomas (2010) describe culturally responsive evaluators as "bringing needed, shared life experiences and understandings to the evaluation tasks at hand" (p. 76). They therefore privilege the shared lived experiences that evaluators have with participants as key to cultural responsiveness. The readiness of evaluators to reflect on their own positionality, and to grow their capability for reflection, may be necessary but is not sufficient to ensure cultural responsiveness. In the Western context, some evaluators asked whether they were in fact the right person to be undertaking an evaluation, and many evaluators in the Western context saw cultural matching as essential to ensure evaluation validity.

This matching was often achieved in indigenous contexts through the inclusion of indigenous community members as guides, advisors, team members, community evaluators, meaning makers, or knowledge translators and disseminators. No one, however, talked about building community evaluative capacity to the point where communities and tribes could take on the evaluation mantle themselves. No evaluators were explicitly working toward making themselves redundant by ensuring that cultural matching was possible and inevitable. Perhaps this is a hallmark of the profession—that it safeguards its own professionalization with certificates and diplomas that are needed before a community can evaluate whether a program is meeting its objectives and its own vision of itself.

Although the processes of self-reflection and of opening themselves up to learning-in-context continued for some throughout the evaluation process, very few evaluators, lifted their gaze to the horizons of their own discipline and practice to question the imposition of Western paradigms in non-Western or minoritized Western contexts. This questioning may threaten their own subjectivity or potentially destabilize their relationship with funders. Whatever the reason, their commitment to being culturally responsive did not push them to a second cycle of reflection. They did not move outside the boundaries of their profession to question whether their approach to evaluation can understand how decisions are made within a given cultural context.

Still, those who were self-reflective were a step ahead of those who did not explain how they fit or did not fit into the cultural context. This assumed "right" to exist in a context culturally different from their own infused some of the evaluations in indigenous and Western contexts, and almost all those in the international development context. In the latter case, we have described evaluators as "creative pluralists" who adapt participatory evaluation approaches to best fit the cultural context. In this sense, these evaluators are technical experts who know how to implement methodological fixes to ensure that data is collected to substantiate their evaluative judgments. While they lean into their context through those who speak the local language, they pull out again once the information is translated back into their own native tongue. Their "play" with culture may seem only skin deep, but these are evaluators whose work has been chosen specifically because it was considered culturally responsive to international development contexts. This should perhaps give some pause for concern about how other evaluators in these contexts are working with local people to assess programs that have been implemented to support their "development." Perhaps they fit into the sixth category of insider-outsider relations proposed by Herr and Anderson (2014): "outsider(s) studies insider(s)" in the tradition of "university-based, academic research" (p. 41).

THE RELATIONAL DIMENSION OF CULTURAL PRACTICE

Culturally responsive approaches to evaluation are deeply relational, reflected most readily in the participatory methodologies chosen by evaluators to ensure that communities are actively engaged in and help support and direct the evaluation. This leads to evaluators and communities collaborating on the selection or development of evaluation methods so that participant voices can be heard. Local people are often brought on board with the evaluation team to create a closer, more concordant data collection in which community members are at ease and able to share in a safe and culturally responsive way.

If evaluators are not known to a community, their journey into a community is often supported by a cultural expert or guide. This is important in cases where the community remembers negative experiences it has had with researchers and evaluators. A person known to and trusted by the community can bridge the gap between the community and evaluators. If the evaluators are not known to the community, the community has little reason to trust them, even if it is being compelled by funders to engage with evaluators. Cultural guides figuratively, and sometimes literally, hold the hands of evaluators on one side of the bridge and the hands of community members on the other side. They then use their knowledge of culturally responsive engagement protocols to bring both groups to the middle of the bridge for meeting and greeting—the start of a relationship.

This is not, however, a means to an end, with the end being the implementation of an evaluation. Across the three contexts explored here, evaluators spoke about trust relationships between communities and evaluators being strengthened throughout the evaluation, with this being particularly prominent where evaluators also expressed their openness to learning and to the reflective adaptation of the evaluation. As Hazel Symonette (2004) explains in her work on "self as evaluator," evaluators must be able to flex and flow with grace and style. For indigenous peoples, a relationship built for an evaluation continues beyond the end of that evaluation. Some evaluators described their long-term relationships with indigenous communities over several evaluations, as well as other formal and informal exchanges of expertise and friendship. Although an anthropologist rather than an evaluator, Keith Basso (1996) described his "enormous and profound . . . debt to the Apache people of Cibecue" spanning 35 years (p. xvii). If evaluators were to think of themselves as in a long-term—possibly lifelong—relationship with the communities they work in, this might well prompt them to learn more, share more of their own knowledge, and do the best they can to support a community's own dreams of its future.

The complexities of being both an insider and an outsider within a community were explored by some indigenous evaluators who were working in either their own tribal homelands or in another indigenous context. When Linda Smith (2012) contemplated her own status as a researcher doing data collection in her tribal homeland, she described herself as an insider in some respects (from the same place, a woman, a mother) and an outsider in other respects (university educated, older, partnered) in relation to the young Māori single female parents she was interviewing. Her work reminds us that we are always someone in relation to others and the someone we are can be negotiated through the acknowledgment of how we are at once the "same as" and "different from" them. How evaluators are positioned as an insider/outsider, in turn, positions them within or across worldviews and thereby informs their framing of epistemology, their methodological decisions, and how they approach axiology or ethics (Herr & Anderson, 2014). Indigenous, tribal, or minority evaluators might also borrow Patricia Hill Collins's (2000) term *outsider within* to describe their own subjectivity within the evaluation profession if and when they query their own belonging to this "family." This may happen should the profession marginalize their own ways of knowing.

In the international context, "expatriates" who returned to undertake evaluation in their communities of origin had to re-establish their relationships and location as insiders rather than as outsiders. Some of the indigenous evaluators who worked back in their own tribal areas talked about a similar process. Their relatives there became familial guides who were able to bind an evaluator back into the context as a local through making explicit the evaluator's genealogical connections. Even then, the evaluators themselves felt their existence to be somewhat liminal since they were in different ways both insiders and outsiders. Like other evaluators, the strengthening of relationships within the community also relied on how well they conducted themselves as professional evaluators. Whereas a genealogical connection could be an entry point into their community, it was their conduct as an evaluator that determined whether their community wanted to be in relationship with them in their capacity as a professional evaluator.

It is this professional relationship that must also be considered when local people are brought into evaluation teams, used as guides, or employed as data gatherers. When local people are asked to enter into professional evaluation relationships with others in their community, it is imperative that their role does not conflict either with the status they have within their community or with the other relationships they have had for much longer than the evaluation period, and this includes their familial relationships. It is important that evaluators pay attention to the advice they are given and to any concerns that are raised. Even if a relationship between evaluators and a community continues beyond the evaluation period, it is those who have been engaged by evaluators to support the evaluation locally who remain living in the community. An evaluation cannot threaten their safety and their support networks.

THE INSTITUTIONAL DIMENSION OF CULTURAL PRACTICE

Many evaluators expressed aspirational aims that informed their culturally responsive approach to evaluation. In the indigenous space, some saw their evaluation work contribute to the broader aims of nation-building, self-determination, and the decolonization of indigenous peoples. Their work was aligned with this bigger agenda, even if the contribution was small. Although other evaluators did not explicitly subscribe to this bigger agenda, the growing knowledge they had about indigenous communities helped them rise above methodological solutions to challenge the evaluation framing of the funders. This occurred when they received strong messages from the community about the inappropriateness of what a funder wanted, or when they realized that a funder was approaching the evaluation based on a conception of indigenous deficit, with a view to getting the community to change rather than challenging the broader system. In at least one case, evaluators believed this push-back was the reason why their funding was not continued for the second stage of the evaluation.

Evaluators in the Western and international development contexts described aspirations related to social justice: improving lives, equity, and community well-being. They provided a range of rationales, and often more than one rationale, for their adoption of a culturally responsive approach in their evaluation. These included validity, relevance, theory building, learning, relevance, empowerment, and transformation. Perhaps most important of all, many reflected seriously on why they wanted to be culturally responsive and on what they hoped to accomplish as a result. Like those in indigenous contexts, these reflections provided them with the guidance and reassurance needed to take a collaborative, participatory evaluation approach, working *with* the community rather than *on* it.

There was widespread recognition that evaluators juggle multiple stakeholder interests. Many authors stressed the importance of having evaluation funders provide the time and resources for evaluators to work in participatory ways. Those in the international context were mindful of the need explicitly to negotiate who should be involved in an evaluation, and what the nature of their involvement should be. This concern did not come to the fore in the other contexts. The lesson from the international context is one of ensuring the inclusion of multiple stakeholder voices in an evaluation.

THE AXIOLOGICAL DIMENSION OF CULTURAL PRACTICE

The detailed knowledge of context required to support the validity and integrity of evaluation was emphasized most strongly by those working in indigenous contexts. Part of the need for evaluators to be "seen" in indigenous communities was so that they could get what the community was about and thereby understand the context more fully. The other side of being seen was for the community get to know the evaluators, and to determine whether a trusting relationship could be established with them. In the international context, a development phase allowed evaluators to spend time in the community for similar purposes: building relationships and an understanding of the cultural context. This is often not the case within Western contexts. One possible explanation for this is that evaluators do not have to travel far to be in context, even if the cultural distance between evaluator and community is great. Distance was key for evaluators in indigenous contexts, especially when they could not be in context as often as they wanted or possibly even felt they needed to be. Although they may be funded to work in international development contexts, evaluators also have to travel great distances to get to evaluation locations.

Overall, evaluators spent little time exploring the importance of language. When language was raised as an issue, evaluators talked about the use of interpreters, with evaluators presumably then using tools developed first in English and undertaking analysis on data that, when necessary, had been translated from local languages to English. Evaluators in the Western context wrote more explicitly about language when they described the nature of translation in their evaluations. This ranged from word-for-word translation to translations based on the nuances and meanings behind words. Evaluators who were bilingual and who spoke the native language had a distinct advantage, as occurred in some of the Māori evaluation contexts. In other indigenous contexts, the multiple languages that were spoken either required settling on a common language for communication or employing local people who could communicate both in their language and in English with the evaluators.

Indigenous evaluators also discussed ethical codes that guided their work. Some talked about getting ethical approval for their evaluation from a tribal governance structure or an indigenous review panel or board. Ethics in the international context touched on the shifts evaluators made in their practice and on their rationales for wanting to undertake culturally responsive evaluation. Generally speaking, evaluators saw cultural responsiveness as an ethical commitment in social inquiry.

THE ONTOLOGICAL DIMENSION OF CULTURAL PRACTICE

The ontological question asked by Guba and Lincoln (1994) is "What is the form and nature of reality and, therefore, what is there that can be known about it?" (p. 108). At its heart, this question concerns how well we can understand another culture, and whether we can understand it well enough to see how people in that culture understand the nature and form of their own reality. Within the literature we have selected, *culture* is an elastic term. Surprisingly, it is often used within culturally responsive approaches with a lower case *c*, to define a small space that people inhabit that is almost inward looking. Culture may be acknowledged by evaluators through demographic descriptions, or by a map of the place the people occupy. When this occurred, the worldview of the people engaged within the evaluation hardly seemed to matter, unless there was a need for language translators or cultural brokers to negotiate the opening of an evaluation space for the outsiders. Even then, the work of these mediators was seen as merely technical rather than relational or ontological. It is almost as if the people in the community are seen by evaluators to have a worldview similar to Westerners, although they speak a different language. Or perhaps their worldview just goes unacknowledged as unimportant for the task at hand because the West is there with its methodologies and instruments to do what the evaluation funder desires.

Within contexts where programs were supporting a community's well-being, culture was sometimes seen merely as something people needed to be reconnected with, as if it were a magic wand that would make them whole and well. This is a deep logical flaw in many indigenous contexts. Here the "problem" with indigenous people is that they are disconnected from their culture by virtue of being urban or young or not actively engaged in cultural activities. The "solution" is to offer programmatic remedies that reconnect people to their culture. This solution is quite different from a program sourced from within the worldview of a community, in which participants can retain their cultural integrity, participating in the program as themselves. The journey of change will be one that the community values.

The difficulty is of course that many of the programs evaluators assess are not local. They have been designed elsewhere and exported to the community by a government agent, a philanthropic organization or a development expert. The program itself may or may not be tailored to fit the local context. A program may not understand the way local people see the world and may reflect an integrationist or assimilationist agenda. The message people receive from such programs is "Don't be yourself, be someone(s) that we here on the outside have decided it's better for you to be." Evaluators who reject this agenda, or who feel their role is to interrogate the rationales of programs—rather than just assess whether intended outcomes have been achieved—may find their evaluation at risk if they raise any concerns with evaluation funders. Yet, as we have argued, evaluators are obliged to question the appropriateness—the validity—of a program with its local, cultural context.

The evaluators we have reviewed talk a lot about their understanding of culture, and about how it situates their evaluation and influences their methodological choices.

Very few talk about whether they are seeking to understand merit and worth, or other evaluative criteria, through a cultural lens. Evaluation as it is practiced is a Western endeavor—some might even call it a Western educational endeavor given its origins within the discipline of education. As such, it is infused with and reflects a Western understanding of the nature of reality. It is not surprising that the most privileged peoples on this planet fail to see the boundedness of their own worldviews, their own realities. Privilege is blind to itself. Echoing the idea of "ex-nomination" in Roland Barthes, Spencer (2006) describes how "whiteness is constructed as natural, innocent and omnipresent . . . in our common-sense reality" (p. 16). White people often remain anonymous because their privilege goes unnamed and unnoticed and the status quo of their society unchallenged (Lakoff, 2000).

> Exnomination is the means by which whiteness avoids being named and thus keeps itself out of the field of interrogation and therefore off the agenda for change . . . One practice of Exnomination is the avoidance of self-recognition and self-definition. (Fiske, 1994, p. 42)

In this way, whiteness becomes a "normality" that does not require people to name themselves as having a race or ethnicity. Even though many of the evaluators we have included in this volume did name themselves, variously, as white, indigenous, tribal, or Western, and may have pondered their status as insiders and outsiders to the community, many others did not. We might give them the benefit of the doubt—that they understood they were different but did not think this was relevant to mention in the context of an academic publication. Or we might assume that they either did not notice their whiteness or, if they did, stood steadfast in their right to undertake evaluations no matter the context. Disappointing as this might be, we should not be surprised if white people do not question the "the legacy of white supremacy, from which they continue to benefit" (Winant, 1997, p. 41). However, culturally responsive approaches can succeed only if evaluators' worldviews, including their understanding of the nature of reality, is subject to critical scrutiny so that the cultural context is not simply subsumed under it.

The answer, presented within the context of practice explored here, is to understand cultural responsiveness as resting not on methodological and technical solutions but on active partnerships between funders, evaluators, and local communities, where, moreover, all parties to an evaluation are prepared to work together and share their knowledge and expertise to build an evaluation that supports community aspirations, let alone those of funders.

CONCLUDING REMARKS

We have moved from how evaluators describe their work in academic journals to how they actually go about practicing culturally responsive approaches to evaluation. We have not asked evaluators themselves but have relied instead on how they represent their work in Western, indigenous, and international development contexts. Undoubtedly, we have ignored disciplinary boundaries and academic fashions by making two key assumptions as we have proceeded.

First, we have assumed that what evaluators have written reflects how they have in fact practiced. This assumption seems safe enough when evaluators have co-written about their practice with local people, since co-authorship serves as something of an accountability mechanism back to the community and people. We know of indigenous students who have attended tertiary education institutions and been the first of their tribes to "discover" that close relatives have been profiled by a white academic without their knowledge and probably without their consent. This wariness of indigenous peoples extends across other minoritized groups who want "nothing about them, without them." It makes sense, then, that local co-authors are a response to this challenge. They provide assurance that what is written is a good representation of what happened on the ground.

Second, we might have overlooked good culturally responsive evaluation practice simply because practitioners have written reports only for funders, or because the articles they have written have failed to find a home.

There is also the possibility that we have homogenized the contexts we have examined, flattening the diversity of the people by not fully acknowledging the differences that arise when the intersections of age, gender, sexuality, health, disability, religion and other characteristics are considered. Programs in these contexts are likewise often tailored for specific subpopulations of people, for example, young people or pregnant women. The conceptual framework invites evaluators to practice in culturally responsive ways when they evaluate these programs, building on the learning and practice of other evaluators. Finding out about context and then working to be responsive to it is a journey of discovery for evaluators, who courageously open themselves up to others' worldviews and then think along with them about how evaluation can best serve their needs and aspirations. If there is one thing we would now encourage evaluators to do, it would be to learn as much as possible about the richness and depth of cultural context: People have a right to have their culture acknowledged, valued, and responded to in its full diversity.

8 CONCLUDING THOUGHTS

"[Is it possible] for social science to be different, that is to forget itself and to become something else . . . [or must it] remain as a partner in domination and hegemony?"
(Said, 1989, as cited in Lather, 1990, p. 315).

"To break a cycle of repetition, it becomes necessary at some point to go past the edge of the familiar and enter a place that is truly unknown."
(Taylor, Gilligan, & Sullivan, 1995, p. 10)

Our goal in this final chapter is to circle back to some of the key concepts and ideas that emerged in our analysis across Western, indigenous, and international development domains and to draw on what we consider key practical and theoretical implications for culturally responsive practice. All three domains of practice discussed in this book bear witness to the challenges of practicing culturally responsive approaches to evaluation amidst economic, political, social, and cultural challenges. There is no simple checklist or eight-step recipe for implementing a culturally responsive practice. The evaluator "toolkit" does not come with a cultural map. Every evaluation context is unique in its historical, social, political, and cultural configuration. There is no blueprint for cultural responsiveness.

Culture is finely stitched into the fabric of methodology. Whether evaluations are located close to home or located in communities across the globe, culture is implicated throughout our evaluation work. How do we construct knowledge in culturally responsive ways when we represent Western research or evaluation? When we use a template rooted in principles of the Enlightenment? How can local knowledge thrive amid historical privilege? Are there methods or approaches better attuned to engage in knowledge construction, in drawing upon local stories and learning the importance of other histories, of other stories told in languages that we cannot understand? Who constructs and tells the story? These questions illustrate the many struggles and challenges we identified in the literature, as evaluators moved in and out and between often unfamiliar spaces, creating, compromising, and casting stories within a cacophony of voices, from near and far, local and distant, old and new.

Our thematic journey across three distinct evaluation landscapes revealed complex and dynamic program and community contexts, highlighting the need to understand the multitiered ecologies, histories and local aspirations, and ontologies of program communities. We envision program contexts as places shaped by the dynamics of practice, by what Massey (2005) describes as a "sphere of a multiplicity of trajectories" (p. 119), a place where time and space unite, as the local and global come together and

135

are, again as Massey describes "mutually constituted" (p. 184). We consider local program sites as socially constructed places shaped by the interactions and relationships among people (Gregory, 2009), as historically dynamic places also shaped by institutional norms and values that reside beyond the local context of practice. Most importantly, we frame our studies as operating within a socially and politically dynamic and highly contested space (Gregory, 2009; Lefebvre, 1991) shaped and configured by the discipline of evaluation, a historically situated and highly institutionalized practice.

As our themes illustrate (see Table 8.1 below), our analysis has identified the challenges with using tools, instruments and approaches that have been designed by others elsewhere for use in local contexts, as well as the challenges of working in an applied social science with implications across cultural milieus—implications that cross epistemological, ontological and ethical spaces. The narrative reflections in our selected studies bear witness to the deeply relational, political, and ecological nature of culturally responsive practice and to the ongoing need for a critical, engaged perspective, since these relations and contexts are so very often sites of ongoing exploitation and injustice (Kincheloe & McLaren, 2000). Whether recognized or named as such, these sites are historical entities situated in what are colonized spaces. Epistemology, from a critical perspective, must thus be considered a historical discipline (Rabinow, 1996).

Knowledge and its construction weave their way through all of our themes, as stories are told, translated, transcribed, and continuously re-inscribed. Who tells these stories? Who constructs and reconstructs these local narratives? Whose voices and perspectives are privileged? Whose are not? Who frames the narratives? Whose voices are absent? As Ladson-Billings (2000) reminds us, epistemology represents more than a "way of knowing" or "another way to view the world" (p. 258); an epistemology, as she states quite clearly, is a *"system of knowing"* (p. 258, emphasis added), that is, an embodied, historicized, and discursive practice. This knowledge system, what Foucault (1972) refers to as the west's "cultural archive," represents and contains all of the West's

TABLE 8.1 ■ A Summary of Themes Across Domains of Practice

Indigenous	Western	International Development
multilayered context	interpretations of culture	contextual complexity
local programming	manifestations of power	temporal dimensionality
a kinship world	complexities of language	participatory strategies
insiders and outsiders	multifaceted identities	methodological dissonance
co-production	temporal dimensionality	beyond the spoken word
methodology	cultural valid measurement	cultural translation
accountabilities	use and influence	ethical imperative

history, philosophy, literature, arts, and science. It is noteworthy as much for what it includes as for what it excludes (Harding, 1991).

Despite the narrow and limited range of perspectives contained within the Western canon (Grosfoguel [2013] identifies five key Western countries), it nonetheless emerges as universally applicable and rendered "sufficient to explain the social/historical realities of the rest of the world" (p. 74). To accomplish this universality, the construction of the Western canon required what Portuguese sociologist Boaventura de Sousa Santos (2007) refers to as "epistemicide," the destruction, eradication and delegitimization of other (non-Western) knowledge and cultural systems. Hall's (1992) description of the "West and the Rest" adds to our understanding here. He argues that the concept of the "West" was not a geographical or historical place but an idea that embodied society as developed, industrialized, urban, and modern. As such, the idea of the "West" functions as more than a mere descriptor. Instead it becomes the standard measure by which all other societies are judged, measured, compared, evaluated, and ranked (Hall, 1992). According to Hall, the identity of the "West" does not merely operate as an internal check but is based on its difference from the "Rest" of the world; the "West" and the "Rest" thus become essential parts of the same globalizing discourse.

Despite the context, program, or evaluation purpose, we observed a constant jockeying between culturally responsive practice and funder and program requirements. We noted an improvisational and performative dimension to evaluation work, as the evaluator's gaze shifted from community to funder, from localized conceptions of knowledge to the broader and more generalizable requirements of the sponsoring agencies. As noted sociologist Erving Goffman (1959) vividly portrays, "The image that emerges of the individual is that of a juggler and synthesizer, an accommodator and appeaser, who fulfils one function while he is apparently engaged in another" (p. 40). For some, this tension led to the search for a technical "fix," whether through culturally matching traits between evaluator and community, hiring interpreters or translators, or finding the "right" combination of methods or the "right" balance between predefined instruments and the local cultural community.

The technification of social, political, and ethical concerns, what Li (2007) refers to as an issue of "rendering technical," ensures a narrowed and circumscribed framing of the problem, essentially a depoliticized "rendering" that orients the evaluator toward certain actions in the search for a technical solution. As Merry (2011) describes, "Political debates about compliance shift to arguments about . . . what should be measured, and what each measurement should represent . . . the political process of judging and evaluating is transformed into a technical issue of measurement and counting" (p. S88). As such, any critical discussion of social, political, economic, and ethical issues is subverted and denied, ultimately replaced with unending consultations about technical merit, categorizations, and expertise. As Dahler-Larsen (2014) makes clear in his discussion of "constitutive effects," this focus on the measurable shapes the social reality, in its sanitized, quantifiable version, that it then purports to measure. The effect of this technical demarcation or framing of the social world into measurable components is thus truly political (Dahler-Larsen, 2014).

By way of example, we were struck by the depiction of language in our studies as primarily an issue of translation, rather than one of interpretation, especially given the centrality of language in the construction of meaning, representation, and culture. According to Hall (1997), meaning and language are connected to culture through our mental representations, which we then use to interpret things in the world. People who share a culture often share these same meanings and constructs of the social world, which they represent through a shared language. Thus, as Hall (1997) argues, "The world is not accurately or otherwise reflected in the mirror of language. Language does not work like a mirror. Meaning is produced within language" (p. 14). Hence translation in culturally responsive practice moves beyond the technical concerns of access and hiring to include the shift (or play) between local and national cultures, perspectives, values, and worldviews. As Temple (1997) explains, "The use of translators or interpreters is not merely a technical matter that has little bearing on the outcome. It is of epistemological consequence as it influences what is 'found'" (p. 614). Although translation was seen primarily as a technical concern, translation involves the active process of interpretation, not merely of words, but of concepts, ideas, and perspectives. Given the multiple points of interpretation within the evaluative encounter, from evaluator to translator, from translator to cultural community, from cultural community back to translator, and from translator to evaluator (who then constructs "findings" based on the data), the process of translation assumes epistemological, ontological, and cultural significance.

While we recognize the strong impetus to shift evaluation practice toward technical expertise and away from its social and moral center, cultivating cultural responsiveness requires thoughtful, critical reflection, what for Maxine Greene (1994) is a wakefulness to our own sensemaking. We need to shift our thinking about evaluation away from its technical focus toward seeing it as a way of being in the world (Schwandt, 2015), to appreciate its potential for opening up and broadening our epistemological, ontological, and ethical perspectives. In the opening Keynote to the Fifth International Center for Culturally Responsive Evaluation and Assessment Conference, Eric Jolly (2019) emphasized the need to rewrite the rules of engagement, to rewrite the scripts we have, to work differently or risk recreating the colonizing past.

Cultural responsiveness in evaluation requires kinetic and creative thinking, a shift away from the methodological allure (and safety?) of the Western canon. We need to listen to community voices and perspectives and have the courage to choose a pathway that may very well take us beyond what we know and understand and that may require us to cross a border and enter into territory that is more familiar to those with whom we work. The courage we need to do this comes from our knowing that we will not be alone on this journey, since it will be fueled by growing trust relationships and by the mutual sharing of knowledge, skills, and expertise. In this sense, we need to share control of the "steering wheel" and open ourselves to the enlightenment that can be gained from others' ways of being and knowing.

REFERENCES

Abes, R. V. (2000). Strengthening citizen participation and democratization in the Philippines: ELF's impact evaluation. In M. Estella, J. Blauert, D. Campilian, J. Gaventa, J. Gonsalves, I. Guijt, & R. Riacafort (Eds.), *Learning from change: Issues and experiences in participatory monitoring and evaluation* (pp. 83–94). Ottawa, ON, Canada: International Development Research Centre.

Adeniyi, D. A., & Dinbabo, M. F. (2016). Evaluating outcomes from stakeholders' perception: evidence from an irrigation project in Nigeria. *Ghana Journal of Development Studies, 13*(2), 26.

Agar, M. (2000). Border lessons: Linguistic "rich" points and evaluative understanding. In R. K. Hopson (Ed.), *How and why language matters in valuation. New Directions for Evaluation,* 86, 93–109.

Agger, B. (1991). Critical theory, poststructuralism, postmodernism: Their sociological relevance. *Annual Review of Sociology,* 17, 105–131.

Alkin, M. C. (Ed.). (2012). *Evaluation roots* (2nd ed.). Thousand Oaks, CA: Sage.

Alkon, A., Tschann, J. M., Ruane, S. H., Wolff, M., & Hittner, A. (2001). A violence prevention and evaluation project with ethnically diverse populations. *American Journal of Preventive Medicine, 20* (IS), 48–44.

American Evaluation Association. (2011). *American Evaluation Association public statement on cultural competence in evaluation.* Fairhaven, MA: Author. Retrieved from https://www.eval.org

American Evaluation Association, Diversity Committee. (2004). *Final report: A cultural reading of the program evaluation standards* (2nd ed.). Retrieved from https://www.eval.org/p/cm/ld/fid=74.

Anderson, B. (1983). *Imagined communities.* London, England: Verso.

Anderson-Draper, M. H. (2006). Understanding cultural competence through the evaluation of "breaking the silence: a project to generate critical knowledge about family violence within immigrant communities." *The Canadian Journal of Program Evaluation, 21*(2), 59–79.

Argyris, C., & Schön, D. (1978). *Organizational learning: A theory of action perspective,* Reading, MA: Addison-Wesley.

Asad, T. (1986). The concept of cultural translation in British social anthropology. In J. Clifford & G. E. Marcus (Eds.), *Writing culture: The poetics and politics of ethnology* (pp. 141–164). Berkeley: University of California Press.

Askew, K., Beverly, M. G., & Jay, M. L. (2012). Aligning collaborative and culturally responsive evaluation approaches. *Evaluation and Program Planning, 35,* 552–557.

Baker, M., Pipi, K., & Cassidy, T. (2015). Kaupapa Māori action research in a Whānau Ora collective: An exemplar of Māori evaluative practice and the findings. *Evaluation Matters— He Take Tō te Aromatawa*i, 1, 113–136.

Baldwin, J. R., Faulkner, S. L., & Hecht, M. L. (2006). Layers of meaning: An analysis of definitions of culture. In J. R. Baldwin, S. L. Faulkner, M. L. Hecht, & S. L. Lindsley (Eds.), *Redefining culture: Perspectives across the disciplines* (pp. 27–52). New York, NY: Routledge.

Bamberger, M. (1991). The politics of evaluation in developing countries. *Evaluation and Program Planning*, 14, 325–339.

Bamberger, M., Vaessen, J., & Raimondo, E. (2016). *Dealing with complexity in development evaluation: A practical approach*. Thousand Oaks, CA: Sage.

Banks, J. A. (1993). The canon debate, knowledge construction, and multicultural education. *Educational Researcher*, 22(5), 4014.

Barth, F. (1994). Enduring and emerging issues in the analysis of ethnicity. In H. Vermeulen & C. Govers (Eds.), *The anthropology of ethnicity: Beyond 'ethnic groups and boundaries'* (pp. 11–32). Amsterdam, The Netherlands: HET SPINHUIS.

Basso, K. H. (1996). *Wisdom sits in places: Landscape and language among the Western Apache*. Albuquerque: University of New Mexico Press.

Bauder, H. (2006). Learning to become a geographer: Reproduction and transformation in academia. *Antipode*, 38, 671–679.

Bauman, Z. (1992). *Intimations of postmodernity*. London, England: Routledge.

Bauman, Z. (2000). *Liquid modernity*. Cambridge, England: Polity Press.

Berends, L., & Roberts, B. (2003). Evaluation standards and their application to indigenous programs in Victoria, Australia. *Evaluation Journal of Australasia*, 3 (new series) (2), 54–59.

Best, S., & Kellner, D. (1987). *The postmodern turn*. New York, NY: The Guilford Press.

Best, S., & Kellner, D. (1997). *The postmodern turn*. New York, NY: Guilford Press.

Bhola, H. S. (2003). Social and cultural contexts of educational evaluation: A global perspective. In T. Kellaghan & D. L. Stufflebeam (Eds.), *International handbook of educational evaluation* (pp. 397–416). Boston, MA: Kluwer.

Bi Niba, J. E., & Green, J. M. (2005). Major factors influencing HIV/AIDS project evaluation. *Evaluation Review*, 29(4), 399–413.

Billig, M. (1978). A social psychological view of the National Front. *European Monographs in Social Psychology 15*. London, England: Harcourt Bruce Jovanovich.

Billig, M. (1978). *Fascists: A social psychological view of the National Front*. London: Harcourt Bruce Jovanovich.

Bishop, R., Berryman, M., Wearmouth, J., Peter, M., & Clapham, S. (2012). Professional development, changes in teacher practice and improvements in indigenous students' educational performance: A case study from New Zealand. *Teaching and Teacher Education*, 28(5), 694–705. doi:10.1016/j.tate.2012.02.002

Blake, E. (2002). Spatiality past and present: An interview with Edward Soja. *Journal of Social Archaeology*, 2, 139–158.

Blignault, I., Haswell, M., & Jackson Pulver, L. (2016). The value of partnerships: Lessons from a multi-site evaluation of a national social and emotional wellbeing program for indigenous youth. *Australian and New Zealand Journal of Public Health* (Special Issue), 53–58. doi:10.1111/1753-6405.12403

Blignault, I., & Williams, M. (2017). Challenges in evaluating Aboriginal healing programs: Definitions, diversity and data. *Evaluation Journal of Australasia*, 17(2), 4–10.

Bocock, R. (1992). The cultural formations of modern society. In S. Hall & B. Gieben (Eds.), *Formations of modernity* (pp. 229–274). Cambridge, England: Polity Press.

Bond, C., Foley, W., & Askew, D. (2016). "It puts a human face on the researched"—A qualitative evaluation of an Indigenous health research governance model. *Australian and New Zealand Journal of Public Health, 40*(Suppl. 1), S89–S95.

Bonvillain, N. (1997). *Language, culture, and communication: The meaning of messages.* Saddle River, NJ: Prentice Hall.

Botcheva, L., Shih, J., & Huffman, L. C. (2009). Emphasizing cultural. *American Journal of Evaluation, 30*(2), 176–188.

Boulton, A., & Kingi, T. (2011). Reflections on the use of a Māori conceptual framework to evaluate complex health policy: The case of New Zealand's Healthy Eating, Healthy Action Strategy evaluation. *Evaluation Journal of Australasia, 11*(1), 5–10.

Bourdieu, P. (1972). *Outline of a theory of practice.* Cambridge, England: Cambridge University Press.

Bowen, M. L., & Tillman, A. S. (2015). Developing culturally responsive surveys: Lessons in development, implementation, and analysis from Brazil's African descent communities. *American Journal of Evaluation, 36*(1), 25–41.

Bowman, N. (2018). Looking backward but moving forward: Honoring the sacred and asserting the sovereign in indigenous evaluation. *American Journal of Evaluation, 39*(4), 543–568.

Bowman, N., & Dodge Francis, C. (2018). Culturally responsive indigenous evaluation: Establishing the legal, cultural, and ethical requirements for conducting evaluations in Indian Country. *New Directions for Evaluation.*

Boyce, A. S. (2017). Lessons learned using a values-engaged approach to attend to culture, diversity, and equity in a STEM program evaluation. *Evaluation and Program Planning, 64,* 33–43.

Boyer, P. (2006). Should expediency always trump tradition? AIHEC/NSF project develops indigenous evaluation methods. *Journal of American Indian Higher Education, 18*(2), 6, 13–15.

Bradley, J. E., Mayfield, M. V., Mehta, M. P., & Rukonge, A. (2002). Participatory evaluation of reproductive health care quality in developing countries. *Social Science & Medicine, 55*(2), 269–282.

Brago Brandão, D., Renato Silva, R., & Codas, R. (2012). Youth participation in evaluation: The Pró-Menino Program in Brazil. *New Directions for Evaluation, 2012*(134), 49–59.

Brandon, P. R., Smith, N. L., Ofir, Z., & Noordeloos, M. (2014). Monitoring and evaluation of African Women in Agricultural Research and Development (AWARD): An exemplar of managing for impact in development evaluation. *American Journal of Evaluation, 35*(1), 128–143.

Brant Castellano, M. (2000). Updating Aboriginal traditions of knowledge. In G. J. Sefa Dei, B. L. Hall, & D. Goldin-Rosenberg (Eds.), *Indigenous knowledge in global contexts: Multiple readings of our world* (pp. 21–36). Toronto, ON, Canada: University of Toronto Press.

Brant Castellano, M. (2004). Ethics of Aboriginal research. *Journal of Aboriginal Health, 1*(1), 98–114.

Brayboy, B. M. (2005). Toward a tribal critical race theory in education. *The Urban Review, 37*(5), 425–446.

Brekhus, W. (1998). A sociology of the unmarked: Redirecting our focus. *Sociological Theory, 16*(1), 34–51.

Browne, J., Thorpe, S., Tunny, N., Adams, K., & Palermo, C. (2013). A qualitative evaluation of a mentoring program for Aboriginal health workers and allied health professionals. *Australian and New Zealand Journal of Public Health, 37,* 457–462.

Buskens, I., & Earl, S. (2008). Research for change: Outcome mapping's contribution to emancipatory action research in Africa. *Action Research, 6*(2), 171–192.

Butty, J. L. M., Reid, M. D., & LaPoint, V. (2004). A culturally responsive evaluation approach applied to the talent development school-to-career intervention program. *New Directions for Evaluation, 101,* 37–47.

Cajete, G. (2000). *Native science. Natural laws of interdependence.* Santa Fe, NM: Clear Light.

Cannella, G. S., Lincoln, Y. S. (2004). Epilogue: Claiming a critical public social science: Reconceptualizing and redeploying research. *Qualitative Inquiry, 10*(2), 298–309.

Capra, F. (1997). *The web of life.* New York, NY: Anchor Books.

Carden, F. (2010). Introduction to the forum on evaluation field building in South Asia. *American Journal of Evaluation, 31*(2), 291–221.

Carden, F. (2013). Evaluation, not development evaluation. *American Journal of Evaluation, 34*(4), 576–579.

Carden, F., & Alkin, M. C. (2012). Evaluation roots: An international perspective. *Journal of Multidisciplinary Evaluation, 8*(17), 108–118.

Carlson, T., Moewaka Barnes, H., & McCreanor, T. (2017). Kaupapa Māori evaluation: A collaborative journey. *Evaluation Matters—He Take Tō Te Aromatawai, 3,* 67–99.

Carspecken, P. F. (1996). *Critical ethnography in educational research: A theoretical and practical guide.* New York, NY: Routledge.

Cavino, H. M. (2013). Across the colonial divide: Conversations about evaluation in indigenous context. *American Journal of Evaluation, 34*(3), 339–355.

Chambers, R. (2007). *From PRA to PLA and pluralism: Practice and theory* (IDS Working Paper 286). Brighton, England: Institute of Development Studies.

Chesterton, P. (2003). Balancing ethical principles in evaluation: A case study. *Canadian Journal of Program Evaluation, 18*(1), 49–60.

Chilisa, B. (2012). *Indigenous research methodologies.* Thousand Oaks, CA: Sage.

Chilisa, B., Major, T. E., Gaotlhobogwe, M., & Mokgolodi, H. (2016). Decolonizing and indigenizing evaluation practice in Africa: Toward African relational evaluation approaches. *Canadian Journal of Program Evaluation, 30*(3), 313–328.

Chino, M., & DeBruyn, L. (2006). Building true capacity: Indigenous models for indigenous communities. *American Journal of Public Health, 96*(4), 596–599.

Chinyowa, K. C. (2011). Revisiting monitoring and evaluation strategies for applied drama and theatre practice in African contexts. *The Journal of Applied Theatre and Performance, 16*(3), 337–356.

Chong, J., Hassin, J., Young, R. S., & Joe, J. R. (2011). Stuck inside the federal-Indian funding relationship: A tale of two evaluations. *Evaluation Review, 35*(5), 523–549.

Chouinard. J. A. (2010). *Understanding cross-cultural evaluation: Making sense of theory and practice.* Unpublished Ph.D. thesis, University of Ottawa.

Chouinard, J. A. (2013). The case for participatory evaluation in an era of accountability. *American Journal of Evaluation, 34*(2), 237–253.

Chouinard, J. A. (2014). Understanding relationships in culturally complex evaluation contexts. *Evaluation, 20*(3), 332–347.

Chouinard, J.A. (2016). Introduction: Demystifying the concept of culture in international development evaluations. *Canadian Journal of Program Evaluation*, 30.3, Special Issue, 237–247.

Chouinard, J. A., & Cousins, J. B. (2007). Culturally competent evaluation for Aboriginal communities: A review of the empirical literature. *Journal of MultiDisciplinary Evaluation*, 4(8), 40–57.

Chouinard, J. A., & Cousins, J. B. (2009). A review and synthesis of current research on cross-cultural evaluation. *American Journal of Evaluation, 30*(4), 457–494.

Chouinard, J. A., & Cousins, J. B. (2015). The journey from rhetoric to reality: Participatory evaluation in a development context. *Educational Assessment, Evaluation and Accountability, 27*(1), 5–39.

Chouinard, J. A., & Hopson, R. (2016). Toward a more critical exploration of culture in international development evaluation. *Canadian Journal of Program Evaluation* (Special Issue), *30*(3), 248–276.

Chouinard, J. A., & Milley, P. V. (2016). Mapping the spatial properties of participatory practice: A discussion of context in evaluation. *Evaluation and Program Planning, 54*, 1–10.

Christie, C. A. (2003). What guides evaluation? A study of how evaluation practice maps onto evaluation theory. *New Directions for Evaluation, 97*, 7–35.

Christie, C. A., & Barela, E. (2005). The Delphi technique as a method for increasing inclusion in the evaluation process. *The Canadian Journal of Program Evaluation, 20*(1), 105–122.

Clayson, Z., Castaneda, X., Sanchez, E., & Brindis, C. (2002). Unequal power-changing landscapes: Negotiations between evaluation stakeholders in Latino communities. *American Journal of Evaluation, 23*(1), 33–44.

Clifford, J., & Marcus, G. E. (1986). *Writing culture: The poetics and politics of ethnography.* Berkeley: University of California Press.

Cockburn, C. (1998). *The space between us: negotiating gender and national identities in conflict.* London, England: Zed Books.

Collins, P. H. (2000). *Black feminist thought: Knowledge, consciousness, and the politics of empowerment* (2nd ed.). New York, NY: Routledge.

Collins, P. H., & Bilge, S. (2016). *Intersectionality.* Malden, MA: Polity Press.

Conlin, S., & Stirrat, R. L. (2008). Current challenges in development evaluation. *Evaluation, 14*(2), 193–208.

Conner, R. F. (1985). International and domestic evaluation: Comparisons and insights. *New Directions for Evaluation*, 25, 19–28.

Conner, R. F. (2004). Developing and implementing culturally competent evaluation: A discussion of multicultural validity in two HIV prevention programs for Latinos. *New Directions for Evaluation, 102*, 51–65.

Cooper, C. W., & Christie, C. A. (2005). Evaluating parent empowerment: A look at the potential of social justice evaluation in education. *Teachers College Record, 107*(10), 2248–2274.

Copeland-Carson, J. (2005). Applying theory and method in evaluation anthropology: The example of the South Bronx's comprehensive community revitalization project. *NAPA Bulletin, 24*, 89–106.

Coppens, N. M., Page, R., & Chan Thou, T. (2006). Reflections on the evaluation of a Cambodian youth dance program. *American Journal of Community Psychology, 37*(3/4), 321–331.

Cornachione, E. B., Trombetta, M. R., & Casa, S. P. C. (2010). Evaluation use and involvement of internal stakeholders: The case of a new non-degree online program in Brazil. *Studies in Educational Evaluation, 36*, 69–81.

Cornwall, A. (2004). Introduction: New democratic spaces? The politics and dynamics of institutionalized participation. *IDS Bulletin, 35*(2), 1–10.

Cornwall, A., & Jewkes, R. (1995). What is participatory research? *Social Science & Medicine, 41*(12), 1667–1676.

Cousins, J. B. (2004). Crossing the bridge: Toward understanding use through empirical inquiry. In M.C. Alkin (Ed.), *Evaluation roots: Tracing theorists' views and influences* (pp. 319–330). Thousand Oaks, CA: Sage.

Cousins, J. B., & Chouinard, J. A. (2012). *Participatory evaluation up close: An integration of research-based knowledge.* Charlotte, NC: Information Age.

Cousins, J. B., & Whitmore, E. (1998). Framing participatory evaluation. In E. Whitmore (Ed.), Understanding and practicing participatory evaluation. *New Directions in Evaluation, 80*, 3–23.

Cram, F. (2005). An ode to Pink Floyd: Chasing the magic of Māori and Iwi providers. (J. S. Te Rito, Ed.). *Tihei Oreore Monograph Series: Policy Seminars, 1*(2), 15–26.

Cram, F. (2015). Harnessing global social justice and social change with multiple and mixed method research. In S. Hesse-Biber & R. B. Johnson (Eds.), *The Oxford handbook of mixed and multiple methods research* (pp. 667–687). New York, NY: Oxford University Press.

Cram, F. (2016). Lessons on decolonizing evaluation from Kaupapa Māori evaluation. *Canadian Journal of Program Evaluation, 30*(3), 296–312.

Cram, F. (2018). Conclusion: Lessons about indigenous evaluation. In F. Cram, K. A. Tibbetts, & J. LaFrance, *Indigenous evaluation. New Directions for Evaluation, 159*, 121–133.

Cram, F., & Hopson, R. (2018). Digging deeper to engage wicked problems through evaluation. In R. Hopson, & F. Cram (Eds.), *Tackling wicked problems in complex ecologies: The role of evaluation* (pp. 234–256). Redwood City, CA: Stanford University Press.

Cram, F., Kennedy, V., Paipa, K., Pipi, K., & Wehipeihana, N. (2015). Being culturally responsive through Kaupapa Māori evaluation. In S. Hood, R. K. Hopson, & H. T. Frierson (Eds.), *Continuing the journey to reposition culture and cultural context in evaluation theory and practice* (pp. 289–311). Charlotte, NC: Information Age.

Cram, F., & Mertens, D. (2015). Transformative and indigenous frameworks for mixed and multi method research. In S. N. Hesse-Biber & B. B. Johnson (Eds.), *The Oxford handbook of mixed and multiple methods research* (pp. 99–109). New York, NY: Oxford University Press.

Cram, F., & Mertens, D. (2016). Negotiating solidarity between indigenous and transformative paradigms in evaluation. *Evaluation Matters—He Take Tō Te Aromatawai, 2*, 161–189.

Cram, F., & Pipi, K. (2000). *Māori/Iwi provider success: Report on the pilot project.* Tamaki Makaurau, Auckland, New Zealand: IRI.

Cram, F., Pipi, K., & Paipa, K. (2018). Kaupapa Māori evaluation in Aotearoa New Zealand. *New Directions for Evaluation: Indigenous Evaluation, 159*, 63–77.

Cram, F., Vette, M., Wilson, M., Vaithianathan, R., Maloney, T., & Baird, S. (2018). He awa whiria—braided rivers: Understanding the outcomes from Family Start for Māori. *Evaluation Matters—He Take Tō Te Aromatawai*, 4, 165–206.

Crang, M., & Thrift, N. J. (Eds.). (2000). *Thinking space*. London, England: Routledge.

Crawford, G. (2003). Promoting democracy from without: Learning from within (Part II). *Democratization, 10*(2), 1–20.

Crazy Bull, C. (1997). A Native conversation about research and scholarship. *Tribal College Journal, 9*, 17–23.

Cronbach, L. J. (1980). *Toward reform of program evaluation: Aims, methods and institutional arrangements*. San Francisco, CA: Jossey-Bass.

Crush, J. (1995). Introduction. In J. Crush (Ed.), *Power of development* (pp. 1–26). London, England: Routledge.

Cullen, A. E., Coryn, C. L. S., & Rugh, J. (2011). The politics and consequences of including stakeholders in international development evaluation. *American Journal of Evaluation, 32*(3), 345–361.

Curtis, E., Townsend, S., & Airini. (2012). Improving indigenous and ethnic minority student success in foundation health study. *Teaching in Higher Education, 17*(5), 589–602.

Daes, E.-I. A. (2000). Protecting knowledge: Traditional resource rights in the new millennium. Keynote address to the "Defining Indigenous Peoples' Heritage" Conference, Vancouver, February 23–26, 2000. Vancouver, BC, Canada: Union of British Columbia Indian Chiefs.

Dahler-Larsen, P., Abma, T., Bustelo, M., Irimia, R., Kosunen, S., Kravchuk, I., . . . & Tshali, C. K. (2017). Evaluation, language, and untranslatables. *American Journal of Evaluation, 38*(1), 114–125.

Dahler-Larsen, P. (2012). *The evaluation society*. Stanford, CA: Stanford University Press.

Dahler-Larsen, P. (2014). Constitutive effects of performance indicators: Getting beyond unintended consequences. *Public Management Review, 16*(7), 969–986.

Dahler-Larsen, P. (2017). Evaluation, language, and untranslatables. *American Journal of Evaluation, 38*(1), 114–125.

Dahler-Larsen, P., & Schwandt, T. A. (2012). Political culture as context for evaluation. In D. J. Rog, J. L. Fitzpatrick, & R. F. Conner (Eds.), *Context: A framework for its influence on evaluation practice*. (New Directions for Evaluation, 135), 75–87.

de Certeau, M. (1984). *The practice of everyday life*. Berkley: University of California Press.

de Sousa Santos, B. 2007. Beyond Abyssal Thinking: From Global Lines to Ecologies of Knowledge." *Eurozine* 33, 45–89.

de Sousa Santos, B. (2014). *Epistemologies of the South: Justice against epistemicide*. Boulder, CO: Paradigm.

Delpit, L. D. (1988). The silenced dialogue: Power and pedagogy in educating other people's children. *Harvard Educational Review, 53*(3), 280–298.

Denzin, N., & Lincoln, Y. (2000). *Handbook of qualitative research* (2nd ed.). Thousand Oaks, CA: Sage.

Dewey, J. (2007). *Human nature and conduct: An introduction to social psychology*. New York, NY: Cosimo. (Original work published 1922)

Dilley, R. M. (2002). The problem of context in social and cultural anthropology. *Language and Communication, 22*, 437–456.

Donaldson, S. I., Azzam, T., & Conner, R. F. (2013). Future directions for improving international development evaluations. In S. I. Donaldson, T. Azzam, & R. F. Conner (Eds.), *Emerging practices in international development evaluation* (pp. 225–241). Charlotte, NC: Information Age.

Donaldson, S. I., & Lipsey, M. W. (2008). Roles for theory in evaluation practice. In I. Shaw, J. Greene, & M. Mark (Eds.), *Handbook of evaluation*. Thousand Oaks: Sage.

Du Bois, W. (1920). The souls of white folk. In N. Huggins (Ed.), *W. E. B. Du Bois: Writings*. New York, NY: Library of America.

Duggan, C. (2012). "Show me your impact": Evaluating transitional justice in contested spaces. *Evaluation and Program Planning, 35*(1), 199–205.

Durham, J., & Tan, B. (2010). Lessons learnt from an evaluation of an unexploded ordnance removal program in Lao PDR. *Evaluation Journal of Australasia, 10*(1), 44–48.

Ebbutt, D. (1998). Evaluation of projects in the developing world: Some cultural and methodological issues. *International Journal of Educational Development, 18*(5), 415–424.

Elkins, C. (2010). Evaluating development interventions in peace-precarious situations. *Evaluation, 16*(3), 309–321.

Escobar, A. (1995). *Encountering development: The making and unmaking of the third world*. Princeton, NJ: Princeton University Press.

Estrella, M., Blauert, J., Campilian, D., Gaventa, J., Gonsalves, J., Guijt, I., & Ricafort, R. (Eds.). (2000). *Learning from change: Issues and experiences in participatory monitoring and evaluation*. Ottawa, ON, Canada: International Development Research Centre.

Eversole, R. (2005). Whose vision, whose rules? A culture and development typology. *Canadian Journal of Development Studies, 26*(2), 294–308.

Fischer, M.J. (2007) Culture and Cultural Analysis as Experimental Systems. Cultural Anthropology, (22)1, 1–65.

Fisher, P. A., & Ball, T. J. (2002). The Indian Family Wellness Project: An application of the Tribal Participatory Research Model. *Prevention Science, 3*(3), 235–240.

Fiske, J. (1994). *Media matters: Everyday culture and political change*. Minneapolis: University of Minnesota Press.

Fleischaker, S. (1999). From cultural diversity to universal ethics: Three models. *Cultural Dynamics, 11*(1), 105–128.

Forrest, R., Taylor, L.-A., Roberts, J., Pearson, M., Foxall, D., & Scott-Chapman, S. (2016). PATU. Fighting fit, fighting fat! The Hinu Wero approach. *AlterNative, 12*(3), 282–297.

Fortun, K. (2009). Foreword to the 25th Anniversary edition. In J. Clifford & G. E. Marcus (Eds.), *Writing culture: The poetics and politics of ethnology* (pp. vii– xx). Berkeley: University of California Press.

Foucault, M. (1972). *The archaeology of knowledge and the discourse on language*. New York, NY: Pantheon Books.

Foucault, M. (1980). *The history of sexuality* (vol. 1). New York, NY: Vintage.

Foucault, M. (1984). Of other spaces, Heteropias. Translated from Architecture, Mouvement, Continuite no. 5, 46–49

Foucault, M. (1991). *The Foucault effect: Studies in governmentality*. Chicago, IL: The University of Chicago Press.

Fraser, N. (2001). Recognition without ethics? *Theory, Culture and Society, 18*(2–3), 21–42.

Fraser, N., & Honneth, A. (2003). *Redistribution or recognition? A political-philosophical exchange*. London, England: Verso.

Freeman, R. (2009). What is "translation"? *Evidence & Policy, 5*(4), 429–447.

Frierson, H. T., Hood, S., & Hughes, G. B. (2002). Strategies that address culturally responsive evaluation. In J. Frechtling (Ed.), *The 2002 user-friendly handbook for project evaluation* (pp. 63–73). Arlington, VA: National Science Foundation.

Frierson, H. T., Hood, S., Hughes, G. B., & Thomas, V. G. (2010). A guide to conducting culturally responsive evaluations. In J. Frechtling Westat (Ed.), *The 2010 user-friendly handbook for project evaluation* (pp. 75–96). Arlington, VA: National Science Foundation.

Geertz, C. (1973). *The interpretations of culture: Selected essays*. New York, NY: Basic Books.

Geertz, C. (1983). The native's point of view: On the nature of anthropological understanding. In C. Geertz, *Local knowledge: Further essays in interpretative anthropology*. New York, NY: Basic Books.

Geertz, C. (1993). *Local knowledge: Further essays in interpretive anthropology*. London, England: Falmer.

Geertz, C. (2000). *Available light: Anthropological reflections on philosophical topics*. Princeton, NJ: Princeton University Press.

Gherardi, S. (2009). Introduction: The critical power of the "practice lens." *Management Learning, 40*(2), 115–128.

Ginsberg, P. E. (1988). Evaluation in cross-cultural perspective. *Evaluation and Program Planning, 11*(2), 189–195.

Giroux, H. A. (2005). *Border crossings: Cultural workers and the politics of education* (2nd ed.). New York, NY: Routledge.

Goffman, E. (1959) *The presentation of self in everyday life*. Garden City, NJ: Doubleday.

Goffman, E. (1997). The under life of a public institution (1961). In C. Lemert & A. Branaman (Eds.), *The Goffman reader*. Malden, MA: Blackwell.

Gordon, E. W., Miller, F., & Rollock, D. (1990). Coping with communicentric bias in knowledge production in the social sciences. *Educational Researcher, 19*(2), 14–19.

Greene, J. C. (1997). Evaluation as advocacy. *American Journal of Evaluation, 18*, 25–35.

Greene, J. C. (2005). Evaluators as stewards of the public good. In S. Hood, R. K. Hopson, & H. T. Frierson (Eds.), *The role of culture and cultural context: A mandate for inclusion, the discovery of truth, and understanding in evaluative theory and practice* (pp. 7–20). Charlotte, NC: Information Age.

Greene, J. C. (2007). *Mixed methods in social inquiry*. San Francisco, CA: Jossey-Bass.

Greene, M. (1994). Epistemology and educational research: The influence of recent approaches to knowledge (Chapter 10). *Review of Research in Education, 20*, 423–464.

Gregory, D. (2009). Space. In D. Gregory, R. Johnston, G. Pratt, M. Watts, & S. Whatmore (Eds.), *The dictionary of human geography* (5th ed., pp. 707–710). Chichester, England: Wiley-Blackwell.

Grey, K., Putt, J., Baxter, N., & Sutton, S. (2016). Bridging the gap both-ways: Enhancing evaluation quality and utilisation in a study of remote community safety and wellbeing with Indigenous Australians. *Evaluation Journal of Australasia, 16*(3), 15–24.

Grosfoguel, R. (2013). The structure of knowledge in westernized universities: Epistemic racism/sexism and the four genocides/epistemicides of the long 16th century. *Human Architecture: Journal of the Sociology of Self-Knowledge, XI*(1), 73–90.

Grover, J. G. (2010). Challenges in applying indigenous evaluation practices in mainstream grant programs to indigenous communities. *Canadian Journal of Program Evaluation, 23*(2), 33–50.

Guba, E. G., & Lincoln, Y. S. (1994). Competing paradigms in qualitative research. In N. K. Denzin & Y. S. Lincoln (Eds.), *Handbook of qualitative research* (pp. 105–117). London, England: Sage.

Guba, E. G., & Lincoln, Y. S. (1989). *Fourth generation evaluation*. Newbury Park, CA: Sage.

Guba, E. G., & Lincoln, Y. S. (2005). Paradigmatic controversies, contradictions, and emerging confluences. In N. K. Denzin & Y. S. Lincoln (Eds.), The SAGE *handbook of qualitative research* (3rd ed., pp. 191–216). Thousand Oaks, CA: Sage.

Gupta, A., & Ferguson, J. (1992). "Culture": Space, identity, and the politics of difference. *Cultural Anthropology, 7*(1), 6–23.

Guzman, B. L. (2003). Examining the role of cultural competency in program evaluation: Visions for new millennium evaluators. In S. I. Donaldson & M. Scriven (Eds.), *Evaluating social programs and problems: Visions for the new millennium* (pp. 167–181). Mahwah, NJ: Lawrence Erlbaum.

Hall, S. (1990). Cultural identity and diaspora. In J. Rutherford (Ed.), *Identity: community, culture, difference* (pp. 222–237). London, England: Lawrence & Wishart.

Hall, S. (1992). The west and the rest: Discourse and power. In S. Hall & B. Gieben (Eds.), *Formations of modernity* (pp. 276–320). Cambridge, England: Polity Press and Open University.

Hall, S. (1996a). Introduction: Who needs identity? In S. Hall & P. Du Gay (Eds.), *Questions of cultural identity* (pp. 1–17). Thousand Oaks, CA: Sage.

Hall, S. (1996b). The question of cultural identity. In S. Hall, D. Held, D. Hubert, & K. Thompson (Eds.), *Modernity: An introduction to modern societies* (pp. 595–634). Oxford, England: Blackwell.

Hall, S. (1997). The work of representation. In S. Hall (Ed.), *Representation: Cultural representations and signifying practices* (pp. 15–64). London, England: Sage.

Hall, S. (2016). *Cultural studies 1983: A theoretical history*. Durham, NC: Duke University Press.

Hamerton, H., Mercer, C., Riini, D., McPherson, B., & Morrison, L. (2012). Evaluating Māori community initiatives to promote Healthy Eating, Healthy Action. *Health. Promotion International, 29*(1), 60–69.

Harding, S. (1991). *Whose science? Whose knowledge? Thinking from women's lives*. NY: Conrell Universty Press.

Harklau, L., & Norwood, R. (2005). Negotiating researcher roles in ethnographic program evaluation: A postmodern lens. *Anthropology and Education Quarterly, 36*(3), 278–288.

Hart, M. A. (2007). *Worldviews, knowledge, and research: The development of an indigenous research paradigm.* Paper presented at the Indigenous Voices in Social Work: Not Lost in Translation Conference, June 4–7. 2007, Makaha, Hawaii.

Hart, R. A., & Rajbhandary, J. (2003). Using participatory methods to further the democratic goals of children's organizations. *New Directions for Evaluation, 2003*(98), 61–75.

Harvey, D. (1973). *Social justice and the city.* Oxford, England: Blackwell.

Haugen, J., & Chouinard, J. A. (2018, September 5). Transparent, translucent, opaque: Exploring the dimensions of power in culturally responsive evaluation contexts. Advance online publication. *American Journal of Evaluation.*

Hay, K. (2010). Evaluation field building in South Asia: Reflections, anecdotes, and questions. *American Journal of Evaluation, 31*(2), 222–231.

Haylock, L., & Miller, C. (2016). Merging developmental and feminist evaluation to monitor and evaluate transformative social change. *American Journal of Evaluation, 37*(1), 63–79.

Henry, E., & Pene, H. (2001). Kaupapa Māori: Locating Indigenous ontology, epistemology and methodology within the academy. *Organisation, 8*, 234–242.

Henry, G. T. and M. M. Mark (2003) `Beyond Use: Understanding Evaluation's Influence on Attitudes and Actions', *American Journal of Evaluation* 24(3): 293–314.

Heron, J., & Reason, P. (1997). A participatory inquiry paradigm. *Qualitative Inquiry, 3*(3), 274–294.

Herr, K., & Anderson, G. (2014). *The action research dissertation: A guide for students and faculty* (2nd ed.). Thousand Oaks, CA: Sage.

Hobart, M. (1986). Introduction: Context, meaning, and power. In M. Hobart & R. H. Taylor (Eds.), *Context, meaning and power in Southeast Asia* (pp. 7–19). Ithaca, NY: Southeast Asia Program.

Holte-McKenzie, M., Forde, S., & Theobald, S. (2006). Development of a participatory monitoring and evaluation strategy. *Evaluation and Program Planning, 29*(4), 365–376.

Hong, Y., Mitchell, S. G., Peterson, J. A., Latkin, C. A., Tobin, K., & Gann, D. (2005). Ethnographic process evaluation: Piloting an HIV prevention intervention program among injection drug users. *International Journal of Qualitative Methods, 4*(1), 1–12.

Hood, S. (1998). *Responsive evaluation Amistad style: Perspectives of one African American evaluator.* In R. Davis (Ed.), *Proceedings of the Stake Symposium on Educational Evaluation.* Urbana: University of Illinois.

Hood, S. (2009). Evaluation for and by Navajos: A narrative case of the irrelevance of globalization. In K. E. Ryan & J. B. Cousins (Eds.), *The SAGE International Handbook of Educational Evaluation* (pp. 447–463). Thousand Oaks, CA: Sage.

Hood, S. & Hopson, R. K. (2008). Evaluation roots reconsidered: Asa Hilliard, a fallen hero in the "nobody knows my name" project, and African educational excellence. *Review of Educational Research, 78*(3), 410–426.

Hood, S., Hopson, R.K., & Kirkhart, K. (2015). Culturally responsive evaluation. In K.E. Newcomer, H.P. Hatry & J.S. Wholey (Eds.), *Handbook of Practical Program Evaluation* (4th Edition) (pp. 281–317). Hoboken, NJ: John Wiley & Sons.

Hood, S., Hopson, R. K., & Kirkhart, K. E. (2016). Culturally responsive evaluation: Theory, practice, and future implications. In K. A. Newcomer, H. P. Hatry, & J. S. Wholey (Eds.), *Handbook of practical program evaluation* (4th ed., pp. 281–317). Hoboken, NJ: Jossey-Bass.

Hopson, R. K. (2000a). Editors notes. In R. K. Hopson (Ed.), *New Directions for Evaluation, 86*, 1–3.

Hopson, R. K. (2000b). How and why language matters in evaluation. R. K. Hopson (Ed.), *New Directions for Evaluation, 86*.

Hopson, R. K. (2003). *Overview of multicultural and culturally competent program evaluation: Issues, challenges and opportunities.* Social Policy Research Associates, Woodland Hills: The California Endowment.

Hopson, R. K. (2009). Reclaiming knowledge at the margins culturally responsive evaluation in the current evaluation moment. In K. Ryan, & B. Cousins (Eds.), *The SAGE international handbook of educational evaluation.* Thousand Oaks, CA: Sage.

Hopson, R. K., & Cram, F. (2018). Tackling wicked problems in complex evaluation ecologies. In R. K. Hopson, & F. Cram (Eds.), *Tackling wicked problems in complex ecologies: The role of evaluation* (pp. 3–24). Redwood City, CA: Stanford University Press.

Hopson, R. K., Kirkhart, K. E., & Bledsoe, K. L. (2012). Decolonizing evaluation in a developing world. Implications and cautions for equity-focused evaluations. In M. Segone & M. Bamberger (Eds.), *Evaluation for equitable development results* (pp. 115–141). New York, NY: UNICEF.

House, E. R. (1993). *Professional evaluation: Social impact and political consequences.* Thousand Oaks, CA: Sage.

House, E. R., & Howe, K. R. (2000). Deliberative democratic evaluation. *New Directions for Evaluation, 85*, 3–12.

Howe, D. (1994). Modernity, postmodernity and social work. *British Journal of Social Work, 24*, 513–532.

International Labour Organisation (2013). Understanding the Indigenous and Tribal Peoples Convention, 1989 (No. 169). Handbook for ILO Tripartite Constituents. Geneva: International Labour Organisation.

Jainullabudeen, T. A., Lively, A., Singleton, M., Shakeshaft, A., Tsey, K., McCalman, J., . . . & Jacups, S. (2015). The impact of a community-based risky drinking intervention (Beat da Binge) on Indigenous young people. *BMC Public Health, 15*, 1319.

Janke, T. (1998). *Our culture, our future. Report on Australian indigenous cultural and intellectual property rights.* Sydney, Australia: Michael Frankel & Co.

Jay, M., Eatmon, D., & Frierson, H. T. (2005). Cultural reflections stemming from the evaluation of an undergraduate research program. In S. Hood, R. K. Hopson, & H. T. Frierson (Eds.), *The role of culture and cultural context: A mandate for inclusion, the discovery of truth, and understanding in evaluative theory and practice* (pp. 201–216). Greenwich, CT: Information Age.

Jolly, E. (2019). Keynote. Presented at the Center for Culturally Responsive Evaluation and Assessment Conference, March 27, 2019, Chicago, IL.

Jones, L. (2008). The distinctive characteristics and needs of domestic violence victims in a Native American community. *Journal of Family Violence, 23*, 113–118.

Jordan, S., Stocek, C., & Mark, R. (2013). Doing participatory evaluation in indigenous contexts—Methodological issues and questions. *Action Learning, Action Research Journal, 19*(1), 12–35.

Jordan, S., Stocek, C., Mark, R., & Matches, S. (2009). Doing participatory evaluation: From "jagged world views" to indigenous methodology. *Australian Journal of Indigenous Education, 38*(Supplement), 74–82.

Kawakami, A., Aton, K., Cram, F., Lai, M., & Porima, L. (2007). Improving the practice of evaluation through indigenous values and methods: Decolonizing evaluation practice—returning the gaze from Hawai'i and Aotearoa. In P. Brandon, & P. Smith (Eds.), *Fundamental issues in evaluation* (pp. 219–242). New York, NY: Guilford Press.

Kawakami, A., Aton, K., Rawlins-Crivelo, L., & Napeahi, L. (2006). *Empowering a Native Hawaiian community: A community-based study*. Manoa: University of Hawaii & INPEACE.

Kelly, J. G. (2006). *Becoming ecological: An expedition into community psychology*. New York, NY: Oxford University Press.

Kemmis, S., Edwards Groves, C., Wilkinson, J. & Hardy, I. (2012). Ecologies of practices: Learning practices. In P. Hager, A. Lee, & A. Reich (Eds.), *Practice, learning and change*. London, England: Springer.

Kennedy, V., Cram, F., Paipa, K., Pipi, K., Baker, M., Porima, L., . . . & Tuagalu, C. (2015). Beginning a conversation about spirituality in Māori and Pasifika evaluation. In S. Hood, R. K. Hopson, & H. Frierson (Eds.), *Continuing the journey to reposition culture and cultural context in evaluation theory and practice* (pp. 151–178). Charlotte, NC: Information Age.

Kincheloe, J. & McLaren , 1998, Rethinking critical theory and qualitative research. In N.Denzin and Y. Lincoln (Eds.), *The landscape of qualitative research: Theories and issues*. Thousand Oaks, CA: Sage.

King, J. A., Nielson, J. E., & Colby, J. (2004). Lessons for culturally competent evaluation from the study of a multicultural initiative. *New Directions for Evaluation, 102*, 67–79.

Kirkhart, K. E. (1995). Seeking multicultural validity: A postcard from the road. *Evaluation Practice, 16*(1), 1–12.

Kirkhart, K. E. (2005). Through a cultural lens: Reflections on validity and theory in evaluation. In S. Hood, R. K. Hopson, & H. Frierson (Eds.), *The role of culture and cultural context: A mandate for inclusion, the discovery of truth, and understanding in evaluative theory and practice* (pp. 21–39). Charlotte, NC: Information Age.

Kirkhart, K. E. (2011). Culture and influence in multisite evaluation. *New Directions for Evaluation, (129)*, 73–85.

Kirkhart, K. E. (2015). Unpacking the evaluator's toolbox: Observations on evaluation, privilege, equity and justice. *Evaluation Matters-He Tō Te Aromatawai, 1*, 7–24.

Kokko, S., & Lagerkvist, C. J. (2017). Using Zaltman metaphor elicitation technique to map beneficiaries' experiences and values: A case example from the sanitation sector. *American Journal of Evaluation, 38*(2), 205–225.

Koller, S. H., Raffaelli, M., & Carlo, G. (2012). Conducting research about sensitive subjects: The case of homeless youth. *Universitas Psychologica, 11*(1), 55–65.

Kothari, U. (2001). Power, knowledge and social control in participatory development. In B. Cook & U. Kothari (Eds.), *Participation: The new tyranny?* (pp. 139–152). London, England: Zed Books.

Kouévi, A. T., Van Mierlo, B., Leeuwis, C., & Vodouhê, S. D. (2013). The design of a contextualized responsive evaluation framework for fishery management in Benin. *Evaluation and Program Planning, 36*(1), 15–28.

Kroeber, A.L. & Kluckhohn, C. (1952). Culture, a critical review of concepts and definitions. Cambridge, MA: The Museum.

Kukutai, T., & Taylor, J. (2016). Data sovereignty for indigenous peoples: Current practices and future needs. In T. Kukutai & J. Taylor (Eds.), *Indigenous data sovereignty: Toward an agenda*. Centre for Aboriginal Economic Policy Research, College of Arts and Social Sciences, The Australian National University, Canberra. Research Monograph No. 38 (pp. 1–22). Canberra: ANU Press.

Kumok, Z. (2017, December 4). How much is your relationship costing you?: The financial realities of a long distance relationship. Retrieved from https://www.moneyunder30.com/the-financial-realities-of-a-long-distance-romance

Kushner, S. (2000). *Personalizing evaluation*. London, England: Sage.

Labonte, R. (2004). Social inclusion/exclusion: dancing the dialect. *Health Promotion International*, *19*(1), 115–121.

Ladson-Billings, G. (1995). Toward a theory of culturally relevant pedagogy. *American Educational Research Journal*, *32*(3), 465–491.

Ladson-Billings, G. (2000). Racialized discourses and ethnic epistemologies. In N. Denzin & Y. Lincoln (Eds.), *Handbook of qualitative research* (2nd ed., pp. 257–277). Thousand Oaks, CA: Sage.

LaFrance, J. (2004, Summer). Culturally competent evaluation in Indian Country. *New Directions for Evaluation*, *102*, 39–50.

LaFrance, J., & Nichols, R. (2009). *Indigenous evaluation framework: Telling our story in our place and time*. Written for the American Higher Education Consortium. Alexandria, VA: American Indian Higher Education Consortium.

LaFrance, J., & Nichols, R. (2010). Reframing evaluation: Defining an indigenous evaluation framework. *The Canadian Journal of Program Evaluation*, *23*(2), 13–31.

LaFrance, J., Nichols, R., & Kirkhart, K. E. (2012). Culture writes the script: On the centrality of context in indigenous evaluation. In D. J. Rog, J. L. Fitzpatrick, & R. F. Conner (Eds.), Context: *A framework for its influence on evaluation practice. New Directions for Evaluation*, *135*, 59–74.

Lakoff, R. T. (2000). *The language war*. Berkeley: University of California Press.

Laperrière, H. N. (2007). Taking evaluation contexts seriously: A cross-cultural evaluation in extreme unpredictability. *Journal of MultiDisciplinary Evaluation*, *3*(4), 41–57.

LaPoint, V., & Jackson, H. L. (2004). Evaluating the co-construction of the family, school, and community partnership program in a low-income urban high school. *New Directions for Evaluation*, *101*, 25–36.

Lather, P. (1988). Issues of validity in openly ideological research: Between a rock and a soft place. *Interchange*, *17*(4), 63–84.

Lather, P. (1990). Postmodernism and the human sciences. *The Humanistic Psychologist*, *18*(1), 64–84.

Lather, P. (1991). *Getting smart: Feminist research and pedagogy with/in the postmodern*. New York, NY: Routledge.

Lather, P. (March 2015). *Against proper objects: Towards diversely qualitative*. Lecture presented at the University of Regina. Retrieved from https://www.youtube.com/watch?v=GePNU9hXwJ8.

Lawrence, A., Haylor, G., Barahona, C., & Meusch, E. (2000). Adapting participatory methods to meet different stakeholder needs: Farmers' experiments in Bolivia and Laos. In M. Estella, J. Blauert, D. Campilian, J. Gaventa, J. Gonsalves, I. Guijt, D. Johnson, & R. Riacafort (Eds.), *Learning from change: Issues and experiences in participatory monitoring and evaluation* (pp. 50–67). Ottawa, ON, Canada: International Development Research Centre.

Lawyers, Guns & Money. (2019, March 7). *Marking the unmarked category.* Retrieved from http://www. lawyersgunsmoneyblog.com/2019/03/marking-unmarked-category

Leal, P. A. (2010). Participation: The ascendancy of a buzzword in the neo-liberal era. In A. Cornwall & D. Eade (Eds.), *Deconstructing development discourse: Buzzwords and fuzzwords* (pp. 89–100). Warwickshire, England: Practical Action.

Lee, K. (2007). *The importance of culture in evaluation: A practical guide for evaluators.* Denver: The Colorado Trust.

Lee, R. M., & Renzetti, C. M. (1993). The problems of researching sensitive topics: An overview and introduction. In C. M. Renzetti & R. M. Lee (Eds.), *Researching sensitive topics.* Newbury Park, CA: Sage.

Lefebvre, H. (1991). *The production of space.* Maiden, MA: Blackwell.

Letichevsky, C. A., & Penna Firme, T. (2012). Evaluating with at-risk communities: Learning from a social program in a Brazilian slum. *New Directions for Evaluation, 2012*(134), 61–76.

Letiecq, B. L., & Bailey, S. J. (2004). Evaluating from the outside: Conducting cross-cultural evaluation research on an American Indian reservation. *Evaluation Review, 28*(4), 342–357.

Li, T. M. (2007). *The will to improve: Governmentality, development, and the practice of politics.* Durham, NC: Duke University Press.

Lincoln, Y. S., & Guba, E. G. (2005). Paradigmatic controversies, contradictions, and emerging confluences. In *The SAGE handbook of qualitative research* (pp. 191–216). Thousand Oaks, CA: Sage.

Long, N. (1992). Introduction. In N. Long & A. Long (Eds.), *Battlefields of knowledge: The interlocking of theory and practice in social research and development* (pp.3–43). London, England: Routledge.

Lum, D. (2003). *Culturally competent practice: A framework for understanding diverse groups and justice issues.* Pacific Grover, CA: Thomas Learning.

Luo, L. P., & Liu, L. (2014). Reflections on conducting evaluations for rural development interventions in China. *Evaluation and Program Planning, 47*, 1–8.

Lustig, R., Ben Baruch-Koskas, S., Makhani-Belkin, T., & Hirsch, T. (2015). Evaluation in the Branco Weiss Institute: From social vision to educational practice. *New Directions for Evaluation, 146*, 95–105.

Lyotard, J. F. (1979). *The postmodern condition: A report on knowledge.* Minneapolis: The University of Minnesota Press.

MacDonald, B. (1976). Evaluation and the control of education. In D. Tawney (Ed.), *Curriculum evaluation today: Trends and implications* (pp. 125–136). London, England: Macmillan.

MacDonald, B., & Parlett, M. (1973). Re-thinking evaluation: Notes from the Cambridge authority, teacher education and educational studies. *Cambridge Journal of Education, 3*(2), 74–83.

Mackey, H. J. (2012). Transformational partnerships: translating research into practice through culturally competent evaluation practices in American Indian communities. *International Journal of Qualitative Studies in Education, 25*(7), 951–968.

Madison, A. M. (1992a). Editor's notes. Minority issues in program evaluation. *New Directions in Program Evaluation, 53*, 1–4.

Madison, A. M. (1992b). Primary inclusion of culturally diverse minority program participants in the evaluation process. Minority issues in program evaluation. *New Directions in Program Evaluation, 53*, 35–43.

Madison, A. M. (2000). Language in defining social problems and in evaluating social programs. In R. K. Hopson (Ed.), How and why language matters in valuation. *New Directions for Evaluation, 86*, 17–28.

Maemura, Y. (2016). Impartiality and hierarchical evaluations in the Japanese development aid community. *American Journal of Evaluation, 37*(3), 408–424.

Makgamata, M. M. (2009). Challenges in implementing a participatory evaluation approach: A case study of the Limpopo Literacy Teaching Evaluation Project. *Education as Change, 13*(1), 91–103.

Manuel, G., & Posluns, M. (1974). *The fourth world: An Indian reality*. Minneapolis: University of Minnesota Press.

Mark, M. M., Henry, G. T., & Julnes, G. (2000). *Evaluation: An integrated framework for understanding, guiding, and improving policies and programs*. San Francisco, CA: Jossey-Bass.

Martinez, A., Running Wolf, P., BigFoot, D. S., Randall, C., & Villegas, M. (2018). The process of becoming: A roadmap to evaluation in Indian country. In F. Cram, K. A. Tibbetts, & J. LaFrance (Eds.), *Indigenous evaluation. New Directions for Evaluation, 159*, pp. 33–46.

Massey, D. (1999). Spaces of politics. In D. Massey, J. Allen, and P. Sarre (Eds.), in *Human geography today* (pp. 279–294). Cambridge, England: Polity Press.

Massey, D. (2005). *For space*. London, England: Sage.

Mathison, S. (Ed.). (2005). *Encyclopedia of evaluation*. Thousand Oaks, CA: Sage.

Mazur, R., & Woodland, R. H. (2017). Evaluation of a cross-cultural training program for Pakistani educators: Lessons learned and implications for program planning. *Evaluation and Program Planning, 62*, 25–34.

Mead, H. M. (2003). *Tikanga Māori. Living by Māori values*. Wellington, New Zealand: Huia.

Merry, S. E. (2011). Measuring the world: Indicators, human rights, and global governance. *Current Anthropology, 52*(3), S83–S95.

Merryfield, M. M. (1985). The challenge of cross-cultural evaluation: Some views from the field. In M. Q. Patton (Ed.), *Culture and Evaluation. New Directions for Program Evaluation, 25*, 3–17.

Mertens, D. M. (2009). *Transformative research and evaluation*. New York, NY: Guilford Press.

Mertens, D. M. (2014). *Research and evaluation in education and psychology* (4th ed.). Thousand Oaks, CA: Sage.

Mertens, D. M. (2016). Assumptions at the philosophical and programmatic levels in evaluation. *Evaluation and Program Planning, 59*, 102–108.

Mertens, D. M., & Hopson, R. K. (2006). Advancing evaluation of STEM efforts through attention to diversity and culture. In D. Huffman, F. Lawrenz (Eds.), *Critical issues in STEM evaluation. New Directions for Evaluation, 109*, 35–51.

Mertens, D. M., & Wilson, A. T. (2012). *Program evaluation theory and practice: A comprehensive guide.* New York: NY: Guilford Press.

Meyer, M. A. (2001). A cultural understandings of empiricism: A Native Hawaiian critique. *Canadian Journal of Native Education, 25*(2), 188–198.

Mills, C. W. (1959). *The sociological imagination.* Oxford, England: Oxford University Press.

Moewaka Barnes, H. (2000). Collaboration in community action: A successful partnership between indigenous communities and researchers. *Health Promotion International, 15*(1), 17–25.

Montgomery, K.E. (2005). *"A better place to live": National mythologies, Canadian history textbooks, and the reproduction of White supremacy.* Unpublished Ph.D. thesis, University of Ottawa

Morgan, P. (2013). Evaluating capacity development. In S. I. Donaldson, T. Azzam, & R. F. Conner (Eds.), *Emerging practices in international development evaluation* (pp. 75–104). Charlotte, NC: Information Age.

Mosse, D. (2013). The anthropology of international development. *Annual Review of Anthropology, 42*, 227–246.

Mustonen, T., & Feodoroff, P. (2018). Skolt Sámi and Atlantic salmon collaborative management of Näätämö watershed: Finland as a case of indigenous evaluation and knowledge in the Eurasian Arctic. In F. Cram, K. A. Tibbetts, & J. LaFrance (Eds.), *Indigenous Evaluation. New Directions for Evaluation, 159*, 107–119.

Nagai, Y. (2001). Developing assessment and evaluation strategies for vernacular elementary school classrooms: A collaborative study in Papua New Guinea. *Anthropology & Education Quarterly, 32*(1), 80–103.

Nandi, R., Nanda, R. B., & Jugran, T. (2015). Evaluation from inside out. *Evaluation Journal of Australasia, 15*(1), 38–47.

NBC News. (2018, May 25). MSNBC's "Everyday racism in America": Real stories of racial bias. Retrieved from https://www.nbcnews.com/news/us-news/everyday-racism-america-real-stories-racial-bias-n877296

Nelson-Barber, S., LaFrance, J., Trumbull, E., & Aburto, S. (2005). Promoting culturally reliable and valid evaluation practice. In S. Hood, R. K. Hopson, & H. Frierson (Eds.), *The role of culture and cultural context: A mandate for inclusion, the discovery of truth, and understanding in evaluative theory and practice* (pp. 61–85.). Charlotte, NC: Information Age.

Newman, K. (2008). Whose view matters? Using participatory processes to evaluate Reflect in Nigeria. *Community Development Journal, 43*(3), 382–394.

Niba, M. B., & Green, J. M. (2005). Major factors influencing HIV/AIDS project evaluation. *Evaluation Review, 29*(4), 313–330.

Nobles, W. (1991). Extended self: Rethinking the so-called negro self-concept. In R. L. Jones (Ed.), *Black psychology* (3rd ed., pp. 295–304). Berkley, CA: Cobb & Henry.

Noblit, G. W., & Jay, M. (2010). Against the majoritarian story of school reform: The Comer Schools Evaluation as a critical race counternarrative. In M. Freeman (Ed.), *Critical social theory and evaluation practice. New Directions for Evaluation, 127*, 71–82.

Noe, T., Fleming, C., & Manson, S. (2003). Healthy nations: Reducing substance abuse in American Indian and Alaska native communities. *Journal of Psychoactive Drugs, 35*(1), 15–30.

Novins, D. K., King, M., & Stone, L. S. (2004). Developing a plan for measuring outcomes in model systems of care for American Indian and Alaska Native children and youth. *American Indian and Alaska Native Mental Health Research, 11*(2), 88–98.

Ofir, Z., & S, Kumar. (2013). Evaluation in developing countries: What makes it different? In S. I. Donaldson, T. Azzam, & R. F. Conner (Eds.), *Emerging practices in international development evaluation* (pp. 11–24). Charlotte, NC: Information Age.

Patton, M. Q. (1982). *Creative evaluation.* Beverly Hills, CA: Sage.

Patton, M. Q. (1985). Cross-cultural non-generalizations. *New Directions for Program Evaluation, 25,* 93–96.

Patton, M.Q. 2000. Overview: Language matters. In R.K. Hopson, How and why language matters in evaluation. *New Directions for evaluation,* No. 86. San Francisco, CA: Josssey-Bass.

Patton, M. Q. (2015). *Qualitative evaluation and research methods* (4th ed.). Thousand Oaks, CA: Sage.

Pihama, L., Cram, F., & Walker, S. (2002). Creating methodological space: A literature review of Kaupapa Māori research. *Canadian Journal of Native Education, 26*(1), 30–43.

Pipi, K., Cram, F., Hawke, R., Hawke, S., Huriwai, T. M., Keefe, V., . . . & Tuuta, C. (2002). *Māori and Iwi provider success: A research report of interviews with successful Iwi and Māori providers and government agencies.* Wellington, New Zealand: Te Puni Kōkiri.

Potvin, L., Cargo, M., McComber, A. M., Delormier, T., & Macaulay, A. C. (2003). Implementing participatory intervention and research in communities: Lessons from the Kahnawake Schools Diabetes Prevention Project in Canada. *Social Science & Medicine, 56,* 1295–1305.

Pouw, N., Dietz, T., Bélemvire, A., de Groot, D., Millar, D., Obeng, F., & Zaal, F. (2017). Participatory assessment of development interventions. *American Journal of Evaluation, 38*(1), 47–59.

Prilleltensky, I., Nelson, G., & Valdes, L. S. (2000). A value-based approach to smoking prevention with immigrants from Latin America: Program evaluation. *Journal of Ethnic & Cultural Diversity in Social Work, 9*(12), 97–117.

Rabinow (1996)

Reagan, T. (1996). *Non-western educational traditions: Alternative approaches to educational thought and practice.* Mahwah, NJ: Erlbaum.

Reid, P., & Robson, B. (2007). Understanding health inequalities. In B. Robson, & R. Harris (Eds.), *Hauora: Māori standards of health IV* (pp. 3–10). Wellington: Te Rōpū Ranaghau Hauora a Eru Pōmare.

Richmond, L. S., Peterson, D. J., & Betts, S. C. (2008). The evolution of an evaluation: A case study using the Tribal Participatory Research Model. *Health Promotion Practice, 9*(4), 368–377.

Ridde, V., Goossens, S., & Shakir, S. (2012). Short-term consultancy and collaborative evaluation in a post-conflict and humanitarian setting: Lessons from Afghanistan. *Evaluation and Program Planning, 35*(1), 180–188.

Robertson, P., Jorgensen, M., & Garrow, C. (2004). Indigenizing evaluation research: How Lakota methodologies are helping "Raise the Tipi" in the Oglala Sioux Nation. *American Indian Quarterly, 28*(3/4), 499–526.

Rogoff, B. (2003). *The cultural nature of human development.* New York, NY: Oxford University Press.

Rosaldo, R. (1989). *Culture and truth: The remaking of social analysis*. Boston, MA: Beacon Press.

Rosaldo, R. I. (2006). Foreword: Defining culture. In J. R. Baldwin, S. L. Faulkner, M. L. Hecht, and S. L. Lindsley (Eds.), *Redefining culture: Perspectives across the disciplines* (pp. ix–xiii). New York, NY: Routledge.

Rowley, K. G., Daniel, M., Skinner, K., Skinner, M., White, G. A., & O'Dea, K. (2000). Effectiveness of a community-directed "healthy lifestyle" program in a remote Australian Aboriginal community. *Australian and New Zealand of Public Health, 24*(2), 136–144.

Ryan, K. E., Chandler, M., & Samuels, M. (2007). What should school-based evaluation look like? *Studies in Educational Evaluation, 33*, 197–212.

Said, E. (1978). *Orientalism*. New York: Pantheon.

Salmond, A. (1975). *Hui: A study of Māori ceremonial gatherings*. Auckland, New Zealand: Reed Books.

Samuels, M., & Ryan, K. (2011). Grounding evaluations in culture. *American Journal of Evaluation, 32*(2), 183–198.

Santamaría, A. P., Webber, M., Santamaría, L. J., Dam, L. I., & Jayavant, S. (2016). Te Ara Hou—A new pathway for leading Māori success as Māori. *Evaluation Matters—He Take Tō Te Aromatawai, 2*, 99–129.

Scheurich, I., & Young, M. (1997). Coloring epistemologies: Are our research epistemologies racially biased? *Educational Researcher, 26*(4), 4–16.

Scheurich, J. J., & Young, M. D. (1997). Coloring epistemology: Are our research epistemologies racially biased? In J. J. Scheurich (Ed.), *Anti-racist scholarship: An advocacy*. Albany: State University of New York Press.

Schick, R. S. (2002). When the subject is difference: Conditions of voice in policy oriented qualitative research. *Qualitative Inquiry, 8*(5), 632–651.

Schmidt, B., Campbell, S., & McDermott, R. (2016). Community health workers as chronic care coordinators: Evaluation of an Australian indigenous primary health care program. *Australian and New Zealand Journal of Public Health, 40*(Suppl. 1), S107–S114.

Schwandt, T. A. (1996). Farewell to criteriology. *Qualitative Inquiry, 2*(1), 58–72.

Schwandt, T. A. (1997). Reading the "problem of evaluation" in social inquiry. *Qualitative Inquiry, 3*(1), 4–25.

Schwandt, T. A. (2002). Traversing the terrain of role, identity and self. In K. E. Ryan & T. A. Schwandt (Eds.), *Exploring evaluator role and identity* (pp. 193–207). Charlotte, NC: Information Age.

Schwandt, T. A. (2007, November 8). *The role of practical knowledge in learning*. Paper delivered at the 21st Annual Conference of the American Evaluation Association, Learning to evaluate, evaluating to learn. Baltimore, MD.

Schwandt, T. A. (2015). *Evaluation foundations revisited: Cultivating a life of the mind for practice*. Stanford, CA: Stanford University Press.

Seidman, S. (2004). *Contested knowledge: Social theory today* (3rd ed.). Maiden, MA: Blackwell.

Sen, A. K. (1999). *Development as freedom* (1st ed.). New York, NY: Knopf Press.

Senese, G. (2005). The PENAL project: Program evaluation and Native American liability. In S. Hood, R. K. Hopson, & H. T. Frierson (Eds.), *The role of culture and cultural context: A mandate for inclusion, the discovery of truth, and understanding in evaluative theory and practice* (pp. 129–147). Charlotte, NC: Information Age Publishing.

SenGupta, S., Hopson, R. K., & Thompson-Robinson, M. (2004). Cultural competence in evaluation: An overview. *New Directions for Evaluation, 102*, 5–19.

Sherwood, J. (2013). An Aboriginal health worker's research story. In D. Mertens, F. Cram, & B. Chilisa (Eds.), *Indigenous pathways into social research: Voices of a new generation* (pp. 203–218). Walnut Creek, CA: Left Coast Press.

Sidersky, P., & Guijt, I. (2000). Experimenting with participatory monitoring in north-east Brazil: The case of AS-PTA's Projecto Paraiba. In M. Estella, J. Blauert, D. Campilian, J. Gaventa, J. Gonsalves, I. Guijt, D. Johnson, & R. Riacafort (Eds.), *Learning from change: Issues and experiences in participatory monitoring and evaluation* (pp. 68–82). Ottawa, ON, Canada: International Development Research Centre.

Simons, H. (2012). *Case study research in practice*. London, England: Sage.

Slater, D. (1999). Situating geographical representations: Inside/outside and the power of imperial interventions. In D. Massey, J. Allen, & P. Sarre (Eds.), *Human geography today* (pp. 62–84). Cambridge, England: Polity Press.

Slater, D., & Bell, M. (2002). Aid and the geopolitics of the post-colonial: Critical reflections on New Labour's overseas development strategy. *Development and Change, 33*(2), 335–360.

Small, S. A., Tiwari, G., & Huser, M. (2006). The cultural education of academic evaluators: Lessons from a university-Hmong community partnership. *American Journal of Community Psychology, 37*, 357–364.

Smeyers, P, & Burbles, N. C. (2006). The changing practices and social relations of education. *Educational Theory, 56*(4), 363–369.

Smith, D. E. (1987). *The everyday world as problematic: A sociology for people*. Toronto, ON, Canada: University of Toronto Press.

Smith, G. (1990). *Research issues related to Maori education*. Paper presented at the NZARE Special Interests Conference, Education Department, University of Auckland. Auckland, New Zealand.

Smith, L. T. (1999). *Decolonizing methodologies: Research and indigenous peoples*. London, England: Zed Books Ltd.

Smith, L. T. (2006). Fourteen lessons of resistance to exclusion: Learning from the Maori experiences in New Zealand over the last two decades of neo-liberal reform. In M. Mulholland, & Contributors (Eds.), *State of the Māori nation. Twenty-first-century issues in Aotearoa* (pp. 247–260). Auckland, New Zealand: Reed.

Smith, L. T. (2012). *Decolonizing methodologies: Research and indigenous peoples* (2nd ed.). London, England: Zed Books.

Smith, L. T. (2018). Indigenous insights on valuing complexity, sustaining relationships, being accountable. In R. Hopson, & F. Cram (Eds.). Redwood City, CA: Stanford University Press.

Smith, L. T., Tuck, E., & Yang, K. W. (2019). Introduction. In L. T. Smith, E. Tuck, & K. W. Yang (Eds.), *Indigenous and decolonizing studies in education: Mapping the long view* (pp. 1–23). New York, NY: Routledge.

Smith, N. J. (1991). The context of investigations in cross-cultural evaluations. *Studies in Educational Evaluation, 17*, 3–21.

Smith, N. J. (2008). Fundamental issues in evaluation. In N. L. Smith & P. R. Brandon (Eds.), *Fundamental issues in evaluation* (pp. 1–23). New York, NY: Guilford Press.

Smith, N. L. (1993). Improving evaluation theory through the empirical study of evaluation practice. *Evaluation Practice, 14*(3), 237–242.

Smith, S. E. (1997). Deepening participatory action research. In S. E. Smith, D. G. Williams, & N. A. Johnson (Eds.), *Nurtured by knowledge: Learning to do participatory action research* (pp. 173–264). New York, NY: Apex Press.

Spencer, S. (2006). *Race and ethnicity. Culture, identity and representation.* New York, NY: Routledge.

Stake, R. E. (1967). The countenance of educational evaluation. *Teachers College Record, 68*(7), 523–540.

Stake, R. E. (1975). To evaluate an arts program. In R. E. Stake (Ed.), *Evaluating the arts in education: A responsive approach* (pp. 13–31). Columbus, OH: Merrill.

Stake, R. E. (1998). When policy is merely promotion, by what ethic lives an evaluator? *Studies in Educational Evaluation, 24*(2), 203–212.

Stake, R. E. (2004). *Standards-based & responsive evaluation.* Thousand Oaks, CA: Sage.

Stanfield, J. H., Jr. (1999). Slipping through the front door: Relevant social scientific evaluation in the people of color century. *American Journal of Evaluation, 20*(3), 415–431.

Sue, D. W., & Sue, D. (1999). *Counselling the culturally different: Theory and practice* (3rd ed.). New York, NY: Wiley.

Sutton, S., Baxter, N., Grey, K., & Putt, J. (2016). Working both-ways: Using participatory and standardised methodologies with Indigenous Australians in a study of remote community safety and wellbeing. *Evaluation Journal of Australasia, 16*(4), 30–40.

Symonette, H. (2004). Walking pathways toward becoming a culturally competent evaluator: Boundaries, borderlands, and border crossings. *New Directions for Evaluation, 102*, 95–109.

Tajfel, H. (1982). Social psychology of intergroup relations. *Annual Review of Psychology, 33*, 1–39.

Tapella, E., & Rodríguez-Bilella, P. (2014). Shared learning and participatory evaluation: The sistematización approach to assess development interventions. *Evaluation, 20*(1), 115–133.

Taskforce on Whānau-Centred Initiatives. (2010). *Whānau Ora: Report of the Taskforce on Whānau-Centred Initiatives*, to Hon. Tariana Turia, Minister for the Community and Voluntary Sector. Wellington, New Zealand: Taskforce on Whānau-Centred Initiatives.

Taylor, J.M., Gilligan, C., & Sullivan, A.M. (1995). *Between voice and silence, women and girls, race and relationship.* Cambridge, Mass: Harvard University Press.

Temple, B. (1997) Watch your tongue: Issues in translation and cross-cultural research. *Sociology, 31*(3), 607–618.

Thomas, J. (1993). *Doing ethnography.* Thousand Oaks, CA: Sage.

Thomas, V. G. (2004). Building a contextually responsive evaluation framework: Lessons from working with urban school interventions. *New Directions for Evaluation, 101*, 3–23.

Thrift, N. (2003). Space: The fundamental stuff of human geography. In S. Holloway, S. Rice, & G. Valentine (Eds.), *Key concepts in geography* (pp. 95–107). London, England: Sage.

Thurman, P. J., Allen, J., & Deters, P. B. (2004). The Circles of Care evaluation: Doing participatory evaluation with American Indian and Alaska Native communities. *American Indian and Alaskan Native Mental Health Research, 11*(2), 139–154.

Torres, D. V. H. (2000). Monitoring local development with communities: The SISDEL approach in Ecuador. In M. Estella, J. Blauert, D. Campilian, J. Gaventa, J. Gconsalves, I. Guijt, I. & R. Riacafort (Eds.), *Learning from change: Issues and experiences in participatory monitoring and evaluation* (pp. 109–123). Ottawa, ON, Canada: International Development Research Centre.

Triandis, H. C. (2000). Cultural syndromes and subjective well-being. In E. Deiner & S. M. Eunkook (Eds.), *Culture and subjective well-being* (Kindle Edition ed., pp. 13–36). Cambridge: MIT Press.

Tsey, K., & Every, A. (2000). Evaluating Aboriginal empowerment programs: The case of family well-being. *Australian and New Zealand Journal of Public Health, 24*(5), 509–514.

Tuck, E., & Yang, K. W. (2012). Decolonization is not a metaphor. *Decolonization: Indigeneity, Education & Society, 1*(1), 1–40.

Tuck, E., & Yang, K. W. (2019). Series editors' introduction. In L. T. Smith, E. Tuck, & K. W. Yang (Eds.), *Indigenous and decolonizing studies in education: Mapping the long view* (pp. x–xxi). New York, NY: Routledge.

Turnbull, D. (2000). *Masons, tricksers and cartographers: Comparative studies in the sociology of scientific and indigenous knowledge.* Amsterdam, The Netherlands: Harwood Academic.

Uhl, G., Robinson, B., Westover, B., Bockting, W., & Cherry-Porter, T. (2004). Involving the community in HIV prevention program evaluation. *Health Promotion Practice, 5*(3), 289–296.

United Nations. (2007). *United Nations Declaration on the Rights of Indigenous Peoples.* Geneva, Switzerland: Author.

United Nations. (2013). Growing gulf between rich and poor "Reproach to the Promise of the United Nations Charter," Secretary-General tells General Assembly during thematic debate. Meetings Coverage and Press Releases. Retrieved from https://www.un.org/press/en/2013/ga11391.doc.htm

Van Vlaenderen, H. (2001). Evaluating development programs building joint activity. *Evaluation and Program Planning, 24*, 343–352.

Verhest, T. G. (1987). *No life without roots: Culture and development* (B. Cumming, Trans.). London, England: Zed Books.

Vo, A. T. (2013). Visualizing context through theory deconstruction: A content analysis of three bodies of evaluation theory literature. *Evaluation and Program Planning, 38*, 44–52.

W. K. Kellogg Foundation. (2017). *The step-by-step guide to evaluation: How to become savvy evaluation consumers.* Battle Creek, MI: Author.

Watts, V. M., Christopher, S., Streitz, J. L., & McCormick, A. K. (2005). Evaluation of a lay health adviser training for a community-based participatory research project in a Native American community. *American Indian Culture and Research Journal, 29*(3), 59–79.

Weedon, C. (1987). *Feminist practice and poststructuralist theory* (2nd ed.). Cambridge, England: Blackwell.

Weiss, C. H. (1993). *Evaluation* (2nd ed.). Upper Saddle River, NJ: Prentice-Hall.

Welle, K. (2014). Monitoring performance or performing monitoring? Exploring the power and political dynamics underlying monitoring the MDG for rural water in Ethiopia. *Canadian Journal of Development Studies, 35*(1), 155–169.

Whatmore, S. (1998). Hybrid geographies: Rethinking the "human" in human geography. In D. Massey, J. Allen, & P. Sarre (Eds.), *Human Geography Today* (pp. 22–40). Cambridge, England: Polity Press.

Willging, C. E., Helitzer, D., & Thompson, J. (2006). "Sharing wisdom": Lessons learned during the development of a diabetes prevention program for urban American Indian women. *Evaluation and Program Planning, 29,* 130–140.

Williams, L., & Cram, F. (2012). *What works for Māori. Synthesis of selected literature.* Wellington, New Zealand: Department of Corrections.

Williams, R. (1981). *Culture & society.* London, England: Fontana Paperbacks.

Williams, R. (1983). *Keywords: A vocabulary of culture and society.* London, England: Fontana Paperbacks.

Wilson, S. (2008). *Research is ceremony. Indigenous research methods.* Black Point, NS, Canada: Fernwood.

Winant, H. (1997). Behind blue eyes: Whiteness and contemporary U. S. racial politics. In M. Fine, L. Weis, L. C. Powell, & L. M. Wong (Eds.), *Off White: Readings on race, power, and society* (pp. 40–53). New York, NY: Routledge.

Woodley, C., Fagan, S., & Marshall, S. (2014). Wadawurrung Dya Baap Ngobeeyt: Teaching spatial mapping technologies. *Campus-Wide Information Systems, 31*(4), 276–287.

Writer, J. H. (2008). Unmasking, exposing, and confronting: Critical Race Theory, Tribal Critical Race Theory and multicultural education. *International Journal of Multicultural Education, 10*(2), 1–15.

Zamir, J., & Abu Jaber, S. (2015). Promoting social justice through a new teacher training program for the Bedouin population in the Negev: An evaluation case study. *New Directions for Evaluation, 146,* 71–82.

Zulli, R. A., & Frierson, H. T. (2004). A focus on cultural variables in evaluating an upward bound program. *New Directions for Evaluation, 102,* 81–93.

APPENDICES

Study	Sample/Context	Approach Stated (note if indigenous led)	Implications for Practice (e.g., inclusion methods)	Cultural Consideration(s), Implications, Critiques, Connections to Framework	Other Relevant/ Interesting Observations/ Conclusions
Baker, Pipi, & Cassidy (2015)	New Zealand: Whānau Ora (Māori family well-being) action research evaluation	Indigenous evaluators, working collaboratively within a government funded indigenous initiative to support Māori whānau (families) achieve their aspirations	Collaborative development of four values-based methods: whānau interviews, logic modeling and rubric development, wānanga (learning gatherings), and group reflective hui (gatherings)	Context of initiative and provider organization described Whānau interviews depicted in pictorial form supported interviewees' comfort with sharing	Importance of relationships between provider organizations and whānau stressed by findings as key to successful practice and whānau transformation Evaluator support for key workers to reflect on and grow their practice and for whānau to reflect on service delivery model

(Continued)

[1] There are actually 32 papers included, but the two papers by Jordan and colleagues are essentially the same.

Appendix 1 ■ (Continued)					
Study	Sample/Context	Approach Stated (note if indigenous led)	Implications for Practice (e.g., inclusion methods)	Cultural Consideration(s), Implications, Critiques, Connections to Framework	Other Relevant/ Interesting Observations/ Conclusions
Berends & Roberts (2003)	Australia: Evaluation standards and their application in Victoria—drug and alcohol programs	Process-oriented evaluation, by nonindigenous evaluators Mixed methods, including the use of face-to-face qualitative methods in site visits	Board members, elders and clients involved Opportunities to review draft reports and recommendations Review of evaluation against AEA utilization guidance Importance of evaluators establishing trustworthiness	A steering group, the Koori alcohol and drug program coordinator, and an extensive consultation phase supported cultural responsiveness Informal support group of Koori community leaders gave evaluators advice about the evaluation and were the guardians of the process	Most programs delivered by community-controlled organizations as part of a range of social and health programs. Koori staff facilitated understandings of cultural influences present in the programs. Potential was opened up for multiple interpretations of findings that responded to stakeholder utilization. Timelines were secondary to due evaluation process.
Bishop, Berryman, Wearmouth, Peter, & Clapham (2012)	New Zealand: Changes in indigenous students' educational performance attributable to a professional development program: Te Kotahitanga	Indigenous evaluators Repeated measures over two different groups of schools, at different times Mixed methods— observation, achievement data	Use of Māori/ indigenous practices and methods as well as wrapping of non-Māori methods within Māori processes	Indigenous-centric analysis of indigenous education disparities Commitment by evaluators to intervention strategies (as also involved in design of initiative)	Intervention is described as a "culturally responsive, relationship-based pedagogy" and a "comprehensive school reform model."

Blignault, Haswell, & Pulver (2016)	Australia: Multisite evaluation of a national social and emotional well-being program for indigenous youth in remote and regional Aboriginal communities	Two-person evaluation teams for site visits consisting of an Aboriginal evaluator and a non-indigenous evaluator	Community informants included participants, their parents, and community leaders and elders. Focus groups held in the form of "yarning circles." Use of Aboriginal well-being measurement tool	Time constraints restricted cultural responsiveness. Reliance on Red Cross managers to ease introduction to sites An outcome was a new sense of Aboriginal identity for young people, increased confidence. Importance of connection to land, family, and community	The program was developed and owned by the community. Program activities were diverse and there was greater participation of community. Evaluators concluded that good working partnerships are essential for achieving positive outcomes.
Blignault & Williams (2017)	Australia: Development of resources to support local indigenous community-based healing programs, within their own worldview and definition of health	Not stated whether indigenous evaluators Indigenous evaluation guide based on Stufflebeam literature review, key informant consultative interviews, national workshop	Good practice guidelines sourced from stakeholders about content and delivery of programs Yarning used as an evaluation method as well as taking photos Importance of taking time	Uses the term *culturally sensitive methodologies and tools* (p. 4) Healing seen as a journey, not an event, that reflects history, culture, and context Challenge of defining healing for outcome purposes	Life precolonization described as "rich in spirituality, lore, relationships and roles, music, art and storytelling" (p. 4) Evaluators distinguish between the "Stolen Generation" and the general indigenous population

(Continued)

Appendix 1 ■ (Continued)					
Study	Sample/Context	Approach Stated (note if indigenous led)	Implications for Practice (e.g., inclusion methods)	Cultural Consideration(s), Implications, Critiques, Connections to Framework	Other Relevant/ Interesting Observations/ Conclusions
Bond, Foley, & Askew (2016)	Australia: Evaluation of the Inala Aboriginal and Torres Strait Islander Community Jury for Health Research	Lead author is indigenous. Methodology informed by phenomenological approach and use of narrative inquiry with those involved in the process	Assessment of national guidelines for ethical health research promoting more inclusive and respectful research	Recognition of initiative as doing important identity work Eight of nine participating researchers interviewed were non-indigenous.	Jury members recognized importance of representing community's strengths. Power of yarning— respectful talk—emerged as key theme of initiative. Also reflected in methodology of evaluation
Boulton & Kingi (2011)	New Zealand: Healthy Eating, Healthy Action Strategy—Māori conceptual framework	Indigenous paper Te Tuhono Oranga Evaluation Framework (seven principles for cultural alignment) Evaluation of whether Māori-specific and general activities improved Māori health outcomes	Practical analytical tool, ensuring rigorous data analysis Linked to wider evaluation of initiative through adaptation of questions and added questions Indigenous analytical approach	Overarching conceptual framework to guide program evaluation included Māori conceptual framework and responsiveness to guiding documents and charters, including Treaty of Waitangi Principle-based evaluation	Strategy developed to reflect New Zealand's "historical, social and environmental context" (p. 6), including recognition of the Treaty of Waitangi Strategy described as "multifaceted and complex" (p. 6)

Carlson, Moewaka Barnes, & McCreanor (2017)	New Zealand: Kaupapa Māori evaluation (KME) of tribally-based Māori health provider	Indigenous evaluators (one from tribe), collaborative evaluation. Evaluation about co-ownership, mutually beneficial outcomes, shared power; that is, prioritizing participant voices to determine effectiveness	Evaluation aims negotiated with provider organization. Tribal advisory group met four times over course of evaluation. All stakeholders invited to help test KME framework.	Importance of face-to-face engagement and also evaluator being known in community, so she could engage with mauri (energy) and wairua (spirit). Evaluator had kin connections with many participants and her relations helped out with hui (meetings). Evaluator's responsibility to prioritize stakeholders' voices, as ones most directly affected by outcomes	Identified issue of no receiving feedback via e-mail from advisory group, and time constraints restricting face-to-face opportunities for receiving feedback. Discussion with advisory board highlighted members' need to increase their understanding of health literacy, as this was a new concept for them.
Chesterton (2003)	Australia: Care options for indigenous children and young people seen as at risk of CAN	Unclear if evaluator is indigenous. Evaluation processes established following discussions with stakeholders. Aboriginal Reference Group	Acknowledgment of structural and cultural factors' impact on care decisions. Highlighted importance of asking questions about who decides what gets evaluated	Committed to being culturally sensitive, including consultation to ensure support and ownership, reference group, flexible responsive methodology, protocols, building trust, sensitive methods. Questions extent to which evaluators advocate for minority indigenous stakeholder voice	Issue of contracted evaluators at sway of commissioners if want future contracts. Evaluators "whitewashing" rather than risking "blacklisting" (p. 57). Ethical tensions for evaluators, in face of values-based interpretations of ethical principles. Evaluation in indigenous contexts is political.

Appendix 1 ■ (Continued)					
Study	**Sample/Context**	**Approach Stated (note if indigenous led)**	**Implications for Practice (e.g., inclusion methods)**	**Cultural Consideration(s), Implications, Critiques, Connections to Framework**	**Other Relevant/ Interesting Observations/ Conclusions**
Chong, Hassin, Young, & Joe (2011)	USA: Evaluation of tribal substance abuse prevention and intervention, two tribes	Not stated if indigenous evaluators Participatory evaluation to counter tribal resistance to evaluators with little experience working with tribes Looking at implementation, effectiveness, and scalability of programs	Cultural competency in evaluation process Tribes need technical support for evaluation process. Big differences between the two tribes, especially stakeholders	Evaluation needs to be culturally responsive while maintaining scientific rigor. Recommendation of tribal participatory evaluation: oversight, facilitation, employment of community members, culturally responsive assessment	Call for funding agencies to invest resources and provide technical assistance for grantees
Curtis, Townsend, & Airini (2012)	New Zealand: Māori and Pasifika tertiary students interviewed to inform institutional development that was then evaluated	Kaupapa Māori and Pasifika Research methodologies 3 phases: needs analysis, intervention, evaluation Critical Incident Technique used	Māori and Pasifika input into research Care taken to ensure process would be culturally safe Acknowledgment of cultural limitations	Rejection of victim blaming, with focus on workforce development, organizational change, and meaningful improvements for indigenous students Interviews started with culturally appropriate engagement protocols.	Designed to address disparities in health science workforce Confirmed importance of "well integrated, culturally appropriate, academic and pastoral support" for Māori and Pasifika students (p. 598)

Fisher & Ball (2002)	United States: Indian Family Wellness (IFW) project, a family-centered prevention intervention for preschool children	Tribal Participatory Research: collaborative researcher—community relationships IFW based on values and traditions of participating tribe and their vision for parenting and well-being of tribal members	Four mechanisms to help ensure culturally responsive practice: tribal oversight, use of a facilitator, training and employment for community members, culturally specific intervention and assessment	Collaboration began with submission of grant proposal and continued for first year after funding received. Development and adoption of tribal research code	All tribal members who completed 9-month research training and wanted employment, were hired on project. Committed to developing tribal models of well-being and assessing whether intervention facilitates these
Forrest et al. (2016)	New Zealand: Group exercise initiative—PATU Aotearoa Hinu Wero (Fat Challenge)	Mixed methods (explanatory sequential design) evaluation of 9-week pilot	Looking for effective intervention to reduce Māori inequities Use of Facebook to promote participant feedback	Initiative developed by Māori, for Māori. Tikanga Māori (cultural) protocols implemented in evaluation, including use of Māori language as well as English.	Indigenous imagery, naming, and concepts used in delivery of program and engagement of participants in the evaluation.
Grey, Putt, Baxter, & Sutton (2016)	Australia: Indigenous Australians' remote safety and well-being following Northern Territory Emergency Response	Participatory (and potentially transformative) mixed-methods approach, with aim to hear from indigenous Australians affected by program	Principles: person-centered approach; preparing for long-term evaluation of change; and building a learning partnership between indigenous people and government	Use of "both-ways" learning model; community capacity building commitment Participatory approach involved community people in all steps of the evaluation, including employing local people as researchers.	Hearing from those affected by a policy contributes to evaluation quality and use Links contextual and cultural relevance to evaluation quality Spending time to build trust was vital.

(Continued)

Appendix 1 ■ (Continued)

Study	Sample/Context	Approach Stated (note if indigenous led)	Implications for Practice (e.g., inclusion methods)	Cultural Consideration(s), Implications, Critiques, Connections to Framework	Other Relevant/ Interesting Observations/ Conclusions
Grover (2010)	United States: AI/AN substance abuse program evaluation	Indigenous evaluator Use of culturally valid processes, methods, and measures	Formation of (fluid) community coalition—open to all—to plan services (needs assessment, planning) Community survey Commitment to community capacity building	Involvement of community must be within context of indigenous cultural values. Evaluator often acts as mediator between program/ community and funder— evaluator disposition important: respectful, honest, tactful Issue of indigenous programs not being seen as "evidence-based" and eligible for funding	Identifies major themes about doing indigenous evaluation: involving and honoring community's goals, respecting self-determination, building trust and respect, being sensitive to traditional mistrust of research and government Communities may not have capacity to deliver a program, so need culturally responsive capacity building models.
Hamerton, Mercer, Riini, McPherson, & Morrison (2012)	New Zealand: Evaluating Māori community initiatives to promote healthy eating and healthy activity	Indigenous and non-indigenous evaluators Process (fidelity check) and short-term outcome evaluation Kaupapa Māori evaluation approach, using case studies	Face-to-face engagement, building relationships of trust, allowing them to report their conceptions, responses, and experiences of program how they wanted to	Evaluator roles included listening respectfully, practicing reciprocity (e.g., koha/gift), and sharing information about successful initiatives. Incorporation of indigenous models of health and well-being in data collection (Te Whare Tapa Whā)	Project REPLACE invited participants to slowly change their behavior to incorporate healthier alternatives. Cultural advisory from district health board were thanked for their support throughout the evaluation.

(Continued)

Jainullabudeen et al. (2015)	Australia: Community-based risky drinking intervention for indigenous young people	Community-driven, participatory intervention, actively engaging young people in design, implementation and evaluation Baseline and post-intervention surveys to target 18- to 24-year-olds	Community sought partnership with researchers for evaluation. Young people from community trained and remunerated for opportunistic surveying.	Input into survey items by local residents, trained as research assistants, who consulted with young people and then collaborated on survey development Findings not disputed by community members.	Three broad themes to program activities that were implemented to coincide with two major and at least 12 minor community events each year Some evaluation capacity building that funded local people and left skills in the community
Jordan, Stocek, Mark, & Matches (2009); Jordan, Stocek, & Mark (2013)	Canada: Evaluation of COOL (Challenging Our Own Limits), after-school care	Indigenous co-author Participatory evaluation with Cree nation of Wemindji in Quebec Participatory evaluation chosen as "closely aligned with Indigenous science" (p. 79)	Changes sought in organizations and groups based on bottom-up consensus. Dialogue with community about community development and social programs Visual evaluation methods	Acknowledgment of colonization and structural inequities as well as technologies of (neo) colonialism, including evaluation Importance of not pathologizing and individualizing social problems in the community that are the legacies of colonization	COOL committee from nation oversaw design and implementation of program—based on values, customs, and traditions = homegrown, autonomous, self-determined Cree program.

Appendix 1 ■ (Continued)					
Study	Sample/Context	Approach Stated (note if indigenous led)	Implications for Practice (e.g., inclusion methods)	Cultural Consideration(s), Implications, Critiques, Connections to Framework	Other Relevant/ Interesting Observations/ Conclusions
Letiecq & Bailey (2004)	United States: American Indian youth-based initiative to improve the quality and quantity of comprehensive, community-based programs for children, youth, and families	Tribal Participatory Research Model: Cross-cultural evaluation, "outside" evaluators Process evaluation, leading to one-group pretest/posttest outcomes evaluation design	Tribal oversight, cultural facilitator, community members hired as on-site staff, culturally specific assessment	"Outsider" evaluators must consider their perspectives and place, analyze power differentials, and rethink evaluation approaches. Respect evaluation resistance and query the "right" way of knowing. Investment in evaluation capacity building	Notes that effects of inequality minimized if intersectionality not at the core of evaluation
Mackey (2012)	United States: Prosocial intervention in 10 schools serving American Indian families	Indigenous evaluator Evaluation aligned with participant-identified tribal values that enables program improvement Student, family, school, and community outcomes Research about cultural responsiveness of the evaluation	Examined participant perceptions of the alignment of evaluation with culturally specific program goals Long-term relationship with evaluator	Bifurcation of values: funder vs. community (accountability vs. legitimacy) Disconnect between evaluated "success" and degree to which participants felt the program was successful Context of school and students not taken into account in evaluation Qualitative evaluation elements often tell the "story" of the program, especially regarding intangible benefits.	Program designed to reflect the culture of community and aligned with tribally determined values and character traits, to protect tribal cultural traditions and enable children to succeed in both tribal and non-tribal worlds (including, but not confined to, academic achievement).

| Moewaka Barnes (2000) | New Zealand: Alcohol-related road traffic accident prevention program for Māori | Indigenous evaluator Collaborative 3-year action project between indigenous communities and researchers Extensive networking, including with elders | Importance of indigenous ownership and empowerment for addressing inequities, community preparation for taking on intervention, and strategies sourced within local cultural context | Longer time frames may be needed for measuring effectiveness of programs. Sharing of program ideas and strategies across communities indicated naturalistic utilization-focused evaluation methodology, with collection of qualitative data from a variety of stakeholders. Use of Māori places (e.g., marae) and meeting protocols important | Decolonization piece pivotal in program at one site Program and evaluation very collaborative and Māori community-centric |
| Novins, King, & Stone (2004) | United States: Overview/summary paper about evaluation of mental health services for American Indian and Alaska Natives children and young people | Not specified whether indigenous evaluators Circles and Care (CoC) planning process, to facilitate "culturally and programmatically relevant approaches to measuring outcomes" (p. 89) | Key questions raised in CoC: What is a positive outcome for children, adolescents, families (and communities)? How should these outcomes be measured? | Desire to focus on strengths, not problems (mainstream) Outcome measurement plans developed with grantees. Outcomes for communities reflected healing process. | Pragmatic approach adopted by grantees because of constraints of time, funder requirements, and mandated outcome measurement plans already in existence in delivery organizations. |

(Continued)

Appendix 1 ■ (Continued)

Study	Sample/Context	Approach Stated (note if indigenous led)	Implications for Practice (e.g., inclusion methods)	Cultural Consideration(s), Implications, Critiques, Connections to Framework	Other Relevant/ Interesting Observations/ Conclusions
Potvin, Cargo, McComber, Delormier, & Macaulay (2003)	Canada: Kahnawake Schools Diabetes Prevention Project, involving an Aboriginal community (Mohawk)	Not stated if indigenous evaluators Describes four principles of community program/public health evaluation that emerged from lessons learned during a participatory project	Principles: (1) Integration of community members as equal partners, (2) Integration of intervention and evaluation, (3) Organizational and program flexibility, (4) Making the project a learning opportunity for all	Replace linear evaluation models with process-oriented ones that capture context and allow for changes in programs during implementation	Public health programs can reduce inequalities if egalitarian, that is, based within genuine/active community engagement as opposed to expert/ outsider-designed programs.
Richmond, Peterson, & Betts (2008)	United States: Promoting healthy relationships project for American Indian Youth evaluation	Tribal Participatory Research Model Initially process and outcomes evaluation; then funder demanded quasi-experimental design focused on outcomes but not feasible Return to rich process evaluation	Collaborative development of culturally relevant data collection methods/tools Equal weight and respect for diverse expertise and knowledge Importance of relationship building and communication with community	Cites LaFrance (2004), that programs need to be evaluated in their own context Program modification process was interactive, involving discussions with project team when they reviewed the evaluation findings.	Conflicts between communities and funder about quasi-experiment evaluation design Concerns expressed over lack of tribal anonymity or confidentiality.

| Robertson, Jorgensen, & Garrow (2004) | United States: Community-based law enforcement program for the Oglala Lakota Nation evaluation | Use of participatory action research and empowerment evaluation models as these seem to mirror a Lakota approach "Tribal control set the stage for local evaluators to use the evaluation as a means of activism for nation building" (p. 508). | Importance of quantitative data, with evaluation evidence a valuable advocacy tool Traditional words sourced for equivalent of tribal evaluation. Challenges also regarding transformative justice system change in face of funding dependency, and measuring progress toward institutional change Evaluation can overburden local support structures. | "Raising the tipi"— incorporates cultural teaching, family responsibility, and tribal duty Completion of funding was not ending of project. Evaluators need to have a "stake" in the community. Putting local researchers "in the driver's seat" for the evaluation for "activism-oriented" evaluation approaches (p. 509). Cites Linda Smith with respect to change in the face of system having limited popular legitimacy: "It necessarily involves the processes of transformation, of decolonization, of healing, and of mobilization as peoples". (2012) Challenge is for evaluation to support this. | Practice of Lakota ways as a means of overcoming colonial oppression, including "processes of knowledge creation" (p. 499) Ends desired by the people include self-determination and sovereignty. Indigenous "nation building" is the process of constructing effective institutions of self-governance that can provide a foundation for sustainable development, community health, and successful political action (p. 500). |

(Continued)

Appendix 1 ■ (Continued)

Study	Sample/Context	Approach Stated (note if indigenous led)	Implications for Practice (e.g., inclusion methods)	Cultural Consideration(s), Implications, Critiques, Connections to Framework	Other Relevant/Interesting Observations/Conclusions
Rowley et al. (2000)	Australia: Evaluation of a community-directed healthy lifestyle program in a remote Aboriginal community	Intervention and control groups "self-selected" and participants followed up for change in outcomes over 24 months Community surveys to assess community change trends	Intervention and evaluation possible because of community buy-in through participatory design of the intervention. Community members employed as diabetes workers and store manager. This improved availability of healthy food and family and team activities.	Researchers provided technical advice, data analysis, feedback on findings, and advocacy to health and funding bodies.	Non-indigenous researchers invited into community to help design program. Aboriginal Health Workers employed when funding gained, with two eventually running program. Shift from program focus on body weight and metabolic control to holistic, community initiative
Santamaria, Webber, Santamaria, Dam, & Jayavant (2016)	New Zealand: Educational leadership development project for principals, to support Māori educational success	Indigenous and non-indigenous evaluators Kaupapa Māori evaluation engaging critical race theory Collaborative	Documenting practices of culturally responsive education leaders Interviews and focus groups, document analysis	Appreciation of role of Māori knowledge, identity, and belief systems in program, and also the schools' engagement with families and tribes Critical analysis of role of culturally responsive pedagogy	Evaluators came with a very informed, culturally responsive lens to critically evaluate the role of culture in a program developed to support Māori students succeed in education as Māori.

Sutton, Baxter, Grey, & Putt (2016)	Australia: Remote community safety and well-being evaluation	Both-ways model—combining indigenous traditions and knowledge with non-indigenous "ways of doing." Participatory research cycle: consent, training local researchers, hearing community voice, giving report back, ownership of report by community	To ensure evaluation meaningful, relevant, and useful to those affected by intervention. Inclusion of core questions in survey so credible for policy making	Acknowledge the privilege of being able to work in indigenous communities. Local people able to make evaluative judgments about importance of changes. Local people trained and mentored in research roles, with support of consultants.	A sign that an evaluation is culturally responsive is that communities are keen to participate. Consultants chosen based on relationship with communities, experience using participatory qualitative methods, understanding of quantitative methods, and experience with Aboriginal team members. Fostered collaboration among consultants
Thurman, Allen, & Deters (2004)	United States: Evaluation of mental health service model for American Indian/Alaska native children and their families	Not specified whether indigenous. Participatory approach, with tribally based activities throughout evaluation 3-year time frame that enabled trust building, community involvement, and data collection and sharing	Evaluation akin to storytelling—used to teach, guide, perpetuate program story, and shape its future. Locally defined outcomes, findings informing local strategies. Extensive body of local knowledge developed	Understanding of mistrust and historical/intergenerational trauma. Culturally grounded definitions of disorders. Dissemination of evaluation findings through cultural venues. Provision of evaluation technical assistance, and two-way learning with grantees. Information sharing across evaluation sites	Circles of Care—Families and communities had "substantial" input into how to address the mental health needs of children, resulting in a culturally responsive program. Acknowledgment of reservation sovereignty. Stressed importance of difference between rural and urban contexts. Importance of evaluator: bravery, spirituality, and acknowledgment of tribal self-determination

Appendix 1 ■ (Continued)					
Study	Sample/Context	Approach Stated (note if indigenous led)	Implications for Practice (e.g., inclusion methods)	Cultural Consideration(s), Implications, Critiques, Connections to Framework	Other Relevant/ Interesting Observations/ Conclusions
Watts, Christopher, Stretiz, & McCormick (2005)	United States: Evaluation of Lay Health Advisor training	Project coordinator is indigenous CBPR process evaluation	Importance of programs acting on feedback given during evaluation Interview guide developed collaboratively with community advisory board and consultants	Culturally appropriate to use qualitative method Insider/outside status of interviewer reflected on in paper's limitations section	Messengers for Health: CBPR project developed after pre-intervention survey interviews (N=101). Training facilitators included American Indian students and American Indian project coordinator.
Willging, Helitzer, & Thompson (2006)	United States: Evaluation of curriculum-based diabetes prevention program for urban American Indian women	Indigenous and non-indigenous design and evaluation team Participatory evaluation Formative evaluation	Evaluation highlighted lack of historical content in program, poor use of indigenous imagery, and over-emphasis on maternal roles. The questions asked about "traditionalism" were critiqued.	Culture conceptualized as "a shared set of beliefs and values, encompassing reliance on family and extended kin in addition to balance and harmony with nature" (p. 132). Evaluation findings stressed need for inclusivity of diversity of women's lived realities.	Consideration of culture in design of program, informed by interviews with young urban American Indian women who requested a "culturally appropriate, healthful, less intensive lifestyle intervention" (p. 131)

Appendix 2 ■ A Summary of Sample Studies in Western Context (n=24)					
Study	Sample/Context	Approach Stated/ Theoretical Orientation	Rationale	Implications for Practice (e.g., methods used for inclusion)	Cultural Consideration(s), Implications, Critiques, Connections to Framework
Alkon et al. (2001)	USA: Violence prevention education program for childcare staff and Hispanic parents	RCT; culturally sensitive approach	Culturally sensitive approaches necessary given diversity of populations; methodologies should reflect local cultures rather than "ethnocentric" standards.	Methods should incorporate emic perspective in each phase of study; need to used mixed methods to enrich process and outcome data; need excellent communication skills; discuss communication styles weekly; instruments not initially validated with local population; implications for validity of data; lots of time and resources required	Discuss complexity of culture; question whether evaluators need to come from same cultural group; discuss community demographic, cultural make up, hire culturally competent staff; characteristics; emic perspective would help account for values and traditions of different ethnic groups

(Continued)

Appendix 2 ■ (Continued)					
Study	Sample/Context	Approach Stated/ Theoretical Orientation	Rationale	Implications for Practice (e.g., methods used for inclusion)	Cultural Consideration(s), Implications, Critiques, Connections to Framework
Anderson-Draper (2006)	Canada: A family violence prevention program in an immigrant community	Participatory evaluation with emphasis on cultural competence; social cognitive theory	Develop shared meaning that is reflective of diversity of stakeholder perspectives	Cultural competence in evaluation requires balance of participatory from consultative to truly participatory; need to spend lots of time building relationships and provide lots of up front training and support; need to include stakeholders throughout and in different ways; need to be flexible and adaptable with less structured agenda; participatory evaluation highlighted as way to gain cultural competence	Defines culture and cultural competence; highlight cultural context (historical, social, political factors that influence all phases of evaluation); lots of examples of reflection-in-action and learning by doing; questions whether evaluator needs to reflect cultural background of community; reflects on her own positionality and need to be open-minded and willing to learn; evaluator (as profession) contains certain assumptions, values, and beliefs; learning takes place both ways

Boyce (2017)	USA: Research Experiences for Undergraduates program housed within an NSF Science and Technology Center	Values-engaged, educative (VEE) draws from responsive and democratic	Enhance understanding of program, commitment to engage with issues of culture and diversity and responsiveness to stakeholder needs and interests	Focus on underrepresentation, participative and lots of continuous dialogue with stakeholders about values and goals; requires deep and sustained engagement and responsiveness, requires patience; use formal and informal opportunities to foster communication; VEE approach helpful	VEE approach encourages attention to diversity and equity and responsiveness to culture and context.
Butty, Reid, & LaPoint (2004)	USA: CRESPAR program: Urban school-to-career intervention program for at-risk middle school students mostly of African American background	Culturally responsive approach (CRE)	To ensure multicultural validity and increase understanding of how and why programs work to ensure increased advocacy, social betterment, and justice	Follow eight steps offered by Frierson et al., (2002) Participative and active stakeholder involvement, triangulation, labor intensive, had to perform multiple roles due to lack of staff, focus on language of instruments and norming them to population	CRE takes full account of culture; evaluators bring shared life experience; CRE defines as culture, context, and responsive evaluation

(Continued)

Appendix 2 ■ (Continued)

Study	Sample/Context	Approach Stated/ Theoretical Orientation	Rationale	Implications for Practice (e.g., methods used for inclusion)	Cultural Consideration(s), Implications, Critiques, Connections to Framework
Christie & Barela (2005)	USA: Student-centered outreach program to increase UCLA admission of underrepresented groups	Delphi technique; social justice and empowerment models	Used to enhance level of involvement of marginalized stakeholders and ensure everyone has a voice; increased program understanding and provided strength-based approach	Need to verify cultural accuracy of methods; Delphi method used to ensure all perspectives included; evaluator controls evaluation and conducts all data collection and analysis; used to eliminate power imbalances Delphi technique gives equal weight to all stakeholders.	Discuss underrepresented people and social justice in evaluation
Clayson, Castaneda, Sanchez, & Brindis (2002)	USA: Three low-income, Latinx community initiatives aimed at building community, strengthening leadership, and enhancing civic engagement at the grassroots level	Context sensitive lens; critical theory approach, constructivist	Provide a more complete analysis; acknowledge role of evaluator and positions evaluation historically, socially, and politically	Three-pronged approach to evaluation: create a multidisciplinary team, design inclusive approach, ensure transparency with stakeholders at all times; multifaceted role of evaluator; methods need to be valid with population; evaluation as a political act	Significant cultural and historical background on population; researcher historically positioned; emphasis on context—macro and micro level understanding required; insider/outsider; conflict between funder/community priorities and needs; power issues made manifest throughout

Clifford, Fischer, & Pelletier (2014)	USA: Veterans Treatment Court Services evaluation with social work evaluators and veteran community leaders	Collaborative, ecological theory and culturally responsive/cross-cultural methods	Approach "encouraged" for veterans; reflects complexity of system for veterans; program improvement	Used four-part typology of themes to analyze perceptions: theory, validity, ethics, and relational approach	Considerations given to values and goals within cultural context and its influence on evaluation; ecological model (micro/meso level systems analysis); focus on relational dimension
Conner (2004)	USA: HIV prevention program in two Latinx communities	Multicultural validity; quasi-experimental design	Cultural sensitivity; validity	Used participatory approach in creating foto-novellas; used Spanish-only speakers; methods and instruments designed for population	Multicultural validity used to get at issue of cultural sensitivity; need to design instruments and approach to fit cultural context; importance of building rapport and trust; importance of speaking literal and figurative language of participants; validity and collaboration linked
Cooper & Christie (2005)	USA: University-sponsored parent education program for low-income Latina mothers	Social justice approach; qualitative case study design	To be inclusive of least powerful	Role of evaluator to make sure voices and perspectives of least powerful shared; need for flexibility in approach throughout; evaluator as advocate played out	Social justice approach is collaborative; need to understand cultural/gender issues to understand stakeholder views and context; social justice approach can also enable educators and evaluators to promote educational equity.

(Continued)

Appendix 2 ■ (Continued)					
Study	Sample/Context	Approach Stated/ Theoretical Orientation	Rationale	Implications for Practice (e.g., methods used for inclusion)	Cultural Consideration(s), Implications, Critiques, Connections to Framework
Copeland–Carson (2005)	USA: Community revitalization project for African American population	Anthropological evaluation; collaborative and empowerment	Address complexity of community initiatives	Strength-based approach; used language people would be familiar with and that would be acceptable to funder; evaluator as advocate; methods and approach evolved throughout based on findings and funder requirements and constraints; worked with "community consultants" for expert knowledge	Methods seen as cultural constructions; anthropological approach interconnected with broader sociocultural systems; influence of power on ways of knowing; evaluator self-aware of theoretical orientation
Coppens, Page, & Chan Thou (2006)	USA: Cambodian youth dance program	Cultural competence	Cultural sensitivity while meeting funder requirements	Struggle balancing needs of all stakeholders; funding came with strings attached and needed to generate data using standardized measures; appropriateness of methods; created diverse advisory committee	Tensions and conflicts using Western methods in Cambodian community; lots of background about community culture and history; communication styles highlighted as issue; relationships as evolving and dynamic; pace of project highlighted

Harklau & Norwood [2005]	USA: A summer college readiness program for African Americans, Asian Americans, and Anglo youth	Postmodern approach for ethnographic evaluation	Focus on researcher reflexivity; provide "other ways of knowing"	From ethnographic position focused on evaluator role and subjectivity; seen as dynamic and negotiated; ethnographic perspective enabled them to become instrumentally more involved in program activities; noted report content steered by stakeholders as focus on accountability and legitimative uses	Focus on evaluator role and influence on power dynamics; intersection of identities and subject positions
Hong et al. [2005]	USA: HIV prevention program targeting African American injection drug users	Ethnographic method	Capture dynamic interactions of stakeholders and cultural relevance	Piloted intervention to ensure cultural relevance and used process evaluation to monitor and assess effectiveness and appropriateness of program; identified opinion leaders and key informants; collaborative spirit enabled evaluators to interact directly with stakeholders to better reflect norms and realities of participants	Links to culture not made explicit apart from fact that worked closely with participants.

(Continued)

Appendix 2 ■ (Continued)					
Study	Sample/Context	Approach Stated/ Theoretical Orientation	Rationale	Implications for Practice (e.g., methods used for inclusion)	Cultural Consideration(s), Implications, Critiques, Connections to Framework
King, Nielson, & Colby (2004)	USA: Four multicultural education initiatives addressing curriculum and individual needs	Culturally competent evaluation; participatory	Culture-focused approach of program influenced decision to adopt culturally competent approach	Participatory approach provides viable means to address complexity of multicultural initiative. Evaluator as facilitator; used multiple methods to ensure capturing all voices and perspectives; create multicultural steering committee; relational focus	Defined culture and cultural competence and challenges with these definitions; started from a position of not knowing or "informed not knower"; recognized complexity of issues and multiple worldviews at play; cultural competence requires continuous process of self- and organizational introspection
LaPoint & Jackson (2004)	USA: Family, school and community partnership program for Black students in a low-income urban high school	Talent Development Model; participatory action research	Reflect local school and popular culture; minimize insider/ outsider status by getting buy-in	Stakeholders became assistant evaluators and received ongoing training; ongoing engagement throughout and piloted all instruments to ensure cultural commensurability.	Made efforts to ensure cultural similarity between program participants and evaluators (racial, ethnic, gender, age, and social class); to minimize insider/outsider status, continued rapport building and buy-in strategies; constantly trying to reduce social distance between evaluators and participants; cultural responsiveness is a paradigm shift that includes an asset-based approach rather than deficit model

Mertens & Hopson (2006)	USA: Increase participation of underrepresented groups at multiple levels in science and engineering fields	Transformative paradigm, culturally responsive and culturally competent approaches	Primarily epistemological; shows genuine respect and active process of becoming aware	Collaborative, evaluation capacity building highlighted; evaluator as advocator	Culturally responsive approach resonates with equity and social mission focus of social agenda and advocacy evaluation models; intention is to serve communities that have been disenfranchised; evaluation positioned as Western construct
Noblit & Jay (2010)	USA: School development program serving developmental needs of Black communities and schools	Critical race theory (CRT); comparative case design	To explore the potential integration of CRT in evaluation; CRT used to create "counter narrative" to majoritarian view	Avoided language of CRT so as not to alienate funder and those outside the academy; also funder wanted assessments of effectiveness and they wanted to "write against that story."	CRT places race at the center of analysis; focus on racial minorities; examines individual, institutional, and cultural aspects of society that sustain oppressive structures; biracial team that was multidisciplinary; used CRT approach to "speak back to power"; focus on language and communication to change discourse
Prilleltensky, Nelson, & Valdes (2000)	Canada: Smoking prevention program for Latin American immigrants	Values-based approach based on participatory community planning, sensitivity to cultural diversity and holistic philosophy of health; PAR; root in Latin America	Help marginalized people experience personal and political empowerment and buy-in, foster community development	Participants involved in formulating and conducting all aspects of inquiry; control of ownership over process shared between evaluator and participants; trained local participants in evaluation research	PAR thought to share power among all; process guided by a sensitivity to cultural diversity; requires cultural competence on part of evaluator; values influence inquiry so need to make them more explicit; matched backgrounds of investigator with community so shared common language, cultural experiences and values; consider it a value-based partnership with each contributing different things to process and no one held absolute power

(Continued)

Appendix 2 ■ (Continued)					
Study	Sample/Context	Approach Stated/ Theoretical Orientation	Rationale	Implications for Practice (e.g., methods used for inclusion)	Cultural Consideration(s), Implications, Critiques, Connections to Framework
Ryan, Chandler, & Samuels (2007)	USA: Culturally responsive school-based initiatives involving four schools considered "at risk" with Native American, Latinx or African American populations	Culturally responsive evaluation; grounded theory for analysis	Aimed at honoring cultural context in which program takes place; values social justice and seeks power balance	Observed organizational constraints in selecting approach, time, and logistics; training in evaluation so could conduct CRE, so strong professional development component; evolving meaning of culture meant that they started looking at data differently (process use)	Struggles with meaning of culture and definition evolved over course of project changed data use; reflection on self as cultural beings
Samuels & Ryan, (2011)	USA: Higher education program designed to diversify teaching profession	Culturally relevant democratic inquiry (CDI)	Designed to enable teachers to "think evaluatively" within a school improvement planning process	Internal evaluation team; approach unfolds in self-reflective cycles of activities; external evaluator serves educative role as capacity builder; this role beyond that of "measurement technician"	Approach explicitly attends to culture at individual, group, and institutional levels and enacts democratic principles; influenced by CRE but proposes more elaborate definition of culture; evaluation team explored its cultural positionality; introduction of culture broadened learning opportunities beyond single-loop learning

Small, Tiwari, & Huser (2006)	USA: Community partnership with Hmong families with early adolescent children to enhance developmental outcomes	Community research and action	Seek to be culturally sensitive, respectful, collaborative, open-minded and flexible	Collaborative approach and created an evaluation subcommittee though evaluation predetermined and externally driven; required by funder to use evaluation instrument that didn't fit culturally and affected the quality of data and relationships	In process of writing became aware of their own privileged status; self-critical in terms of process learned as the evaluation progressed; need to be aware of racial, gender, age, institutional, and other power and status dynamics; need to recognize cultural differences in communication, coping, and relational styles; need to challenge traditional processes and products of academic knowledge that comes from historically White, Western and masculine worldview
Thomas & Parsons (2016)	USA: Reflections on a case example of an evaluation of a STEM education program	Culturally responsive evaluation, systems-oriented evaluation	Explore interconnections between these two evaluation approaches	By blending two approaches likely to design more relevant evaluation, increase stakeholder participation and enhance usefulness of evaluation; spent lots of time getting to know setting and stakeholders, what they call "front loading"; create diverse group of stakeholders to develop and plan evaluation; need funder and staff buy-in	Approaches help situate project and stakeholders within sociocultural, historical, political, and organizational context; promotes social justice by challenging traditional norms in evaluation; can require paradigm shift for staff and fund as emphasis not only on outcomes

(Continued)

Appendix 2 ■ (Continued)					
Study	Sample/Context	Approach Stated/ Theoretical Orientation	Rationale	Implications for Practice (e.g., methods used for inclusion)	Cultural Consideration(s), Implications, Critiques, Connections to Framework
Uhl et al. (2004)	USA: HIV prevention intervention program for African American women	Tenets from community psychology and ecological perspective; drew from empowerment and utilization-focused evaluation	Increase relevance and appropriateness of evaluation by respecting cultures other than evaluators' own; understanding community	Challenges involving community due to time and resources; hired and trained staff from African American community; improved quality of study and practical value of intervention; contributed to buy-in; improved participant recruitment and retention	Strove to increase cultural sensitivity, community acceptance, and relevance through collaboration; identified evaluators' own values and recognized influence on process
Zulti & Frierson (2004)	USA: Outward Bound program for African Americans	Culturally responsive evaluation	Used CRE based on nature and design of program	Culturally responsive through questions posed and methods used; hired staff from similar backgrounds as program participants (stated that it influenced success); used interviews, focus groups, and questionnaires to determine extent to which cultural aspects built into program	Cultural factors considered critical organizational factors; hired people from same cultural group to ensure program success; no discussion of relationships or self as research instrument

Appendix 3 ■ A Summary of Sample Studies in International Context (n=25)

Study	Sample/Context	Approach Stated	Implications for Practice (e.g., methods used for inclusion)	Cultural Consideration(s), Implications, Critiques, Connections to Framework
Abes (2000)	Philippines: Reflection on the participatory evaluation of a leadership training program, Philippine-Danish Folk School. 23 communities	Participatory impact evaluation	Methodological focus on cultural context, norms, and values	Focus on Filipino cultural context as vital to evaluation process, particularly in terms of methods and norms for validation, but also in terms of data collection and interview/focus group protocols; used understanding of Filipino psychology and the identification of eight levels of culture characterizing how Filipinos interact with others (based on a spectrum of insider/outsider status); evaluators thus needed to spend time becoming "insiders" and learning to be respectful of community norms and values; identified a "bridge" person to help with introductions to the community
Bi Niba & Green (2005)	South Africa: Analysis of five communication-based projects implementation/evaluation in the area of HIV/AIDs	Participatory evaluation	Evaluators facilitated reflection with project coordinators after three stages of the project (preparation, training, and implementation) to gauge perceptions of processes and outcomes; peer educators became part of program staff: educating and facilitating learning with others.	It was noted that evaluators differed from program beneficiaries in terms of gender, race, language, and age; evaluators worked closely with managerial program staff to conduct focus groups in first language of students and beneficiaries; language was viewed as primary limitation to effective evaluation.

(Continued)

Appendix 3 ■ (Continued)				
Study	**Sample/Context**	**Approach Stated**	**Implications for Practice (e.g., methods used for inclusion)**	**Cultural Consideration(s), Implications, Critiques, Connections to Framework**
Botcheva et al. (2009)	Zimbabwe: Reflection on case study of evaluation of HIV/AIDS education projects for youths	Process-oriented, culturally competent evaluation approach	Collected narrative data to reflect cultural emphasis on art and storytelling. Cultural competence is described as a process of collaboration (learning from stakeholders), reflective adaptation (recognizing personal subjectivities), and contextual analysis (recognizing an ecological context).	Emphasized an awareness of cultural differences between evaluators and stakeholders; acknowledged the influence of the evaluator's own "ethnocentric biases and assumptions"; presented evaluation team's backgrounds (e.g., ethnicity, knowledge of program area and population)
Bowen & Tillman (2015)	Brazil: Provides lessons learned on culturally responsive surveys in the context of international education	Culturally responsive evaluation, democratic, and participatory	Community leaders provided input in developing survey questions; focus groups helped in collecting background information and better understanding local context. Cultural context informed development and planning of evaluation, the training of those collecting data, and the content and format of data collection instruments.	Provide historical background of local community and common perceptions of the community in the national culture. Relationships built through local partners, initial focus groups, and ongoing conversations generated meaningful feedback and revisions to survey instrument; position their evaluation efforts within a historical context that has left local communities without basic citizenship rights and access to public programs.

Brago Brandao et al. (2012)	Brazil: Reflections on the evaluation of an educational program for youth who have been convicted of violent crimes	Participatory evaluation	Focus of the evaluation was on training peer evaluators with shared experiences with participants; used comic book to initiate conversations around sensitive topics in interview settings	Peer evaluators were viewed as a way to mitigate power differentials between evaluators and program participants; they sought to address social stigmas of youth crime and the potential concerns of participants of further punitive action by using peer evaluators with shared language and experiences. Dialogue, reflection, and relationship building among peer evaluators, mentors, and primary investigators were important in managing conflicts and maintaining peer evaluator engagement.
Brandon et al. (2014)	Africa: Reflection by multiple evaluators on an evaluation of program for African Women in Agriculture Research and Development (AWARD)	Monitoring and evaluation, developmental, empowerment, realistic, contribution, analysis	A theory of change approach was used as a template for evaluation, and elements of empowerment evaluation were applied to align the program goals with the framework of the evaluation; theory of change was most beneficial in promoting institutional and sector-level improvement, rather than individual changes.	Power dynamics between supervisors (mostly men) and participants (all women) were noted, as were cultural differences among participants from countries across sub-Saharan Africa; the implications were primarily methodological (e.g., keeping sensitive information confidential and reviewing data aggregation strategies); they discuss the accountability-driven nature of most developmental evaluations, citing their explicit attempt to view programs as "open systems" with complex consequences (both positive and negative) and at individual and institutional levels.

(Continued)

Appendix 3 ■ (Continued)

Study	Sample/Context	Approach Stated	Implications for Practice (e.g., methods used for inclusion)	Cultural Consideration(s), Implications, Critiques, Connections to Framework
Buskens & Earl (2008)	Southern Africa: Reflections on a case study of an evaluation of the Infant Feeding Research Project related to the reduction in the role of pediatric HIV/AIDS	Combination of outcome mapping, emancipatory action research, utilization-focused, and appreciative inquiry	Appreciative inquiry focuses the analysis on positive aspects, avoiding deficit framing; evaluators identified "boundary partner" groups to compartmentalize stakeholder meetings and focus on salient indicators of effectiveness.	Evaluators acknowledged negative public perceptions of public health in the region, adapting their approach to promote transformation rather than further critique; problematic relationships between staff and participants were recognized during the research project, leading to plans for revising counseling and training formats; power dynamics were considered, such as perception of researchers as experts, positioning participants as victims and negating their influence/power.
Chinyowa (2011)	Africa: Critique of the traditional M&E application in theatre for community action (TCA) public health intervention and illustration of participatory M&E approach in a second intervention	Participatory monitoring and evaluation (PM&E)	Evaluation activities are integrated into the language of drama and theatre. Evaluative indicators are communicated and analyzed through "play" as participants take on new roles and engage in an immersive, artistic style of learning; an emphasis on public dialogue creates space for local community members to engage in a "process of negotiation" with external experts and evaluators to generate knowledge.	Authors question the "modernization framework" of developmental evaluation, which attempts to mold developing countries in a Western image; questions how evaluators can align indicators with local knowledge systems, saying that the relevance of these indicators dictates the extent to which the evaluation becomes meaningful and valid; insider/outsider dynamic of evaluators is raised as a challenge in establishing the evaluation agenda.

Durham & Tan (2010)	Laos: Reflective case study of an evaluation of an unexploded ordinance clearance program	Theory-based, mixed methods evaluation, realistic	Two advisory/reference groups were established early in the evaluation to provide feedback on evaluation design, process, and language; interviews were conducted with assistance from "cultural brokers" who assisted with verbatim and cultural translation; analysis was initially conducted in respondents' first language by co-researcher.	Reflections on outsider status of evaluator and working with insiders in conducting the evaluation; a mixed methods approach which led to epistemological tension regarding the role of language in data collection and analysis
Elkins (2010)	Iraq & Afghanistan: Reflection on conducting evaluations in peace-precarious countries	Result-oriented/ impact evaluation	Evaluators highlight challenges in getting participant buy-in, planning, and defining the project before implementing the evaluation; highlights multiple dimensions that will influence evaluation in peace-precarious contexts: implementation elasticity, cost elasticity, situational interests, stakeholder complexity, and political sensitivity.	Focuses on the security threats faced by programs and evaluations in "peace-precarious" situations (caused by war, destabilization, or other violent power struggles); risk of violence impacts willingness of funders and pool of evaluators/ program coordinators; can lead to additional uncertainty and instability within program; acknowledges social, political, and economic dimensions that make peace-precarious situations challenging for evaluation

(Continued)

Appendix 3 ■ (Continued)

Study	Sample/Context	Approach Stated	Implications for Practice (e.g., methods used for inclusion)	Cultural Consideration(s), Implications, Critiques, Connections to Framework
Hart & Rajbhandary (2003)	Nepal: Reflections on use of participatory methods in the evaluation of Nepalese children's clubs	Democratic/deliberative evaluation, participatory, empowerment	Participatory methods were tailored to children in programs who often had not attended school and were not literate; used performance methods (e.g., skits, dance) to capture children's perspectives on program functioning, activities, and power dynamics of the clubs.	It was noted that children often waited on responses of their "leaders" before speaking, presenting a challenge for participatory methods and gathering authentic perspectives.
Haylock & Miller (2016)	Africa, Central America, and Asia: Reflections of an evaluation of a women's rights and gender equality program co-funded by Canadian governmental and NGO sources	Feminist Learning System informed by developmental and utilization-focused approaches	Created reflective spaces for partner organizations to discuss their capacity for gender-justice work, simultaneously generating qualitative and quantitative data that met accountability outcome purposes; participatory tools such as outcome mapping and accountability surveys each required significant adaption to align with transformative goals of evaluation (e.g., feminist approach)	Reflected on evaluator–partner power dynamics that led to the creation of additional ways for partners to design and steer processes

There was a tension between the results-based management framework of evaluation (with predetermined outcomes) and program goals of changing gender and power relationships. |

Holte-McKenzie et al. (2006)	Kenya: Reflections on the process of developing an evaluation strategy involving a community-based organization dedicated to empowering girls and young women	Participatory monitoring and evaluation	Key informant interviews were an initial step in identifying current organizational needs, appropriate participatory methods, and cultural considerations; participants helped define what empowerment looked like in reference to core principles of organization.	Criteria for the trustworthiness of data was its accurate reflection of the study setting; participatory approach was viewed in contrast to national culture in which girls are given limited voice and independence.
Laperrière (2007)	Brazil: Reflection on an HIV prevention program for sex workers	Ethnographic, goal-free	The approach recognizes and values local knowledge of what is feasible regarding social change and allows community members to drive action and recommendations.	Authors say that analysis of focus group responses are dependent on the political and social context in which the communication occurred; they cite the complexity of context as limiting the predictability of outcomes and researcher control typically expected in Western methodologies; communication and social networks within the community and the program were described as an important variable in the success of a participatory approach.
Lawrence et al. (2000)	Bolivia & Laos: Reflections on the experiences of monitoring and evaluating impacts of new conservation technology in two countries	Participatory monitoring and evaluation	Participatory approaches were implemented differently in each context to ensure local relevance; less knowledge of participatory approach required more active evaluator role.	Gender issues identified as relevant across both contexts with need identified to devise ways to ensure inclusion of women; identified assumption that external researchers always think that participatory evaluation approaches will be useful for local stakeholders and that they will benefit from the knowledge generated; note that perhaps more a question of "process use" benefit than one based on evaluation results

(Continued)

Appendix 3 ■ (Continued)

Study	Sample/Context	Approach Stated	Implications for Practice (e.g., methods used for inclusion)	Cultural Consideration(s), Implications, Critiques, Connections to Framework
Luo & Liu (2014)	China: Reflections (by two internal evaluators) on the evaluation of a sustainable agricultural biodiversity management project	Participatory Rural Appraisal; culturally responsive evaluation	Identified need to ensure that evaluation needs to be culturally responsive and that the evaluation design be rooted in the cultural context of the program; PRA and use of participatory visualization and diagramming helped farmers present their reality and needs; make connection between inclusion and cultural responsiveness; note that methods that don't take account of cultural context as invalid and unreliable	They see evaluation as culturally and contextually bound; language and cultural translation were described as cultural influences on evaluation; evaluation was a product of donor and evaluator perspectives, when goal was to capture perceptions of local community members.
Lustig et al. (2015)	Israel: Reflections on an evaluation with an NGO that operates a network of schools intended to reduce educational gaps for at-risk students in Israel's "social and geographic periphery"	Participatory and responsive evaluation	Emphasized a strong partnership between program directors and facilitators, with openness and dialogue at the core of understanding how to promote development and education for beneficiaries; internal evaluators serve as a "bridge" between outcome-focused funders and organizational aims of promoting learning and professional development.	Provides an overview of the current culture of evaluation in NGOs in Israel (e.g., limited resources, increasing focus on achievement); evaluation is tailored to program culture (addressing socioemotional skills of individual students) although student perceptions and cultural identities are not considered.

Nagai (2001)	Papua New Guinea: Curriculum project in an elementary school in a Maiwala community	Participatory Action Research; ethnography	Through the participatory process, the evaluator worked as a facilitator, while school teachers engaged in discussions of values, assessment, and evaluation, comparing school life and home life; data was given back to the community to foster empowerment and ownership over the evaluation process.	Previous experiences with expatriates led community members to be initially dependent on the evaluator, expecting her take a lead role in developing curriculum and designing instruction; evaluator positions herself as an active participant in the development of the program, and as someone living in the community and immersed in the culture, although with an outsider perspective of an expatriate; makes efforts to avoid introducing and promoting Western ideas.
Nandi et al. (2015)	India: Evaluation of a government program for the development and empowerment of adolescent girls through a health and nutrition program	Participatory and appreciative approaches	Used a "gender responsive analysis" to examine the conditions and experiences of women and men, and how policies and programs affect them; evaluators acted as facilitators, working to build evaluation capacity among stakeholders and participants; interpreters facilitated focus groups and translated audio so participants could speak in their preferred language.	Suggest that the evaluation community does not give enough attention to how gender inequities shape programs, participants, and evaluation activities; diversity (girls from different religions) created tensions.

(Continued)

Appendix 3 ■ (Continued)

Study	Sample/Context	Approach Stated	Implications for Practice (e.g., methods used for inclusion)	Cultural Consideration(s), Implications, Critiques, Connections to Framework
Newman (2008)	Nigeria: Reflections on the evaluation of *Reflect*, a participatory approach to social and community change	Transformative participatory evaluation	Evaluation team sought critical feedback from participants through workshops; evaluators used information gathered from site visits to create an initial list of key program outcomes but created space for participants to elaborate or go in a different direction.	Recognized and sought to avoid a certain evaluation culture, or "traps" of evaluation. Particularly cognizant of NGO needs to provide evidence of "progress" and their contribution to that progress; reflects on personal identity of evaluator as a white outsider from the West
Pouw et al. (2017)	Ghana and Burkina Faso: Evaluation of rural development programs; NGOs and research institutions partner in a test case of an approach to participatory evaluation	Participatory assessment of development, gender, and equity lens	Apply an intersubjective approach to understanding the history of development initiatives in the area—synthesizing multiple perspectives to understand what role development organizations/programs have played	Key component of approach is multiday workshops with community members to assess the development history of the area; cultural context includes participant culture, history, and interactions with development interventions; when agencies were compared, a competitive environment formed around evaluation.
Sidersky & Guijt (2000)	Brazil: Evaluator's and nonprofit reflection on participatory process in an agricultural development program	Participatory monitoring and evaluation	Action research process involves local stakeholders for more accurate and relevant data and for capacity building. Strong accountability focus	Identify need to design methods for collecting and recording data relevant to indicators and local cultural context

Author (Year)	Title	Methodology	Description	Context
Tapella & Rodríguez-Bilella (2014)	Guatemala: Reflection on the sistematizacion approach to assess development experiences	Sistematizacion: a multistakeholder approach to evaluation	Involvement of multiple and diverse SH groups essential to capture all political, social, economic, and cultural dimensions; participation primarily occurs through meetings and workshops; they describe a risk in complicating and overburdening the evaluation by including too many stakeholders, or trying to include as many stakeholders as possible "just because"	Gathering demographic and sociopolitical information on youth; describing key, relevant national political events; describing laws, policies, violence, and social stigmas affecting youth in the current political climate. Stakeholders with differing ideas risked creating a "boxing ring" where people defend their perceptions of the truth.
Torres (2000)	Ecuador: Reflection on use of participatory approach for community development	SISDEL: A planning, monitoring, and evaluation system based on participatory monitoring and evaluation approaches	Participatory and grassroots development framework that prioritizes beneficiary participation, going beyond donor requirement; PE approaches used to strengthen local institutional capacity	Recognize importance of local culture and thus use methods that are compatible with local customs and conditions. Control of project cycle must be shared between external and local.
Zamir & Abu Jaber (2015)	Israel: Evaluation of a teacher-training program for women in a Bedouin community	Developmental Evaluation, cultural sensitivity, feminist methodology	Focused on creating a joint evaluation process, building trust between evaluators and stakeholders, and building evaluation capacity. Evaluation team sought to help local teacher mentors to come to common understandings of program goals, particularly emphasizing feminist issues with male mentors.	Brief description of the historical and social circumstances surrounding the Bedouin community—primarily creation of Israel and subsequent urbanization efforts that have challenged traditional norms and values of the community

INDEX

Abes, R. V., 191
Abu Jaber, S., 112, 201
Aburto, S., 16
Accountability to community, 63–65
Advisory groups, 62, 83, 105, 123
African drama and theatre project, 95–96
Agar, M., 110
Agriculture biodiversity project in
    China, 96
Airini, ?? 61, 168
Alkon, A., 86, 179
Allen, J., 64, 177
American Evaluation Association (AEA),
    6, 7, 86
American Indian Higher Education
    Consortium (AIHEC), 6–7, 66
Analysis strategies, 37–38
Anderson, Benedict, 21–22
Anderson, G., 128
Anderson-Draper, M. H., 72, 77, 180
Applied drama project in Africa, 95–96
Askew, D., 52, 54, 55, 166
Aton, K., 60, 67
Axiological dimension of culture, 30t,
    31–32, 131

Bacon, Francis, 20
Bailey, S. J., 50, 55, 56, 63, 172
Baker, M., 163
Baldwin, J. R., 20
Ball, T. J., 49, 59, 169
Banks, J. A., 11
Barahona, C., 197
Barela, E., 182
Barthes, Roland, 10
Basso, Keith, 129
Bauman, Z., 23
Baxter, N., 48, 62, 63, 169, 177
Bélemvire, A., 101, 200
Ben Baruch-Koskas, S., 198
Berends, L., 164
Berryman, M., 164
Best, S., 12
Betts, S. C., 55, 64, 174

Bias, 11
Billig, Mick, 21
Binaries as Western concept, 115
Bi Niba, J. E., 191
Biodiversity project in China, 96
Bishop, R., 164
Blignault, I., 165
Bockting, W., 190
Bond, C., 52, 54, 55, 166
Botcheva, L., 104, 192
"Both ways" method, 62
Boulton, A., 166
Boundary partners, 111
Bowen, M. L., 97, 103, 192
Boyce, A. S., 181
Boyer, P., 66
Brago Brandão, D., 106, 109, 193
Brandon, P. R., 106, 193
Brazilian land rights project, 96–97
Breaking the Silence project, 71–72
Bricolage, 13
Brindis, C., 81, 85, 182
British, colonization by, 40
Buskens, I., 194
Butty, J. L. M., 83, 181

Cajete, G., 13
Cambodian youth dance program, 72–73
Capacity building, 7, 127
Cargo, M., 49, 59, 174
Carlson, T., 51, 54, 58, 61, 62, 167
Cassidy, T, 163
Castaneda, X., 81, 85, 182
Cavino, H. M., 56, 67
Challenging Our Own Limits (COOL), 41–42
Chandler, M., 88, 188
Chan Thou, T., 73, 87, 184
Cherry-Porter, T., 190
Chesterton, P., 64–65, 167
Chilisa, Bagele, 40, 51
Chinese sustainable agriculture
    biodiversity project, 96
Chinyowa, K. C., 96, 106, 107, 110, 194
Chong, J., 49–50, 52, 53, 168

Christie, C. A., 84, 182, 183
Christopher, S., 56, 178
CIRCLE (Community Indian Resources for
    Community and Law Enforcement)
    Project, 41
Civilizational racism, 10–11
Clapham, S., 164
Clayson, Z., 81, 85, 182
Clifford, Fischer, & Pelletier ?? 183
Cockburn, C., 90
Co-construction of knowledge,
    79–80, 136. See also Participatory
    methodology
Codas, R., 106, 109, 193
Code of Research Ethics, development
    of, 54
Colby, J., 77, 88, 186
Collaboration, 57–60, 79–80, 123. See also
    Participatory methodology
Colonization
    by British, 40
    ecological views and, 47
    evaluation and, 66, 67
    international development context and,
        97–98, 108
Communicentric bias, 11
Community empowerment, 60–63
Community Indian Resources for
    Community and Law Enforcement
    (CIRCLE) Project, 41
Community ownership of evaluation,
    59–60
Community participatory methods, 63
Competence building, 56
Conceptual use of findings, 87
Confidentiality, 54
Connectedness in indigenous context,
    13–15, 51–55, 121, 129
Conner, R. F., 81, 183
Constitutive effects of evaluation, 91
Consultation, 58
Convention No. 169 (ILO), 39, 39t
COOL (Challenging Our Own Limits), 41–42
Cooper, C. W., 84, 183
Copeland-Carson, J., 81, 184
Coppens, N. M., 73, 87, 184
Co-production of design and
    implementation, 57–60
Cornwall, A., 14
Coryn, C. L. S., 105
"The Countenance of Education
    Evaluation" (Stake), 4
Cram, F., 31–32

Crazy Bull, C., 47
Creative pluralists, 105, 106–107, 128
Cree nation, 41–42, 50
CRIE (culturally responsive indigenous
    evaluation), 8–9
Critical geography, 14–15
Critical subjectivity, 31. See also Personal
    dimension of culture
Critical turn, 22
Cullen, A. E., 105
Cultural archive, 10
Cultural brokers, 109–110, 111
Cultural competence, 2
Cultural differences, depth of, 1
Cultural facilitators, 82–83
Cultural guides, 128–129
Cultural identities, 23, 82–83, 90
Cultural informants, 83
Culturally responsive evaluation (CRE)
    assumptions about, 1
    history of, 3–9, 3n, 8f
    implications for, 135–138, 136t
    indigenous peoples and, 8–9
    need for, 119
    terminology issues, 2–3
    transformational potential of, 103
Culturally responsive evaluation
    framework, 7–8, 8f
Culturally responsive indigenous
    evaluation (CRIE), 8–9
Cultural matching, 82–83, 127
Cultural process use of findings, 88
Cultural responsiveness, 13
Culture
    conceptualization of, 19–24, 19n,
        132–133
    etymological roots of, 20
    as everywhere, 119
    methodology tied to, 135
    Western context and, 76–78
    See also Dimensions of culture
Culture of power, 80
Curtis, E., 61, 168
Customary practices, 53

Dahler-Larsen, P., 81–82, 91, 100, 137
Dam, L. I., 176
Daniel, M., 176
Databases searched, 34
Data ownership, 59–60, 63
de Certeau, M., 14
Decolonization, 9, 47, 67
Decolonizing Methodologies (Smith), 6

de Groot, D., 101, 200
Delormier, T., 49, 59, 174
Delpit, L. D., 80
de Sousa Santos, Boaventura, 137
Deters, P. B., 64, 177
Developing country lens, 104
Dietz, T., 101, 200
Dimensions of culture
    axiological dimension, 131
    ecological dimension, 46–48, 46n,
        48f, 122–124
    epistemological dimension, 91, 120–122
    institutional dimension, 130–131
    ontological dimension, 132–133
    overview, 24–32, 26–30t, 119–120,
        133–134
    personal dimension, 127–128
    political dimension, 60, 114
    relational dimension, 40, 128–130
    See also Methodological dimension
        of culture
Discourse concept, 12
Distance, issues due to, 123, 126, 131
Domains of practice. See Indigenous
    context; International development
    context; Western context
Du Bois, W. E. B., 10
Durham, J., 195

Earl, S., 194
Eastern Door, 8
Ecological dimension of culture, 25, 26t,
    46–48, 46n, 48f, 122–124
Edwards Groves, C., 89
Elkins, C., 102, 195
Empirical research, importance of, 16
Epistemicide, 137
Epistemological dimension of culture, 25,
    26t, 91, 120–122
Epistemological ethnocentrism, 25, 91
Epistemological racism, 12
Epistemology, 136–137
Ethical codes, development of, 54, 131
Ethic of engagement, 112, 113
Ethics, international development context
    and, 112–113
Ethnicity, importance of disclosing, 56–57
Ethnic matching, 82–83, 127
Evaluation influence, 88
Evaluators
    as creative pluralists, 105, 106–107, 128
    matching by ethnicity or culture,
        82–83, 127

positionality and, 55–57, 88, 90, 103, 115,
    128, 129
relationship building by, 51–55
role as fluid, 84
self-reflection by, 31, 127–128
using local people for, 53–54, 56, 58, 83,
    109, 130
Eversole, R., 115
Evidence-based programs, limits of, 49
Ex-nomination, 10, 57, 133
Exploitation, 55

Face time, 53
Facilitators, 82–83
Family, School, and Community
    Partnership Program (FSCPP), 72
Fascists: A Social Psychological View of the
    National Front (Billig), 21
Faulkner, S. L., 20
Findings, use of, 59–60, 87–89, 123–124
Fisher, P. A., 49, 59, 169
Fiske, J., 57
Foley, W., 52, 54, 55, 166
Food, engagement practices and, 54–55
Forde, S., 197
Forrest, R., 169
Fortun, K., 24
Foucault, Michel, 10, 12, 14, 90–91
Foxall, D., 169
Freeman, R., 111
Frierson, H. T., 83, 127, 190
FSCPP (Family, School, and Community
    Partnership Program), 72
Funders
    conflict with culturally responsive
        evaluation and, 64–65, 137
    deficit view of indigenous people
        and, 130
    epistemological dimension and, 121
    evaluative measures and cultural
        appropriateness, 85–86, 125
    power and, 79

Gann, D., 81, 185
Garrow, C., 41, 175
Geertz, Clifford, 21
Genealogy concept, 12
Geopolitical context, 114
Global South. See International
    development context
Goffman, Erving, 137
Green, J. M., 191
Greene, Maxine, 10

Grey, K., 48, 62, 63, 169, 177
Grover, J. G., 62, 63, 170
Guba, Egon G., 132
Guijt, I., 200
Guzman, B. L., 81

Hall, S., 22, 23, 90, 137
Hamerton, H., 43, 53, 55, 170
Hardy, I., 89
Harklua, L., 185
Hart, M. A., 60
Hart, R. A., 196
Hassin, J., 49–50, 52, 53, 168
Haswell, M., 165
Haylock, L., 196
Haylor, G., 197
Healthy Eating Healthy Action program, 42–43
Hecht, M. L., 20
Helicopter evaluation, 66
Helitzer, D., 50n, 62, 178
Herr, K., 128
Hierarchy of social forces, 25. *See also* Ecological dimension of culture
Hirsch, T., 198
Hittner, A., 86, 179
Hobart, M., 115
Holte-McKenzie, M., 197
Hong, Y., 81, 185
Hood, Stafford, 3, 6, 24, 127
Hopson, Rodney K., 1, 2, 3, 24
Howe, D., 23
Huffman, L. C., 104, 192
Hughes, G. B., 127
Huser, M., 77, 189

Identities, 23, 82–83, 90
Imagined Communities (Anderson), 21–22
Implicit bias, 12
Indigenous context
    accountability to community and, 63–65
    axiological dimension and, 131
    co-production of design and implementation and, 57–60
    descriptive analysis, 45
    ecological dimension and, 46–48, 46n, 48f, 122
    epistemological dimension and, 121–122
    evaluators as both insiders and outsiders and, 55–57
    implications for practice in, 65–67
    institutional dimension and, 130

integration and synthesis, 46
local programming and, 49–51
methodological dimension and, 124, 125–126
ontological dimension and, 132
overview, 39–43, 39t, 67
power-sharing and, 60–63
relationships as important in, 13–15, 51–55, 121, 129
sample for, 43–45, 44f, 163–178
themes from, 136, 136t
Indigenous Evaluation Framework, 7
Initial consultation, 58
Inner core, 23
Institutional dimension of culture, 29t, 31, 130–131
Instrumental use of findings, 87
Intergroup perspective on culture, 21–22
International development context
    axiological dimension and, 131
    characterization of, 97–98
    contextual complexity and, 100–102
    descriptive analysis, 99–100
    ethics and, 112–113
    implications for practice in, 113–116
    institutional dimension and, 130–131
    integration and synthesis, 100
    methodological dimension and, 107–108, 124–125, 126
    overview, 95–97, 117
    participatory methodology, 104–107
    relational dimension and, 129–130
    sample for, 98–99, 99f, 191–201
    themes from, 136, 136t
    time dimension and, 102–104, 114–115
    translation of language and culture issues, 110–111
International Labour Organisation (ILO) Convention No. 169, 39, 39t
Interpretation, 81–82, 110–111, 131, 138
Intersectionality, 58–59

Jackson, H. L., 72, 186
Jackson Pulver, L., 165
Jacups, S., 59, 171
Jainullabudeen, T. A., 59, 171
Jargon, 81
Jay, M., 81, 187
Jayavant, S., 176
Joe, J. R., 49–50, 52, 53, 168
Jolly, Eric, 138
Jordan, S., 42, 50, 61, 171

Jorgensen, M., 41, 175
Journals, literature review and, 34–35.
    See also Selection of studies
Jugran, T., 106, 199

Kaupapa Māori, 6, 42, 51
Kawakami, A., 60, 67
Kellner, D., 12
Kemmis, S., 89
Kincheloe, J., 22
King, J. A., 77, 88, 186
King, M., 173
Kingi, T., 166
Kirkhart, Karen, 6, 24, 66, 101
Knowledge construction, 79–80, 136
Kumar, S., 104
Kumok, Z., 126–127
Kushner, S., 91

Labonte, R., 46
Ladson-Billings, Gloria, 4, 136
LaFrance, Joan, 6–7, 16, 48, 51, 52, 65,
    66, 101
Lakota people, 41
Land rights in Brazil project, 96–97
Languaculture, 110
Language use, 53, 80–82, 109–110,
    131, 138
Laperrière, H. N., 197
LaPoint, V., 72, 83, 181, 186
Lather, P., 12
Latkin, C. A., 81, 185
Lawrence, A., 197
Leal, P. A., 108, 115
Legitimzed versus subjugated
    knowledge, 12
Letiecq, B. L., 50, 55, 56, 63, 172
Li, T. M., 137
Limitations of articles reviewed, 38
Lincoln, Yvonna, 132
Literature review, 34–35. *See also*
    Selection of studies
Liu, L., 96, 102, 110, 198
Lively, A., 59, 171
Local engagement practices, 54–55
Local language, 53
Local programming, importance of, 49–51
Luo, L. P., 96, 102, 110, 198
Lustig, R., 198

Macaulay, A. C., 49, 59, 174
MacDonald, Barry, 4–5

Mackey, H. J., 172
Madison, Anne Marie, 5, 80
Makhani-Belkin, T., 198
Māori people, 7, 42–43
Mark, R., 42, 50, 61, 171
Massey, D., 115, 135–136
Matches, S., 42, 50, 61, 171
McCalman, J., 59, 171
McComber, A. M., 49, 59, 174
McCormick, A. K., 56, 178
McCreanor, T., 51, 54, 58, 61, 62, 167
McLaren, ?? 22
McPherson, B., 43, 53, 55, 170
Mercer, C., 43, 53, 55, 170
Merry, S. E., 137
Mertens, Donna, 6, 11, 25
Metanarratives, 116
Methodological dimension of culture
    decolonization of, 67
    in international development context,
        104–108
    methodological eclecticism, 92
    overview, 25, 27t, 124–125
    participatory methodology, 36, 41–43,
        51, 61, 104–107
    power-sharing methodology, 60–63
    validity and, 85–86
    Western view of, 116
Methodological eclecticism, 92
Methodological validity, 85–86
Meusch, E., 197
Millar, D., 101, 200
Miller, C., 196
Mills, C. Wright, 9–10
"Minority Issues in Evaluation"
    (Madison), 5
Mitchell, S. G., 81, 185
Moewaka Barnes, H., 51, 54, 58, 61,
    62, 167, 173
Montgomery, K. E., 12
Morrison, L., 43, 53, 55, 170
Muticultural validity, 6

Nagai, Y., 103, 199
Nanda, R. B., 106, 199
Nandi, R., 106, 199
Napeahi, L., 60, 67
National Front, 21
Nation building, 41
Nelson, G., 82–83, 187
Nelson-Barber, S., 16
Neutrality as impossible, 12

New Directions for Program Evaluation, 5, 74
Newman, K., 200
Nichols, Richard, 6–7, 48, 65, 66, 101
Nielson, J. E., 77, 88, 186
Nigawchiisuun, 41–42
Noblit, G. W., 81, 187
"Nobody Knows My Name" Project, 3
Noordeloos, M., 106, 193
Northern Door, 8–9
Northern Territories Emergency
    Response Program, 47–48, 48f
Norwood, R., 185
Novins, D. K., 173

Obeng, F., 101, 200
O'Dea, K., 176
Ofir, Z., 104, 106, 193
Oglala Lakota people, 41
Ontological dimension of culture, 30t, 32,
    132–133
Outsider populations, 40. *See also*
    Colonization
Ownership of evaluation, 59–60, 63

Page, R., 73, 87, 184
Paradigms, 11
Participatory methodology, 36, 41–43, 51,
    61, 104–107
Patton, Michael Quinn, 5, 11, 101
Pearson, M., 169
Pedagogy, cultural relevance of, 4
Peer review as criteria, 35
Personal dimension of culture, 28t, 31,
    127–128
Peter, M., 164
Peterson, D. J., 55, 64, 174
Peterson, J. A., 81, 185
Pipi, K., 31–32, 163
Political dimension of culture
    evaluation and, 60
    international development context
        and, 114
    overview, 28t, 30–31, 125–127
Political power, 79
Positionality
    indigenous context and, 55–57, 128, 129
    international development context and,
        103, 115
    Western context and, 88, 90
Postmodernism, 22–23
Potvin, L., 49, 59, 174
Pouw, N., 101, 200

Power, 78–80, 116
Power-sharing methodology, 60–63
Prilleltensky, I., 82–83, 187
Process use of findings, 87, 88
Program evaluation, purposes of, 1
Program Evaluation Standards (AEA), 7
Project REPLACE, 42–43
Public Sector Finance Act (1989), 6
*Public Statement on Cultural Competence in
    Evaluation* (AEA), 7, 86
Putt, J., 48, 62, 63, 169, 177

Quilombos project, 96–97

Racism, 10–11, 12
"Raising the tipi," 41
Rajbhandary, J., 196
Rawlins-Crivelo, L., 60, 67
Reflective case narratives, 33, 35, 36
Regimes of practice, 90–91
Reid, M. D., 83, 181
Relational dimension of culture, 29t, 31,
    40, 128–130
Relationship building, 51–55, 128–129
Remedial strategy, 46–47
Renato Silva, R., 106, 109, 193
"Rendering technical," 137
Respectful talk, 52–53
Responsive evaluation, 4
Revitalising and Strengthening Our
    Traditional Philosophies and
    Principles Towards Building Strong
    Governance, Administration and
    Accountability Systems project, 50
Richmond, L. S., 55, 64, 174
Riini, D., 43, 53, 55, 170
Rituals of encounter, 13
Roberts, B., 164
Roberts, J., 169
Robertson, P., 41, 175
Robert Stake Retirement Symposium, 6
Robinson, B., 190
Rodríguez-Bilella, P., 106, 108, 201
Rowley, K. G., 176
Ruane, S. H., 86, 179
Rugh, J., 105
Ryan, K. E., 88, 188

Samuels, M., 88, 188
Sanchez, E., 81, 85, 182
Santamaría, A. P., 176
Santamaría, L. J., 176

Scheurich, I., 10, 11, 12
Schick, R. S., 80
Schwandt, T. A., 91, 100, 112, 113
Scott-Chapman, S., 169
SDGs (Sustainable Development
    Goals), 98
Seagull evaluation, 66
Selection of studies
    indigenous context, 43, 45
    international development context, 98
    overview, 33–36, 36–37f, 38, 134
    Western context, 73–74
Self-reflection, 31, 127–128. *See also*
    Personal dimension of culture
Semiotic approach to culture, 21
SenGupta, S., 24
Sensitivity, 53–54
Shakeshaft, A., 59, 171
Shih, J., 104, 192
Sidersky, P., 200
Singleton, M., 59, 171
Situational responsiveness, 5, 101–102
Skinner, K., 176
Skinner, M., 176
Small, S. A., 77, 189
Smith, Dorothy, 116
Smith, Linda
    case study, 41
    civilizational racism, 11
    co-production and, 57
    cultural underpinnings of Westernized
        research methods, 10
    data ownership and, 63
    Decolonizing Methodologies, 6
    helicopter evaluation and, 66
    positionality and, 129
    understanding versus
        measurement, 115
Smith, N. L., 106, 193
Smith, S. E., 41
Social inquiry, as cultural product, 9–15
Social justice, 112, 130
Sociological imagination, 9–10
Southern Door, 8
Space concept, 14–15, 77, 115
Spencer, S., 133
Stake, Robert, 4
Standardized measures, 85–86, 91, 96
Stanfield, J. H., Jr., 11, 12–13
Statement on Cultural Competency (AEA), 7, 86
Steering committees, 62, 83, 105, 123
Stocek, C., 42, 50, 61, 171

Stone, L. S., 173
Streitz, J. L., 56, 178
Studies, selection of. *See* Selection of
    studies
Subjugated versus legitimized
    knowledge, 12
Sustainable agriculture biodiversity
    project in China, 96
Sustainable Development Goals
    (SDGs), 98
Sutton, S., 48, 62, 63, 169, 177

Talent Development Model, 72
Tan, B., 195
Tapella, E., 106, 108, 201
Taylor, L.-A., 169
Technification of concerns, 137
Technocracy, 115–116
Temple, B., 138
Theatre project in Africa, 95–96
Theobald, S., 197
Thick description, 21, 112
Thomas, V. G., 127
Thomas & Parsons ?? 189
Thompson, J., 50n, 62, 178
Thompson-Robinson, M., 24
Thurman, P. J., 64, 177
Tillman, A. S., 97, 103, 192
Time dimension, 83–85, 102–104, 114–115,
    123, 125
Tiwari, G., 77, 189
Tobin, K., 81, 185
Torres, D. V. H., 106, 201
Townsend, S., 61, 168
Transformative paradigm of Donna
    Mertens, 6, 25
Translation, 81–82, 110–111, 131, 138
Tribal participatory research model
    (TPRM), 61
Tribal peoples, 39t, 41, 41–42, 50. *See also*
    Indigenous context
Trumbull, E., 16
Trust, 128–129
Tschann, J. M., 86, 179
Tsey, K., 59, 171
Tuck, E., 65

Uhl, G., 190
Untranslatables, 81–82

Valdes, L. S., 82–83, 187
Validity, 6, 85–86, 132

Watts, V. M., 56, 178
Wearmouth, J., 164
Webber, M., 176
"West and the Rest," 137
Western canon, 11, 137
Western context
  axiological dimension and, 131
  conceptualization of culture in, 76–78
  descriptive analysis, 75–76
  ecological dimension and, 122–123
  epistemological dimension and, 120–121
  evaluative measures and cultural
    appropriateness, 85–86
  identities and, 82–83
  implications for practice in, 89–91
  institutional dimension and, 130
  integration and synthesis, 76
  language and, 80–82
  methodological dimension and, 125, 126
  overview, 71–73, 92
  personal dimension and, 127
  power and, 78–80
  sample for, 73–75, 74f, 179–190
  themes from, 136, 136t

  time dimension, 83–85
  use and influence of findings, 87–89
Western Door, 8
Westover, B., 190
White, G. A., 176
Whiteness
  as "natural," 10, 57, 133
  racial supremacy and, 11
  Western context and, 77
Wicked problems, 1
Wilkinson, J., 89
Willging, C. E., 50n, 62, 178
Williams, M., 165
Wilson, Shawn, 40
Winant, H., 133
Wolff, M., 86, 179

Yang, K. W., 65
Young, M., 10, 11, 12
Young, R. S., 49–50, 52, 53, 168

Zaal, F., 101, 200
Zamir, J., 112, 201
Zulli, R. A., 83, 190